EUROPEAN ADMINISTRATIVE LAW IN THE CONSTITUTIONAL TREATY

This book presents an integrated approach to general questions of European administrative law and offers some possible solutions to the problems that it poses, with the Treaty establishing a Constitution for Europe as the point of reference. Under the Treaty, general questions of administrative law are no longer addressed merely in a fragmented or incidental way but as a discipline that governs the exercise of sovereign powers by a supranational entity. This calls for a detailed examination of the fields that comprise European administrative law, and the book therefore examines in some detail the key areas of rulemaking powers and normative instruments, the implications of the Charter of Fundamental Rights for European and national administrations, administrative procedure, and judicial protection within the European Union.

Modern Studies in European Law: Volume 12

Modern Studies in European Law

1 Soft Law in European Community Law *Linda Senden*
2 The Impact of European Rights on National Legal Cultures *Miriam Aziz*
3 Partnership Rights, Free Movement and EU Law *Helen Toner*
4 National Remedies Before the Court of Justice: Issues of Harmonisation and Differentiation *Michael Dougan*
5 The National Courts Mandate in the European Constitution *Monica Claes*
6 EU Environmental Law: Challenges, Changes and Decision-Making *Maria Lee*
7 European Union Law and Defence Integration *Martin Trybus*
8 Principles of European Constitutional Law *Armin von Bogdandy & Jürgen Bast*
9 EU International Relations Law *Panos Koutrakos*
10 Free Movement, Social Security and Gender in the EU *Vicki Paskalia*
11 The Regulation of the State in Competitive Markets in the EU *Erika Szyszczak*

European Administrative Law in the Constitutional Treaty

Eva Nieto-Garrido and Isaac Martín Delgado

·HART·
PUBLISHING

OXFORD AND PORTLAND, OREGON
2007

Published in North America (US and Canada) by
Hart Publishing
c/o International Specialized Book Services
920 NE 58th Avenue, Suite 300
Portland, OR 97213-3786
USA
Tel: +1 503 287 3093 or toll-free: (1) 800 944 6190
Fax: +1 503 280 8832
E-mail: orders@isbs.com
Website: www.isbs.com

Hart Publishing, 16C Worcester Place, OX1 2JW
Telephone: +44 (0)1865 517530 Fax: +44 (0)1865 510710
E-mail: mail@hartpub.co.uk
Website: http://www.hartpub.co.uk

British Library Cataloguing in Publication Data
Data Available

ISBN: 978-1-84113-512-0

Typeset by Hope Services, Abingdon
Printed and bound in Great Britain by
Lightning Source UK Ltd

To my parents and to Ana Beliu and David

E. N. G

To my family, from whom I learnt everything that I am

I. M. D

Foreword

In the year 2006, just as the European Union was planning its 50th birthday party, the powerful and prestigious American Bar Association circulated the first fruits of a major restatement of European Community law. Whether the ABA is a non-profit-making organisation, I am not aware; but it is hardly a philanthropic institution. Why then should this massive project have seen the light of day?

One reason is that transatlantic political relationships are becoming closer. We have already experienced joint action in the field of security, with questions raised about legality, as with 'rendition' in breach of due process requirements or, in the case of air travellers, their data protection rights. There is a need for policy convergence, raising questions about participation in the EU rulemaking process. No wonder that Americans, faced with the labyrinthine comitology, work towards a European Administrative Procedures Act. Vicious battles have already taken place in the shadow of the WTO, for example, over imports of bananas or the use of hormones in industrial agriculture. At a more mundane level, any nation wishing to do business with the EU is likely to come into contact with the rules of its competition law, central to the evolution of European administrative procedures, and with its public procurement law, both of which have transformed national laws of administrative contract. What these examples have in common is that all touch on central, areas of administrative law. This is in itself good reason for the ABA's interest.

In its 50-year life span, EU administrative law has grown very rapidly to the point where it is capable of influence well beyond the European Union and its Member States. Indeed at a global level, some see the EU system, with its necessary emphasis on the reconciliation of disparate and divergent legal orders, as the prototype for a global administrative law. The only real rival in this field is American administrative law, as no doubt the ABA also realises. Listing its sources, Professor Jurgen Schwarze, doyen of EU public law studies, originally prioritised the jurisprudence of the Court of Justice, though over the years he began to note the extent to which jurisprudence was being overtaken by a substantial body of regulation and 'soft law', much of it procedural. The Court's contribution, which remains significant, rests on flimsy foundations. Paragraph 2 of TEC Article 288 (ex 215), allowed the courts to develop the law in compensation claims ' in accordance with the general principles common to the laws of the Member States'. In time this became the basis for the development by the Court of an ambitious set of general principles for an EU public law and procedural norms. From its very inception, therefore, EC law has been dedicated to harmonisation while at the same time out of respect for pluralism and diversity; cross-fertilisation rather than centralisation has been the general rule.

This is an area in which administrative lawyers across the European Union should be knowledgeable and open to each other's ideas. But although it is a subject of great importance, EU administrative law has until fairly recently attracted little sustained academic interest. There are, for example, few academic courses devoted to it and EU public law normally focuses on the institutions, with special reference to the Court. One reason for this may be the emphasis on trade and commerce, which has directed scholars towards the commercial subjects: competition, monopolies and state aids. (The failure to characterise these regulatory processes as a form of administrative law is in itself surprising). Language has also undoubtedly been a major problem. It was several years before Professor Jurgen Schwarze's epic comparative study of general principles was translated into English, today on its way to becoming the lingua franca of European studies, while the innovative treatise of Professors Mario Chiti and Giorgio Gaja, has, I suggest, been undeservedly pushed to the sidelines because it is available only in Italian. All the more reason then to welcome the present work by two Spanish scholars.

This work is emphatically not, however, a student text or straightforward administrative law treatise but something much more original and ambitious. At the heart of the book lie two constitutional texts, which the authors see as central to European public law. The first is the ill-fated Constitutional Treaty, which may or may not come into force. Whether or not it does is not, however, a matter of much moment to the authors. Their interest in the Constitutional Treaty lies mainly in its approach to EU lawmaking. EU lawmaking processes are probably the most complex in existence, while the hierarchy of its legal norms is such as to leave all rational public lawyers (as well as those who need to operate them) in despair. The authors argue strongly for simplification and see the way forward as that proposed in the Constitutional Treaty. This would put in place a structure at European level akin to that found in the Member States. There would be European laws and framework laws and, in addition to the implementing powers that have given rise to the comitology, there would be a power to make delegated legislation. Whether or not the Constitutional Treaty ever proceeds to ratification, these normative instruments, the authors believe, would transform European administrative law.

The Charter of Fundamental Rights and Freedoms is the second constitutional text seen by the authors as significant for the future of EU administrative law. Whether or not this will be made binding depends, possibly, on whether the Constitutional Treaty comes into force. However this may be, the Charter will certainly impinge on the EU's administrative organs and processes as well as on its courts. Focusing on the right to good administration in the Charter, the authors set out to consider what its impact might be. These are difficult and delicate questions, with effects at every level of the complex, multi-level European decision-making process. Is it really going to be possible, for example, to confine the ambit of the Charter to cases where Member States 'are implementing Union law'? Will there not be an inevitable 'over-spill effect', bringing conflicts of jurisdiction such as those which have in the past bedevilled relationships between the Court of Justice and the German Constitutional Court? And will there be new conflicts between the two transnational European courts, Luxembourg and Strasbourg?

Transparency in the form of access to official information now figures in the index of nearly all texts on administrative law. A link as yet less commonly recognised is that between freedom of information and data protection. These authors have chosen to highlight the potential clash between rights to know and rights of privacy, placing data protection firmly on the administrative law agenda, where it has not usually featured. This is a matter of the greatest importance at a time when the EU is building giant data banks and making them widely accessible across Member States and, perhaps even less wisely, to states and bodies outside the European Union. It is good too to see that the authors go beyond the Community (or First Pillar) administrative agencies to deal with the accountability of Council agencies and more specifically Europol and Eurojust. If administrative law is about control—and most public lawyers agree that it is—then it must be significant that the competence of the Community Courts in matters of justice and home affairs remains attenuated. As administrative lawyers, we are right to be suspicious in matters of justice and home affairs; they are the more dangerous because they are less well -controlled.

To end on a curmudgeonly note, as a British administrative lawyer, born and bred in a common law system, my only dissent from the priorities of my continental colleagues concerns what they call the 'old issue' of a European code of administrative procedures. In recent years, as the practice of harmonisation has evolved through soft law methods and experiments with the Open Method of Coordination, I have been happy to see this hoary old chestnut fall from the agenda, to be replaced by a call from the private lawyers for a European codification of contract law. (Academics must have something to do). I have much sympathy with the work of the European Ombudsman in developing principles of good administration, in seeing them published and in monitoring their implementation. We need, however, to bear in mind the arguments of those who, like Giandomenico Majone, see the legitimacy of the European project as deriving from 'output legitimacy'. To put this differently, we need to consider whether respect does not depend rather on effective policy-making than on institution-building and constitution-drafting. Surely the lawmaking processes and governance of the European Union are sufficiently sclerotic without a code of administrative procedures as a further target for attack by multinational enterprises and their skilful in-house lawyers?

Professor Carol Harlow
March 2007

Preface and Acknowledgements

The aim of this book is to analyse current problems in European administrative law, many of which are reflected in the on-going reform process of the European Treaties. The Treaty establishing a Constitution for Europe has served as the point of reference for this study. The provisions of the Treaty contain the seeds of future projections of European administrative law which are currently scattered throughout the Community legal system—under a particular policy area or as an annex to the rules of the common market—or through the general principles of Community law elaborated by the Court of Justice of the European Communities. Due to the paralysis of the ratification process, the Brussels European Council of June 2007 agreed to convene an Intergovernmental Conference (IGC) to draft a Treaty of Reform of the existing Treaties. According to the Conclusions of the Presidency (CONCL 2, 11177/07, Brussels, 23 June 2007) the IGC must draw up a Reform Treaty that will introduce into the existing Treaties the innovations resulting from the 2004 IGC, which drafted the Constitutional Treaty. It is expected that the Guidelines to the Constitutional Treaty will provide a blueprint for the drafters of the Reform Treaty. For instance, the mandate contained in the Conclusions of the Presidency declares that the terms 'law' and 'framework law' will be abandoned in the new Reform Treaty, but the IGC will maintain the distinction between what is legislative and what is not and the consequences thereof; the European Charter of Fundamental Rights will have binding force; and the current Third Pillar matters (police and judicial cooperation in criminal matters) will be put into the Title on the Area of freedom, security and justice in the modified EC, such that the competence of the Community Courts will be extended to these sensitive matters. These examples highlight the main questions faced by European administrative law today and which are analysed in this book.

The book is divided into five chapters. Chapters 1, 2 and 5 were written by Eva Nieto Garrido, while Isaac Martín Delgado wrote Chapters 3 and 4.

The first chapter analyses the complexity surrounding the sources of law of the European Union, the problems relating to the different effects of these sources depending on their material scope (the first or the second and third pillars), and the hierarchy of norms established by the Constitutional Treaty as a way of simplifying the current sources. The second chapter presents a study on the impact of the Charter of Fundamental Rights of the European Union on the Community administration were it to have binding force, specifically with regard to the right to good administration, access to documents and the protection of personal data. It analyses whether the binding effects of those rights, once the Charter enters into force, will create new obligations for the Community administration or whether it will simply facilitate enforcement of the rights by making them more visible for citizens of the Union. The same approach is adopted in the third chapter, this time with respect to national administrations; that is, the extent to which the fundamental rights (and especially the rights to good administration, access to documents and protection of personal data) are applicable to acts of the administrations of the Member States. To this end, it is useful to provide a theory of what it means by implementing Union Law based on the case law of the Court of Justice of the European Communities and the provisions of Community law. The fourth chapter argues for the need to create a law on common administrative procedure, as a catalogue of basic rules aimed at the citizens and Member States of the Union, which is necessary given the evolution of European administrative law and the multiple procedures used in Community administration. The introduction of a legal basis for the adoption of a future European law on common administrative procedure in the Constitutional Treaty, and the express recognition of the right to good administration, are the arguments used in this analysis. The fifth and final chapter deals with the reform of the limited jurisdiction of the Court of Justice in sensitive areas from the point of view of human rights, such as those contained in the third pillar (asylum, visas and immigration, and judicial co-operation in civil matters), as well as the problems that this limitation implies for the possibility of challenging decisions adopted by organs of the Union such as Europol and Eurojust. Moreover, it focuses specifically on the necessary reform of the rule on the standing of individuals before the Court of First Instance, especially where a general provision which does not require action at the national level in order to give it effect is challenged.

The authors wish to express their gratitude to all those who helped to make this book possible. From an institutional point of view, we wish to thank the European University Institute, especially the Robert Schuman Centre for Advanced Studies where, as a Jean Monnet fellow and a member of the European Forum on Constitutionalism in Europe, Eva Nieto had the opportunity to attend various seminars which enriched this work.[1] At the same time, the University of Castilla-La Mancha also deserves particular mention for always supporting our projects, such as the workshops on the Constitutional Treaty and Community Administrative Law, which were generously funded in collaboration with the Spanish Centre for Political and Constitutional Studies.[2] Furthermore, the Centre for European Studies[3] and the people associated with it were invaluable during the research stage of the book. On a personal level, we would like to express our gratitude to Professor Luis Ortega Álvarez, who is a constant source of encouragement; to Professors Bruno de Witte and Paul Craig, who made many helpful suggestions with regard to this book; to Dr Clemens Ladenburger, whose thoughts as a member of the Secretariat of the European Convention were decisive for the development of the

[1] Eva Nieto Garrido was Jean Monnet Fellow at the EUI in 2003–4.

[2] Research Project of the Ministry of Education, Science and Technology entitled *Una evolución sustancial de la política ambiental europea, de los principios a la armonización de los procedimientos* (SEJ2005-09249), of which this Project forms a part.

[3] Isaac Martín Delgado was a researcher in the Centre for European Studies of the University of Castilla-La Mancha from 1998 to 2000 and is also an active collaborator in its activities.

study; to Professor José Luis Piñar Mañas, for his help in drafting the section on the protection of personal data; to Professor Luis María Díez-Picazo for his constant support; to Professor Carol Harlow, who encourage us to publish this work and wrote the Foreword; and to Gordon Anthony, Rachael Craufurd-Smith and Eva Moreno who helped us at different stages of the project.

We would also like to thank Cormac Mac Amhlaigh for his help with language, and Richard Hart and Hart Publishing for publishing the book.

These pages are dedicated to our families, for their efforts and the sacrifices they made while we were writing the book.

Contents

Abbreviations

AG	Advocate General
Art	Article
CFI	Court of First Instance
CFSP	Common Foreign and Security Policy
CIS	Customs Information System
CML Rev	*Common Market Law Review*
CONV	Convention
EC	European Community
ECHR	European Convention on Human Rights
ECJ	European Court of Justice
EEC	European Economic Community
ELJ	*European Law Journal*
EL Rev	*European Law Review*
EU	European Union
GC	Grand Chamber
IGC	Intergovernmental Conference
JHA	Justice and Home Affairs
MLR	*Modern Law Review*
NGO	Non Governmental Organisation
NYU	New York University
OHIM	Office for Harmonisation in the Internal Market
OJ	Official Journal of the European Union
OJLS	*Oxford Journal of Legal Studies*
para	paragraph
QMV	Qualify Majority Voting
RSCAS	Robert Schuman Centre for Advanced Studies
SEA	Single European Act
SIS	Schengen Information System
TEU	Treaty on European Union
ToA	Treaty of Amsterdam
UPA	Unión de Pequeños Agricultores

1

Legislative Powers and Normative Instruments

I. INTRODUCTION

This chapter focuses on the modifications introduced by the Constitutional Treaty in relation to the rule-making powers and normative instruments of the European Union. It focuses on the simplification of its normative instruments, analysing the new legal instruments, in particular the various types of secondary law, the consequences of choosing primary or secondary law, and some problems which the Constitutional Treaty leaves unresolved.

The Conclusions of the Presidency of the Council of the European Union (CONCL 2, 11177/07, Brussels, 23 June 2007, p 22) declared that the denominations 'law' and 'framework law' will be abandoned in the new Treaty of reform. Nonetheless, the IGC that will draw up the new draft will maintain the distinction between what is legislative and what is not and the consequences thereof. To that end, three Articles will be introduced after Article 249 EC on, respectively, acts which are adopted in accordance with legislative procedure, delegated acts and implementing acts. Thus, this Chapter may provide useful insights for the Treaties reform process.The principles of transparency and democratic participation led to the introduction of the principle of hierarchy of norms within the EU's legal system, with a clear division between legislative and executive instruments. This 'process of simplification' is part of the transformation that European administrative law is experiencing, similar to that undergone in the United States in the 1960s.

The chapter is divided into the following sections: firstly, this introduction; secondly, a section that gives a brief description of the current EU legal system and its problems. The third section shows the link between the transformation of the legal system in the Constitutional Treaty and the transformation of European administrative law. The fourth section provides an analysis of normative instruments, especially secondary law and its scope and functions. The fifth section analyses a type of European regulation that is not mentioned expressly in the provision of the Constitutional Treaty that establishes the sources of law. Finally, the sixth section deals with some consequences and problems that derive from the clear-cut division between legislative and non-legislative instruments introduced into the EU's legal system by the Constitutional Treaty.

II. LEGISLATIVE POWERS AND NORMATIVE INSTRUMENTS UNDER THE CURRENT TREATIES

This section analyses two elements of the Union's normative system: the legislative powers and the normative instruments envisaged under the current Treaties. Its aim is to highlight their deficiencies and show how the Constitutional Treaty attempts to correct them.

As regards rule-making powers, the Community must act within the limits of the powers conferred on it by the Treaties. It needs a legal basis established by the Treaties for every legal act it adopts. The aim of the legal basis requirement is to guarantee the distribution of power established by the Treaties among EU institutions.[1] The legal basis indicates the author and, sometimes, the procedure to be used for adopting a normative act. However, in most cases the legal basis does not indicate the normative instruments that should be used.

With respect to the distribution of power among the institutions, the Treaties do not establish a system of separation of powers, the judicial power being the only power that resides in one body.[2] Legislative power is shared among the Council, the European Parliament (as co-legislator in some cases or with a consultative role in others) and the Commission, that has the exclusive prerogative of legislative initiative. The distribution of competences among these rule-making powers is based on the principle of balance of powers, which guarantees the participation of all the institutional actors in the legislative process.[3] The legitimacy of the Union's rule-making powers has been debated for a long time, and in this respect the Commission is in the weakest position as compared with the other institutions.[4] Most authors justified the Commission's right of initiative by saying that this institution represents the Community interest in the legislative process[5] and that this arrangement avoids biased initiatives emanating from Member State self-interest. It does not enhance the Commission's position because the executive

[1] Díez-Picazo (2005) 181. On the concept of legal basis see *ibid*, 173–6. See also Case C-45/86 *Commission v Council* [1987] ECR 1493; Case C-158/80 *Rewe-Handelsgesellschaft Nord mbH et Rewe-Markt Steffen v Hauptzollamt Kiel* [1981] ECR 01805; Case C-300/89 *Commission v Council* [1991] ECR I-02867; Case C-271/94 *European Parliament v Council* [1996] ECR I-01689; Case C-269/97 *Commission v Council* [2000] ECR I-02257; Case C-491/01 *British American Tobacco* [2002] ECR I-11453, on the possible use of two legal bases.

[2] With regard to the institutions, the basic principle is that of the balance of powers and not the separation of powers. The observance of the principle of balance of powers means that 'each of the institutions must exercise its powers with due regard for the powers of the other institutions. It also requires that it should be possible to penalize any breach of that rule which may occur': Case C-70/88 *European Parliament v Council* [1990] ECR 1-02041, para 21.

[3] On the principle of balance of powers see Lenaerts and Verhoeven (2002) 35–49. For an argument demanding wider participation in the legislative process, see Smismans (2002). On the principle as a constitutional foundational principle of the Union, see Jacobs (2004).

[4] This forms part of a wider debate on the democratic legitimacy of the Union, which is not the focus of this book. On the democratic deficit of the Union see Bellamy and Castiglione (2000).

[5] See Craig (1998) 48–49; Lenaerts and Verhoeven (2002) 70–71.

power, including the power to dictate implementing rules, is determined on a case-by-case basis during the legislative process.[6]

Furthermore, the EC does not distinguish between the power to adopt general implementing rules for legislative acts and the power to enforce laws through implementing acts. Both cases are covered by the term 'implementation'.[7] The use of implementing acts that reflect basic policy choices have sparked criticism due to a lack of democratic legitimacy.[8] Although the Constitutional Treaty makes a clear-cut distinction between legislation and implementing acts, the criterion used to determine the adoption of a legislative act is not clear. Sometimes it seems that the measure should contain basic policy choices but, at other times, it seems that the measure may affect fundamental rights.

To sum up, the variety and complexity of the current decision making-processes, due in part to the legal basis requirement, has been criticised for its lack of democratic pedigree and its unsuitability in the context of a growing Union.[9] Some authors have justified this complexity by reference to the originality of the integration system and the lack of pre-existing models.[10] Nonetheless, although the decision-making processes have evolved to give an increasingly important role to the European Parliament, their democratisation and simplification would require the establishment of a legislative procedure for the adoption of normative acts of a legislative nature (primary law). Currently, there are not one but several basic legislative procedures, and the adoption of a particular procedure is not based on any systemic logic but seems to depend on diplomatic negotiation during the successive reforms of the Treaties. Within the First Pillar, nine procedures have been identified as

[6] According to Art 202 EC, the Council delegates power to the Commission to implement rules laid down by the Council, but it may also reserve the right to exercise implementing powers itself in specific cases. The Commission has not hidden its wish to eliminate the system of scrutinising its implementing activities, especially the Regulatory Committee's activities. The committee procedure is considered to be unnecessarily cumbersome and far from being a simplifying measure to enable the Council to confer third-level legislation functions on the Commission. During 2000, 1,742 acts were referred to the committees. On the current scrutiny requirement see *The Legal Instruments: Present System*, CONV 162/02, 13 June 2002, 15.

The Regulatory Committee is considered by the Commission to be an inconvenient interference in its implementing powers, a vision shared by the European Parliament, which considers the system to be an undue restriction on the Commission's regulatory powers and a system which reduces the Parliament's role in monitoring the implementing acts of the legislative measures adopted by the co-decision procedure. See Dehousse (2002) 212–13.

The Council Decision laying down the procedures for the exercise of implementing powers conferred on the Commission, commonly known as Comitology, establishes four committees which scrutinise the measures proposed by the Commission depending on its nature (Management Committee, Regulatory Committee, Regulatory Procedure with Scrutiny Committee or Advisory Committee). The Constitutional Treaty's choice of the co-decision procedure as the ordinary legislative procedure should end the activities of the Regulatory Committee and the Regulatory Procedure with Scrutiny Committee. According to the Constitutional Treaty, the European law or framework law that will authorise delegation to the Commission will establish the mechanism of control to be used by the Council and the Parliament to monitor the execution of such delegation (Art I-36(2)).

[7] Arts 202 and 211 EC covered both cases under the term 'implementation'.

[8] Lenaerts and Desomer (2003) 108.

[9] Díez-Picazo (2002) 181.

[10] Bieber and Salomé (1996) 917–919 and 926–927.

depending on the system of voting in the Council and participation by Parliament.[11] This diversity is seen as an obstacle to the transparency that is so desirable in the legislative process, which becomes obscure for citizens and even for the majority of specialists. To avoid this, Working Group IX proposed a simplification of the legislative procedure, adopting the co-decision procedure as the ordinary legislative procedure with public sessions satisfying the principle of transparency in European Governance.[12] The choice of this procedure as the ordinary legislative procedure must be welcomed, while bearing in mind the fact that it has many exceptions and that there will be areas in which it is not used (competition law, state aid, etc).[13]

With respect to normative instruments, Article 249 of the EC contains the classic list of the Community's legal instruments (regulations, directives, decisions, recommendations and opinions), describing their scope and normative force or judicial enforceability. But this provision does not give us any indication of the author of the measure[14] or of the procedure that should be used to adopt it. Moreover, Article 249 does not say anything about the nature of the measure (executive or legislative). In the absence of any provision explicitly establishing a hierarchy between normative instruments, the order of priority among them should be provided for by the foundational regulation or directive of a Community policy in a particular area. Other norms may be made pursuant to this policy, although in developing the policy the same legal instrument may be used.[15]

Numerous acts of secondary legislation have been added to the original classification in Article 249 of the EC, sometimes using the same terms provided for in Article 249 EC but with different characteristics (see below). At other times, some instruments of doubtful legal nature have gained acceptance through use.[16] Such acts of secondary legislation come not only from the provisions of the TEU on CFSP and JHA.[17] 'Guidelines' on economic co-ordination or employment policy and the 'framework programme' in the environment field have also been added to the list of Article 249, to mention just two types. Moreover, other instruments with different

[11] Qualified majority with co-decision, qualified majority with co-operation (even if residual), qualified majority with assent, qualified majority and straight opinion, qualified majority without involvement by the Parliament, unanimity with codecision, unanimity with assent, unanimity with straight opinion, and unanimity without participation by the Parliament (CONV 162/02, n 6, 11). The Final Report on Simplification mentioned 30 procedures in general (taking into account the three pillars) that could be reduced to 5, on which the Group IX works for making the proposals to the Convention (Final Report of Working Group IX on Simplification, CONV 424/02, 29 November 2002, pp 13–14).

[12] In the Report, the Working Group proposed that some modifications be introduced to the co-decision procedure prior to adoption as the ordinary legislative procedure: CONV 424/02, *ibid*, pp 14–15.

[13] See section V below.

[14] The author could be the Council acting alone, the Council and the European Parliament acting together, the Commission, etc.

[15] See Craig and de Búrca (2003) 112.

[16] Such as guidelines, codes of conduct or statements by the Council and the Presidency of the Union. See CONV 162/02 (n 6) 4.

[17] Arts 12 and 34 of the TEU mention principles and general guidelines, common strategies, joint actions, common positions, framework decisions, decisions and conventions. Furthermore, Art 17 of the same Treaty mentions 'decisions' with different meaning to those of Art 249 EC, and other instruments such as guidelines, codes of conduct and statements by the Council and the Presidency of the Union have been accepted.

legal value have been developed, such as inter-institutional agreements, conclusions, resolutions, Council resolutions and Council conclusions, statements by the Member States and declarations attached to certain legal acts by the institutions. The lack of definition of the normative scope and judicial enforceability of some of these instruments in the Treaties has been said to have been caused by a lack of connection between the choice of legal instrument and the intensity of action undertaken by the Union. This situation has contributed to the perceived lack of transparency and legal certainty in the functioning of the Union.[18]

Even within the acts listed by Article 249 it is interesting to note how their meaning and effects are not always the same. One of the most interesting examples is the decision. Article 249 states that a decision is 'binding in its entirety upon those to whom it is addressed'. However, in practice there are decisions without addressees, of normative character and general scope, approved according to the procedure established by Article 251 of the EC and published in the Official Journal, such as the Comitology Decision,[19] the Decision on Resources of the Community[20] and the Decision on the Socrates Programme.[21] Something similar has occurred with regulations. According to Article 249 of the EC, 'a regulation shall have general application. It shall be binding in its entirety and directly applicable in all Member States'. However, in the agricultural sphere, for instance, there are regulations that affect only a very small group of people and are operative for only a short period of time.[22]

The use of regulations as executive or administrative acts and the use of decisions as a norm of general scope without an addressee has two consequences: first, when a regulation is used as an executive act, its content is usually too detailed, making the procedure for its adoption slower and its provisions less flexible in terms of adapting to future changes in the economic sector. Secondly, its provisions are directly applicable to Member States and individuals, and therefore their executive measures are immunised against challenges from individuals who are not directly and individually concerned by the measure, according to the case law of the ECJ.[23]

To conclude, when the Working Group began its analysis, it saw a normative system in which, on the one hand, there were no links between the author of the measure and its procedure of adoption and, on the other, there were no links between the author, the procedure of its adoption and the nature of the measure (legislative, normative or executive). Whereas the diversity of procedures and legal instruments could have been perceived at the beginning as introducing flexibility and autonomy into the everyday workings of the Union, they are now perceived as factors causing extreme complexity and lack of transparency, legal certainty and

18 Lenaerts and Desomer (2003) 108.

19 Council Decision 99/468/EC of 28 June, laying down the procedures for the exercise of implementing powers conferred on the Commission [1999] OJ L184/23. This was modified by Decision 2006/512/EC of 17 July 2006 [2006] OJ L200/11.

20 Council Decision 2000/597/EC (Euratom) of 29 September 2000, on the system of the European Communities' own resources [2000] OJ L253/42.

21 European Parliament and Council Decision 819/95/EC of 14 March 1995, establishing the Community action programme 'Socrates' [1995] OJ L87/10.

22 See references in ch 5.

23 See ch 5.

democratic legitimacy in the decision-making process. The need to simplify and democratise the Union's normative system led the Working Group to introduce the principle of hierarchy of norms, linking the form of the act and its scope with the procedure for its adoption and establishing a clear distinction between legislative and implementing acts. Although there were some areas in which Member States did not want to share their normative power with the European Parliament, this attempt at rationalisation should facilitate the enforcement of the principles of subsidiarity and proportionality by the institutions in their everyday activities.

III. SIMPLIFICATION OF THE UNION'S NORMATIVE INSTRUMENTS AND THE TRANSFORMATION OF EUROPEAN ADMINISTRATIVE LAW

The debate on the introduction of the principle of hierarchy of norms within the normative system of the Union has arisen on several occasions. Article 202 of the EC was introduced by the SEA for the purpose of relieving the legislator of excessively technical and detailed matters. However, currently Community legislation is still considered to be too technical and too detailed. In different Intergovernmental Conferences (IGCs) the introduction of a principle of hierarchy of norms was proposed that would allow the legislator to focus on the adoption of primary law (second-level rules under the Treaties), leaving the details and technical issues to secondary law (third-level rules). For instance, at the Maastricht IGC, Italy and the Commission proposed the introduction of a hierarchy of norms, with instruments classified as 'law' being those adopted by the European Parliament and the Council at the top of the hierarchy and leaving the adoption of regulations and decisions for its implementation to the Commission.[24] On that occasion the co-decision procedure was introduced into the Treaty on European Union, whereas the introduction of a hierarchy of norms was postponed.

The debate on the simplification and rationalisation of the normative system has been on the Commission's agenda for years, and recently it received support from the European Council.[25] It was accepted that the debate on the normative system should be included in a broader debate on European governance.[26]

Prior to the White Paper on European Governance, the Inter-Institutional Declaration of 1993 explicitly linked the concepts of democracy, transparency and subsidiarity within the European Community.[27] In this Declaration the institutions

[24] CONV 162/02 (n 6) 14.

[25] The European Council, in the framework of the Lisbon process, called on the European institutions and the Member States to establish a strategy to simplify the regulatory environment, including the performance of public administration, at both the national and the Community level (CONV 162/02 (n 6) 16). On this debate see Bieber and Amarelle (2000).

[26] Dehousse (2002).

[27] Inter-Institutional Declaration on democracy, transparency and subsidiarity adopted by the Council, the Parliament and the Commission on 25 October 1993 [1993] OJ C329/132.

committed themselves to increasing transparency in their daily operations.[28] For instance, the European Parliament adopted an internal regulation confirming the public character of its sessions, the Council adopted measures to open up some of its debates and give access to its archives, and the Commission guaranteed better public access to its documents.[29]

The institutional reports produced for the 1996 IGC dealt again with improving efficiency, democracy and transparency with a view to making the Union more transparent and bringing it closer to its citizens.[30] Transparency was understood in five different ways:[31] firstly, making access to information held by the institutions easier; secondly, provision of information to experts and to society in general before any substantial legislative proposal is adopted; thirdly, provision of information to national parliaments with enough time to allow them to make comments; the fourth dealt with opening up the workings of Community institutions, in particular the Council and the Commission; and, finally, the fifth was simplification of EC law itself with the aim of rendering it more accessible.

In spite of institutional proposals to improve the efficiency, democracy and transparency of the Union, the Irish 'no' in the referendum on the Nice Treaty highlighted the fact that many people had lost confidence in the face of a complex and poorly understood system of delivering policies at European Union level. That and the decreasing turnout at European Parliament elections made the reform of European Governance one of the four strategic aims of the Commission at the beginning of 2000.[32] The White Paper on European Governance proposed the opening up of the policy-making process with the aim of getting more people and organisations involved in 'shaping and delivering EU policy'.[33] The changes proposed by the White Paper were based on five principles: openness, participation, accountability, effectiveness and coherence (policies and action must be coherent and easily understood). The idea was that the application of these five principles would reinforce the principles of proportionality and subsidiarity.[34] The guidelines of the reform proposed by the White Paper were based on the five principles mentioned above. These guidelines were, first, to encourage more involvement on the part of social and institutional (national, regional and local) actors in shaping and implementing EU policy, and secondly, to improve policies, regulation and delivery to society. The third was to increase the EU's contribution to global governance, and the fourth, to refocus policies and institutions (revitalising the Community method) within a clearer political project for the Union.

[28] Transparency is understood as a way of bringing democracy into European governance. In the words of Curtin (1998), 'information and accessibility to information is the currency of democracy' in our days (p 107).

[29] *Ibid*, 133–4.

[30] Craig (1998) 50.

[31] *Ibid.*

[32] White Paper on European Governance, COM (2001) 428 final, 25 July, pp 1–2 and 6.

[33] *Ibid*, 2.

[34] According to the White Paper, before launching an initiative, it is essential to check systematically whether the action is necessary, whether the European level is the most appropriate and whether the measure chosen is proportionate to those objectives: *ibid*, 9–10.

As regards the EU's normative system, the White Paper requested that it be simplified and rationalised. The main criticisms were the increased complexity of the EU's legislation and its unnecessary level of detail, due to the reluctance of the Council and the European Parliament to leave more power to the Commission to execute policies.[35] Furthermore, the level of detail of EU legislation makes it more difficult to adapt quickly to technical or market changes, thereby impeding the effectiveness of the legislation. Therefore the Commission's proposal on the EU legislation reform emphasises the need to improve the quality, effectiveness and simplicity of the regulatory act, avoiding the opacity of the expert committees' system and the attendant lack of information with respect to how they work.[36]

In the opinion of the author, the proposals set out in the White Paper on European Governance, which are at the root of the modification of European administrative law introduced by the Constitutional Treaty, reveal a process similar to that described by those who have studied the transformation of American rule-making power in the 1960s and 1970s.[37] Shapiro asserted, 'this transformation was triggered by the internal dynamics of administrative law, with a wave of anti-technocratic and pro-democratic sentiment'.[38]

In the American system, the traditional model of administrative law—where agencies acted in theory as transmission belts for implementing legislative directives in particular cases—was substituted by the model of interest representation.[39] The traditional model failed with respect to the agencies' statutes, which did not effectively dictate agency action in cases where it was often broad and non-specific. Agency discretion was seen as favourable to organised interest (to the industry or client firms). Moreover, the crisis with the traditional model of administrative law occurred at a time when agency action was expanding to new areas in which the agencies traditionally do not act, such as health care and education. Judicial will for controlling agency action implied the expansion of judicial review going beyond reviewing the illegal administrative action. With the aim of guaranteeing the participation and considering the wishes of all interested parties in the decision-making process by the agency, judges made the rules regarding the standing of individuals wider when challenging agencies' decisions and recognised the participation rights of all interested parties in the decision-making process.[40] The rule-making process of American agencies had to be perfect, pluralist, democratic, transparent and widely participative.[41] Judges and lawyers acted together to bring agency discretion as a rule-maker within a sort of procedural and substantive norm. The extremely aggressive judicial review process in the US provoked agencies to spend enormous amounts of time and resources on rule-making in order to avoid

[35] *Ibid*, 18.

[36] The White Paper on European Governance mentions seven factors for achieving this, including a clear-cut distinction between legislation and implementation measures, n 32 (pp 20–21).

[37] On this topic see Stewart (1975).

[38] Shapiro (2002b) 15.

[39] See RB Stewart 'The Reformation of American Administrative Law' (1995) 1675–756.

[40] *Ibid*, 1748.

[41] *Ibid*.

the risk of judicial reversals. The current criticism of the pluralist transformation of American administrative law highlights the fact that the rule-making process takes too long and costs too much and, therefore, agencies are not making the rules they need.[42] According to Shapiro, 'both transparency and participation are reduced as agencies move to *sub rosa* policy-making to avoid the costs of rule-making'.[43]

As we have seen, the principles of democracy, transparency and participation are included in every document on European governance. Observance of these principles is required not only in the rule-making process but also in all decision-making processes. The introduction of these principles is driving the transformation of European administrative law. This transformation comes not only from the institutional sphere; the European courts are helping with the transformation process. For instance, they are deriving from Member States' legal traditions a duty of good administration or due diligence on the part of the Commission and the obligation to provide reasons.[44] Nonetheless, European judicial review is far from being as aggressive as the American version. The different foundation of the European judicial system, being based mostly on a civil law tradition, and the negative consequences experienced within the American system may explain this self-restraint.

In spite of the European courts' actions, the process of transforming European administrative law is mainly a top-down process, with the political impulse coming from the institutions in order to gain citizens' support for the European project. The Constitutional Treaty contributes to this process, following the guidelines proposed by the White Paper on European Governance. The simplification of the Union's legal instruments is just one element of this wider process in which the principles of democracy, transparency, participation and accountability are the crucial elements.[45]

IV. NEW NORMATIVE INSTRUMENTS UNDER THE CONSTITUTIONAL TREATY

EU legislation has been criticised for its complexity and its inability to respond to technical or market changes, damaging the effectiveness of the Union's policies. One reason explaining the degree of detail and technicality of Union legislation is the lack of a level of secondary law under that of regulations and directives. The Treaties do not contain a principle relating to the hierarchy of norms and, therefore, there are no second level rules. The Treaty on European Union modified the EC, authorising the Council to delegate powers to the Commission in order to implement rules laid down by the Council.[46] The Council imposed a duty on the Commission to pass the implementing measure through one of the committees

42 For more detailed criticism of the model of interest representation see Stewart, *ibid*, 1770–81.

43 Shapiro (2002b) 18.

44 See Nehl (1999) 1; see also Lenaerts and Corthautm (2004), vol 1, 43–63.

45 On these principles and EU governance see, *inter alia*, Arnull and Wincott (2002); Harlow (2002).

46 EC, Arts 202 and 211.

created by the Comitology Decision.[47] Since the Comitology system's inception, it has been considered unsatisfactory by various actors.[48] With respect to the procedure before the Regulatory Committee, the Commission considers it too long and complex. The European Parliament does not like it either. In spite of the European Parliament's role as co-legislator together with the Council, the European Parliament does not have control over the implementing measures adopted by the Commission through the Regulatory Committee. Decision 2006/512/EC introduced the regulatory procedure, in which the European Parliament increases its capacity for control of measures of general scope designed to amend non-essential elements of a basic instrument, adopted in accordance with the procedure referred to in Article 251 of the EC, by deleting some of those elements or by supplementing the instruments by adding new non-essential elements.[49]

The Comitology system has been criticised for its lack of transparency.[50] The goal of making the Union more transparent and bringing it closer to its citizens was incompatible with both very technical legislation, and with a legal system in which implementing measures are adopted by obscure committees and in which there is no clear procedure for adopting basic policy choices. When Working Group IX received the mandate on the simplification of the Union's legal instruments, it defined its aims in the following terms: to simplify means 'to make comprehensible, but also to provide a guarantee that acts with the same legal/political force have the same foundation in terms of democratic legitimacy'.[51] Democratic legitimacy in a Union founded by States and peoples was understood by Working Group IX as legislative acts coming from bodies that represent those States and peoples (mainly the Council and the Parliament). Taking into account the criticism of the current legal system and the principle of democratic legitimacy of the Union, the Working Group decided to review the legislative procedures with the aim of ensuring that 'acts which have the same nature and the same legal effect . . . [are] produced by the same democratic procedure'.[52]

The simplification process was dictated by this idea and by the introduction of the principle of hierarchy of norms. The principle of hierarchy of norms would enable, first, a clear-cut distinction to be made between legislative and implementing measures, preserving the legislation for basic policy choices and areas in which fundamental rights are at stake. Secondly, the legislators may thus focus on the essential elements of a policy, leaving the details and technicalities to secondary norms. The legislative procedure would take less time and the legislative act would be more understandable by the people.

In spite of these good intentions, the normative instruments adopted by Working Group IX and eventually by the Constitutional Treaty reveal a complicated system

[47] See n 19. On the Committees see Vos (1999), (1997); Andenas and Türk (2000); Craig (2006) 99–113.

[48] See n 6 . [49] See n 19.

[50] CONV 162/02 (n 6) 3 and 16.

[51] CONV 424/02 (n 11) 2. On the drafting history of the Constitutional Treaty on legal instruments see Bering Liisberg (2006) 11–26.

[52] *Ibid.*

in which there are three levels of acts: legislative, delegated and implementing acts. They have various roles within the system that are only easy to describe in theory. Legislative acts will be adopted on the basis of the Treaty and contain the essential elements of an area, whereas delegated acts flesh out the detail or amend certain elements of a legislative act under the authorisation of the legislator.[53] Implementing acts implement legislative, delegated acts and acts provided for in the Constitutional Treaty itself.[54]

Before explaining the types of acts contained within these three levels and their roles, two ideas should be borne in mind. The first is that the current EC says nothing about the nature of regulations and directives, so a regulation or directive may have a legislative or executive nature depending on the legislator's choice. The Working Group decided to maintain this feature in the Constitutional Treaty, and therefore it is possible to find the concept of the directive in legislative[55] and delegated acts.[56] The second idea is that the Working Group introduced into the Union's legal system three levels of normative acts that reflected the sources of law of some Member States. For instance, in the Spanish legal system there are primary laws that regulate the essential elements of a matter, primary laws that authorise the Government to codify legislation in a field or which establish the basis of a regulation and authorise the government to produce an articulate text, and, finally, regulations, which are not legislative acts but develop the elements of the law establishing the details and technicalities.[57] Nonetheless, the three levels of normative acts established by the Constitutional Treaty do not correspond exactly with the Spanish legal instruments described here. The non-legislative nature of delegated acts and the unclear role of implementing acts of the Union (in which, according to the principle of subsidiarity, the implementation function usually corresponds to the Member States) does not allow us to draw parallels.

To understand the three levels of norms introduced by the Constitutional Treaty, the following sections will explain their nature, scope and adoption procedure.

1. Legislative Level: European Law and Framework Law

The European law has taken the concept of primary law from the Member States. It is a legislative act of general application, binding in its entirety and directly applicable in all Member States.[58] The concept of European law is the same as the concept of regulation of Article 249 EC but specifies its legislative nature.

[53] *Ibid*, 9.

[54] *Ibid*.

[55] European law or framework law.

[56] Art I-33(1)(4) of the Constitutional Treaty reads: '*A European regulation shall be a non-legislative act of general application for the implementation of legislative acts and of certain provisions of the Constitution.* It may either be binding in its entirety and directly applicable in all Member States, or be binding, as to the result to be achieved, upon each Member State to which it is addressed, but shall leave to the national authorities the choice of form and methods' (emphasis added).

[57] We are referring to the *Ley, Decretos Legislativos and Reglamentos ejecutivos.*

[58] Constitutional Treaty, Art I-33(1).

The European framework law will be the current directive with a legislative nature. According to the Constitutional Treaty, a European framework law will be 'a legislative act binding, as to the result to be achieved, upon each Member State to which it is addressed, but [which] shall leave to the national authorities the choice of form and methods'.[59]

European laws and framework laws will be adopted directly on the basis of the Constitutional Treaty and will contain the essential elements and the fundamental policy choices in a certain field.[60] It will be the legislator that determines the degree of detail of a legislative act included within the law, when regulation of the details is delegated, and the mechanisms of control on the fulfilment of such delegation.[61]

The legislative nature of the act will determine the procedure to be used. The procedure of co-decision with minimal modifications is, according to the Constitutional Treaty, the ordinary legislative procedure established by Article III-396. The establishment of a legislative procedure by which all legislative acts of the Union are adopted was, as we saw above, a condition *sine qua non* for introducing a democratic element to the simplification process.

2. Delegated European Regulations

Delegated European regulations are a new normative instrument described as a non-legislative act adopted by the Commission when authorised by a European law or framework law. In spite of their non-legislative nature, they may supplement or amend certain non-essential elements of the law or framework law.[62] This role is not compatible with the nature of the delegated European regulation for non-legislative acts. Formally they are not legislative acts but substantively they amend or supplement primary law. The question is why the Working Group decided to exclude them from the list of legislative acts. Taking into account the fact that the Group was creating a new normative instrument, it could have included the delegated act within primary law, as is the case in some Member States' legal systems.[63] It is submitted that the reason for this exclusion from the list of legislative acts relates to one of the guidelines that led the reform of the Union's normative instruments, according to which legislative acts should be approved by the same procedure (co-decision procedure) with the participation of both of the legislators

[59] *Ibid.*

[60] CONV 424/02 (n 11) 10.

[61] On the mechanisms of control, see below.

[62] Constitutional Treaty, Art I-36(1). The role of amended or supplemented European laws or framework laws has given rise to doubt as to their legislative nature. See Craig (2004), vol 1, 80 and Craig (2006) p 126

[63] In the Spanish legal system there is a category of primary law adopted by the Government under the authorisation of the Parliament called *Decretos legislativos* (Arts 82–85 Spanish Constitution of December 1978).

(the Council and the European Parliament). In order to respect this guideline, delegated European regulations could not be of a legislative nature since they must be approved by the Commission.

(a) On Requirements and Limits

The Constitutional Treaty requires, first, that the law or framework law explicitly provides for delegation to the Commission and, second, that the law expressly stipulates 'the objectives, content, scope and duration of the delegation'.[64]

Article I-36(2) lays down the limits of delegation, providing that delegated regulations cannot affect the essential elements of European laws or framework laws. The essential aspects of a given matter will be regulated exclusively by a European law or framework law. The jurisprudence of the ECJ has elucidated upon this concept with regard to the essential elements of particular subjects. For example, in the *Köster* case[65] the Court held that the basic elements of a particular area (the Common Agricultural Policy) should be adopted according to a specific procedure contained in Article 43 (now Article 37) of the EC.[66] The judgment showed that the basic elements of a subject were those which involved a specific policy decision.[67] Therefore, only the exercise of executive competence can be delegated.[68]

In the *Meroni* case, the ECJ held that the exercise of discretionary powers could not be delegated to bodies other than Community institutions.[69] The only competences that can be subject to delegation are specifically defined executive competences which are under the control of the Commission.[70]

Both requirements, as well as the abovementioned limits, can be subject to the control of the ECJ, which can annul the delegated regulation as being *ultra vires*.

(b) Mechanisms of Control

The second paragraph of Article I-36 of the Constitutional Treaty obliges the legislator to establish the conditions to which the delegation is subject.[71] Through delegated acts the legislator delegates one of its own powers and therefore it must be sure of being able to monitor its use. The Working Group considered the introduction of three possible mechanisms of control:[72]

[64] Constitutional Treaty, Art I-36, s 2 (1)(2).
[65] Case C-25/70 *Köster* [1970] ECR 01161.
[66] *Ibid*, para 6.
[67] Lenaerts and Desomer (2003) 110.
[68] Haibach (2000) 58.
[69] Case C-9/56 (para III(c) and (b)) and Case C-10/56 *Meroni* [1957–8] ECR 133. Also in para III(b), the Court found that competences which were not attributed to an institution under the Treaty could not be delegated by that institution.
[70] *Ibid.*
[71] Art I-36(2) establishes that for the adoption of these mechanisms of control, the European Parliament shall act by a majority of its component members and the Council by a qualified majority.
[72] CONV 424/02 (n 11) 11.

— The right to call-back, that is, 'the ability to retrieve the power to legislate on the subject' when the delegated powers are exceeded or when the issue is of major political significance or has major financial implications.
— A period of tacit approval, where after a certain period the delegated act will enter into force if the legislator has not expressed any objection.
— A sunset clause, by which the delegation is of limited duration and when the deadline has passed the delegation should be renewed by the legislator.

The Constitutional Treaty introduced the first and second mechanisms but not the sunset clause.[73] The proposed system of control has been criticised for being of questionable efficiency because it transforms what was originally *ex ante* control (exercised by the Member States through the Committees) to a possible *ex post* control, which must be established by European laws on a case-by-case basis.[74] It is difficult to compare the mechanisms of control of delegated acts established by the Constitutional Treaty with the current control established by the Comitology Decision, which is based on the delegation authorised by Article 202 of the EC. The creation of new normative instruments with the aim of simplifying EU legislation and reducing primary law to the essential elements of a given area should be accompanied by the introduction of simpler but effective mechanisms of control. Although the procedure of control before the Regulatory Committee, composed of representatives of the Member States and presided over by a representative of the Commission, would have been effective in terms of substantive results, it has been criticised for its opacity and lack of transparency.[75] Furthermore, the Commission wanted to have greater autonomy over this area and the European Parliament as co-legislator wanted to have the power to monitor the amendment or substitution of a European law and framework law. Indeed, Decision 2006/512/EC modified the Comitology Decision in order to increase the European Parliament's control over measures of general scope designed to amend the non-essential elements of instruments adopted in accordance with the procedure referred to in Article 251 of the EC. To this end, Decision 2006/512/EC established the regulatory procedure, in which the European Parliament has similar powers to those of the Council acting as a legislator.

The mechanisms of control of delegated acts in the Constitutional Treaty are not unknown in national legal systems. It is not possible to know in advance how effective they will be, but it is true that they are simpler and more transparent than the Regulatory Committee procedure and the Regulatory procedure. Eventually it will fall to the ECJ to declare void a delegated act which exceeds the objectives, content, scope and duration set out by the European law or framework law.

[73] The Praesidium decided to delete the last mechanism of proposed control because some members of the Convention considered that 'the sunset clause' could be a source of uncertainty and cause problems for legal security (CONV 724/02, Annex 2, 93).

[74] Craig (2004) describes the system of control established by Art I-36 of the Constitutional Treaty as 'difficult to monitor and enforce' (pp 82–83). According to him, neither the Council nor the Parliament may have the necessary know-how or time to define precisely the parameters that will have to be developed by the delegated regulations. Nor is it possible to predict whether the ECJ will develop a jurisprudence which will allow for the annulment of measures which exceed the limits of the delegation.

[75] CONV 162/02 (n 6) 3 and 16.

With respect to the argument that delegated and implementing acts may go against the principle of the balance of powers guaranteed by the current Treaties, it is submitted that the Constitutional Treaty contains elements that counterbalance the strengthening of the Commission's powers.[76] First of all, it must be borne in mind that the principle of the balance of powers is not a static but a dynamic principle, which can be altered by subsequent amendments to the Treaties.[77] The system of distribution of powers between the institutions of the Community established in the Treaties, as well as the competences and tasks assigned to each institution, can be subject to later amendment.

The key to maintaining the principle of balance of powers in the Constitutional Treaty, specifically with regard to the reform of the Commission contained in the Constitutional Treaty, can be found in the way in which the Parliament has been granted more control over the Commission.[78] The strengthening of the powers of the Parliament, which will become the ordinary co-legislator with the Council, and the control that can be exercised over the Commission might reinforce the principle of balance of powers in the Union legal system. The Constitutional Treaty gives the Parliament control over the European Commission in three essential ways:[79] (1) in nominating the President; (2) in the composition of the College; and (3) continued supervision for the duration of the term of the Commission. To sum up, the Constitutional Treaty tries to maintain the principle of institutional balance of powers, given that the strengthening of the Commission is counteracted by the European Parliament's increase in political control over the institution.

3. Implementing Acts

Implementing acts come third in the hierarchy of the Union's normative system. They are not of a legislative nature, either formally or substantively. They take the form of European implementing regulations or European implementing decisions[80] and, currently, they are the equivalent of those approved by the Commission according to Article 202 of the EC using the Committees' procedures.[81] However, the Constitutional Treaty introduces a novel test for conferring implementing powers to the Union. These implementing powers are usually within the

[76] Nieto Garrido (2004).

[77] On the principle of balance of powers see Lenaerts and Verhoeven (2002); Guillermin (1992); Lenaerts (1991); Pescatore (1978).

[78] Jacqué (2004) has pointed out the extent to which the history of the Community is marked by the progressive growth of the powers of the Parliament to the detriment of those of the two other institutions. An example is Decision 2006/512/EC, which amends the Comitology decision in order to increase the European Parliament's powers of control over the Commission's acts.

[79] Nieto Garrido (2004) 16–17.

[80] Constitutional Treaty, Art I-37(4).

[81] Art 202(3) EC reads: 'To ensure that the objectives set out in this Treaty are attained the Council shall, in accordance with the provisions of this Treaty: . . . confer on the Commission, in the acts which the Council adopts, powers for the implementation of the rules which the Council lays down. The Council may impose certain requirements in respect of the exercise of these powers. The Council may also reserve the right, in specific cases, to exercise directly implementing power itself.'

competence of the Member States.[82] But, according to the principle of subsidiarity, which is strengthened by the Constitutional Treaty, the Union will have implementing powers 'where uniform conditions for implementing legally binding Union acts are needed'.[83] These legally binding acts 'shall confer implementing powers on the Commission or, in duly justified specific cases and in the cases provided for in Article I-40, on the Council'.[84] The test for conferring implementing powers on the Commission imposes stricter requirements than the mandate to the Council contained in Article 202(3) of the EC. The strengthening of the subsidiarity principle and the introduction of a new normative instrument as the delegated act makes justifying the implementing power of the Commission more difficult. According to the new test included within Article I-37(2) of the Constitutional Treaty, the purpose of and justification for these implementing acts would be to establish uniform conditions of implementation for the obligatory acts of the Union, that is, of European laws and European framework laws as well as regulations and decisions of the Union. Taking into account the functions of these legal instruments, Paul Craig has questioned the utility of these implementing acts established by the Constitutional Treaty.[85] However, although it is recognised that it is not easy to determine the scope of these implementing acts, the following sections will provide some examples of their utility and will deal with their form and mechanisms of control as foreseen by the Constitutional Treaty.

(a) *Areas where Implementing Acts might be Used*

The Final Report of the Working Group on Simplification enables us to see how these acts will allow the Commission to introduce technical specifications that guarantee the effectiveness of Union legislation.[86] Along with the examples contained in the current Treaties, the Constitutional Treaty itself provides some further examples regarding the areas where implementing acts could be used,[87] such as in the area of

[82] The Constitutional Treaty, Art I-37 first para lays down the presumption as to Member States' implementing powers.

[83] Constitutional Treaty, Art I-37(2).

[84] *Ibid.*

[85] Craig analyses the possibility of implementing acts establishing uniform conditions of implementation in areas regulated by a European law, and arrives at the conclusion that, given the nature of the latter which are equivalent to current Community regulations, it should be for the Member States to set down the necessary conditions to ensure their effectiveness. In Craig's opinion it would be more apt to use implementing acts to implement European framework laws, which would be the equivalent of the current Community directives. However, in this case, the adoption of uniform implementing measures by the Commission would contravene the character of European framework laws, that is, the discretion granted to the Member States to choose the measures to adopt with the aim of achieving the objectives specified in the legal norm. These arguments, opposing the passing of implementing acts of the Commission for the establishment of uniform conditions for the implementation of European Laws and of European framework laws, have been used by Craig to question the utility of these legal instruments when the issue at hand deals with the implementation of European regulations described by Art I-33(1)(4) Constitutional Treaty. See Craig (2004) vol 1, 86–88.

[86] CONV 424/04 (n 11) 8.

[87] Apart from the aims contained in the Final Report of the Working Group (n 11), some commentators have identified in the EC provisions that would facilitate the Commission's use of the abovementioned legal instruments. Thus, for example, the adoption by the Council of acts for the

Freedom, Security and Justice. As for judicial co-operation in civil matters, a provision establishes that the Union might adopt measures 'for the approximation of the laws and regulations of Member States'.[88] These measures shall be adopted by European laws and framework laws for ensuring, among other things, the mutual recognition and enforcement among Member States of judgments and decisions in extrajudicial cases and the cross-border service of judicial and extrajudicial documents.[89] The Commission drafting a European law might observe a lack of uniform conditions among Member States which could undermine the purpose of the European law. Under these circumstances the law might delegate power to the Commission to adopt an implementing act. For instance, the Union has adopted regulations establishing uniform conditions among Member States for the effectiveness of its asylum policy: in order to apply the Dublin Convention,[90] it was necessary to establish the identity of applicants for asylum and of persons apprehended in relation to unlawfully crossing the external borders of the Union. To this end, it was necessary to set up a system to compare the fingerprints of applicants for asylum. That system is called Eurodac: a central unit established by the Commission which operates as a computerised central database of fingerprint data. A Council Regulation of 2000[91] created Eurodac and laid down rules as to how Member States shall collect and transmit fingerprint data (eg, they shall transmit to the Central Unit fingerprint data relating to all or at least the index fingers or the prints of all other fingers if indexes are missing[92]). The procedure as regards the collection, transmission and comparison of fingerprints is established by Council Regulation No 407/2002.[93] This Regulation sets up a definition of transmission and establishes rules governing the comparison and transmission of results. It also establishes rules on communication between Member States and the Central Unit in the Commission.

Under the Constitutional Treaty, some of these rules and definitions might be established by an implementing act in the form of European implementing regulations or European implementing decisions. In this way, a degree of flexibility is introduced into the European normative system: a Council regulation will not be necessary to establish or to modify technical details.

purposes of Arts 87 and 88 EC regarding aid granted by Member States referred to in Art 89 EC, will in future be regulated by the adoption of European laws and European framework laws through the ordinary legislative procedure, which, in turn, can authorise the Commission to adopt acts (delegated regulations) which may contain the legal basis for further Commission action in specific cases in the form of implementing acts. These and other examples can be seen in Lenaerts and Desomer (2003) annex, 128–31.

88 Constitutional Treaty, Art III-269(1).

89 *Ibid*, Art III-269(2)(a)(b).

90 Convention determining the State responsible for examining applications for asylum lodged in one of the Member States of the European Communities, signed in Dublin on 15 June 1990 (hereafter 'Dublin Convention') [1997] OJ C254/1.

91 Council Regulation (EC) No 2725/2000 of 11 December 2000, establishing Eurodac for the comparison of fingerprints for the effective application of the Dublin Convention [2000] OJ L316/1.

92 *Ibid*, Art 11(2).

93 Council Regulation (EC) No 407/2002 of 28 February 2002, laying down certain rules to implement Regulation (EC) No 2725/2000 concerning the establishment of 'Eurodac' for the comparison of fingerprints for the effective application of the Dublin Convention [2002] OJ L62/1.

(b) The Form and Mechanism for the Control of Implementing Acts

With regard to the form of these instruments, Article I-37(4) of the Constitutional Treaty provides that 'Union implementing acts shall take the form of European implementing regulations or European implementing decisions'.[94]

The Constitutional Treaty better reflects the real concept of decision, which is wider than that contained in Article 249 of the EC. Currently a European decision may be an administrative act with specific parties but can sometimes be of a normative character, such as the Comitology Decision.[95] A decision under the Constitutional Treaty may apply to specific parties or may apply more widely. The decision which does not apply to specific parties may be used in the area of CFSP,[96] and also to implement binding acts of the Union in that and in other areas.[97]

With regard to the mechanisms for control of implementing acts of the Union, the Constitutional Treaty refers to the establishment in a European law of norms and principles of control.[98] That European law will replace the current Comitology Decision of the Council Article I-37(3) of the Constitutional Treaty is consistent with the decision of the Convention on the Future of Europe to adopt the co-decision procedure as the ordinary legislative procedure: the Parliament will participate as a co-legislator, not only delegating power to the Commission to adopt delegated regulations and implementing acts, but also establishing in advance the mechanisms for control of these measures in a European law. The mechanism or system of control will depend on the political implications of implementing acts. The options will range from acts of a consultative committee which advises the Commission, to cases where the Council of Ministers itself exclusively implement the act (situations relating to the implementation of CFSP, amongst other things).[99]

V. A THIRD TYPE OF EUROPEAN REGULATION

The title of this section was suggested by the wording of Article I-34 of the Constitutional Treaty adopted by the Convention on the Future of Europe and submitted to the President of the European Council on 18 July 2003. This provision read:

> The Council of Ministers and the Commission shall adopt European regulations or European decisions in the cases referred to in Articles 35 [delegated regulations] and 36 [implementing acts] and in the cases specifically provided for in the Constitution . . .

[94] Decisions are defined in Art 249 EC as binding in their entirety upon those to whom they are addressed. The majority of decisions are executive acts, but it must not be forgotten that certain decisions have a normative character, such as the Comitology decision (see n 19).

[95] Constitutional Treaty, Art I-33(1).

[96] CONV 424/02 (n 11) 4; Constitutional Treaty, Art III-294(3)(b).

[97] Constitutional Treaty, Art III-295(3) on the Decisions implementing the CFSP.

[98] *Ibid*, Art I-37(3).

[99] *Ibid*, Art I-37(2) *in fine*.

The wording of this provision pointed out a third type of European regulation but was modified and renumbered in the last version of the Constitutional Treaty, signed in Rome on 29 October 2004. The provision in Article I-35(2) reads:

> The Council and the Commission, in particular in the cases referred to in Articles I-36 and I-37, and the European Central Bank in the specific cases provided for in the Constitution, shall adopt European regulations and decisions.

This modification seems to limit the cases where the Council and the Commission may adopt European regulations and decisions to those contained in Articles I-36 and I-37 (delegated and implementing acts). However, some provisions contained in the third part of the Constitutional Treaty authorise the Council, after consulting the Parliament, to adopt regulations and decisions. Therefore, although the wording of Article I-35(2) changed, giving the impression that it limited the types of European regulations and decisions adopted by the Council and the Commission to those foreseen in Articles I-36 and I-37, the third part of the Constitutional Treaty does not give such an impression.

Consequently, the aim of this section is to analyse the cases specifically providing for the adoption of regulations by the Council and the Commission in the third part of the Constitutional Treaty that are not included in the concept of delegated and implementing regulations.

1. Competition Policy

Under the current Treaties, this policy is developed by Council Regulations according to Article 83 of the EC.[100] During the Convention on the Future of Europe there was no clear idea as to the normative position of this policy. Should it be regulated by European regulations or European laws? European laws would seem to be more appropriate, taking into account the importance of this policy within the Union. However, Member States were reluctant due to the intervention of the European Parliament through the legislative ordinary procedure. They preferred that the Council maintain control over this policy. Therefore, the Constitutional Treaty[101] confers on the Council the power to adopt European regulations, on a proposal from the Commission, to give effect to the principles of this policy set out in Articles III-161 and III-162 (current Articles 81 and 82 EC). The role of the European Parliament in shaping competition policy will be, as it is currently, only a consultative one, because the Council shall consult the European Parliament before acting.[102]

[100] Among others, Council Regulation (EC) No 1/2003 of 16 December 2002 on the implementation of the rules on competition laid down in Arts 81 and 82 of the Treaty [2004] OJ L1/1. See Baño León (2006) 10–11.

[101] Constitutional Treaty, Art III-163.

[102] *Ibid.*

2. State Aids

Under the EC the Council has the power to adopt European regulations, acting on a proposal from the Commission and after consulting the European Parliament, for the application of Articles 87 and 88 of the EC.[103] The Constitutional Treaty preserves this power for the Member States represented in the Council without the intervention of the European Parliament. The Council will be able to adopt European regulations after consulting the European Parliament. The Parliament will have a merely consultative role, as it has under the EC.[104]

3. Economic and Monetary Policy

This policy is another example of where the role of the European Parliament is very limited. The Constitutional Treaty, following current practice, confers powers on the Council to adopt European regulations mainly on monetary policy,[105] but also on economic policy.[106]

4. Area of Freedom, Security and Justice

In this area it is possible to appreciate the logic of the normative system under the Constitutional Treaty. Due to the sensitive policies included in this area that may touch on fundamental rights, they will be developed mainly by European laws or framework laws.[107] Nonetheless, the Council will adopt European regulations to ensure administrative co-operation among the relevant departments of the Member States in the policies included under the Area of Freedom, Security and Justice. It shall act on a Commission proposal or on the initiative of a quarter of the Member States and after consulting the European Parliament.[108]

[103] EC, Art 89.

[104] Constitutional Treaty, Art III-169.

[105] Art III-186(2), second para, reads: 'The Council, on a proposal from the Commission, may adopt European regulations laying down measures to harmonise the denominations and technical specifications of coins intended for circulation to the extent necessary to permit their smooth circulation within the Union. The Council shall act after consulting the European Parliament and the European Central Bank.' Art III-187(4) reads: 'The Council shall adopt the European regulations and decisions laying down the measures referred to in Article 4, Article 5(4), Article 19(2), Article 20, Article 28(1), Article 29(2), Article 30(4) and Article 34(3) of the Statute of the European System of Central Banks and of the European Central Bank. It shall act after consulting the European Parliament: (a) either on a proposal from the Commission and after consulting the European Central Bank; or (b) on a recommendation from the European Central Bank and after consulting the Commission.'

[106] Art III-183 Constitutional Treaty reads: 'The Council, on a proposal from the Commission, may adopt European regulations or decisions specifying definitions for the application of the prohibitions laid down in Arts III-181 [credit facilities in favour of Union institutions or national governments] and III-182 [financial facilities] and in this Article. It shall act after consulting the European Parliament.'

[107] See Arts III-265(2), III-266(2) and III-267(2) regarding policies on border checks, asylum and immigration; Art III-269(2) regarding judicial co-operation in civil matters; Art III-270(1) regarding judicial co-operation in criminal matters; and Art III-275(2) regarding police co-operation.

[108] CONV 424/02 (n 11) 22.

Whereas in policies such as competition, state aids and economic and monetary issues the Constitutional Treaty preserves the status quo with respect to the current Treaties and confers powers on the Council for their development, the dynamic of the normative system changed when the provisions concerning the area of Freedom, Security and Justice were created. The elimination of the pillar structure and the introduction of the principle of hierarchy of norms has the result that in areas where fundamental rights are at stake, the relevant matter will be regulated by European law or framework law. According to this criterion, norms that may have an impact on fundamental rights will be established through the ordinary legislative procedure in which the Council and the Parliament will act as co-legislator.

The logic of the Union's normative system in this field enables us to draw the conclusion that the criterion to be used in deciding which normative instrument should be used in a particular policy will not only depend on whether the act contains a basic policy choice, but also on whether the act may have an impact on fundamental rights.

After seeing the cases in which the Constitutional Treaty specifically provided for the use of European regulations (the third type of European regulation together with delegated regulations and European implementing regulations), the question remains as to why the Constitutional Treaty contains this type of regulation. The existence of delegated and implementing acts was justified by the need to focus primary law on the establishment of basic policy choices, leaving the details and technicalities to secondary law. Delegated regulations will amend and supplement primary law and European implementing regulations will establish uniform conditions among Member States when the implementation of the legally binding acts of the Union so requires. However, Article I-35(2) of the Constitutional Treaty does not attempt to justify to the existence of the third type of regulations adopted directly on the basis of the Constitutional Treaty.

The reason for this, which is clearer in the first draft of the Constitutional Treaty, is a historical one. Under the EC, powers to regulate competition policy, State aids and economic and monetary policy were conferred on the Council of Ministers acting as the governmental authority. When drafting the Constitutional Treaty, Member States did not want to lose control of these policies in favour of a more active role for the European Parliament. Therefore, the solution was to reserve these areas for the Council, establishing a third type of European regulation.

The European Parliament will have only a consultative role as regards this third type of regulation, as it currently has under the policies mentioned above.

VI. THE CHOICE BETWEEN PRIMARY LAW AND SECONDARY LAW: CONSEQUENCES

The principle of hierarchy of norms introduced into the Union's legal system by the Constitutional Treaty will divide normative instruments into legislative and non-legislative instruments. This section focuses on the consequences that the regulation of a policy by European law or framework law will have and on the consequences of its regulation by secondary law, that is, delegated regulations, European implementing regulations or European regulations. Moreover, the section explores how the principle of hierarchy of norms helps to solve the overlapping of legal bases in the same areas that the Union's legal system may encounter them within the Constitutional Treaty

As regards the consequences of the use of primary law or secondary law to regulate an area of Union action, the first consequence concerns the procedure to be used and its implications in terms of transparency and democracy. Primary law (European laws or framework laws) will be adopted via the ordinary legislative procedure with the intervention of the European Parliament as co-legislator. The Constitutional Treaty establishes that documents relating to this procedure shall be available to the public, whereas secondary law (delegated regulations, European implementing regulations and European regulations) will be adopted by the Council where, where there is no public access to documents.[109] Moreover, following the recommendations on simplification of the Working Group, sessions of the European Parliament and the Council working as co-legislator should be open to the public, but not when the Council adopts secondary law.[110]

The second consequence of using primary law or secondary law relates to the standing of a non-privileged applicant who wants to challenge the validity of the EU's act. Under the rule of standing established by the Constitutional Treaty, individuals and private parties do not in general have standing to challenge the validity of a European law or framework law. They will have to prove that they are *individually and directly concerned* by the law in order to be regarded as having standing in an annulment action.[111] However, any natural or legal person may challenge 'a regulatory act which is of direct concern to him or her and does not entail implementing measures'.[112] The term 'regulatory act' was chosen instead of 'act of general application' to avoid any confusion on this point. The discussion circle's aim was to make clear that the flexibility introduced as regards the rule of standing for non-privileged applicants would not be used to challenge European laws and framework laws. The EU's primary law follows the constitutional traditions of the Member States, such that individuals usually do not have standing to challenge the validity of primary laws, although they may have standing when the law violates their fundamental rights guaranteed by their national Constitution.

Finally, one problem that the Union's legal system under the Constitutional Treaty may experience relates to the overlapping of legal bases on the same matter. It is known that the Constitutional Treaty introduces some new legal bases, for instance Article III-122 regarding services of general economic interest. According to this provision,

[109] Constitutional Treaty, Art III-399(2).
[110] CONV 424/02 (n 11) 22.
[111] See ch 5.
[112] Constitutional Treaty, Art III-365(4).

> Without prejudice to Articles I-5, III-166, III-167 and III-238, and given the place occupied by services of general economic interest as services to which all in the Union attribute value as well as their role in promoting its social and territorial cohesion, the Union and the Member States each within their respective competences and within the scope of application of the Constitution, shall take care that such services conditions, in particular economic and financial conditions, which enables them to fulfil their mission. European laws shall establish these principles and set these conditions without prejudice to the competence of Member States, in compliance with the Constitution, to provide, to commission and to fund such services.[113]

This legal basis may overlap with that contained in Article III-166(3) on services of general economic interest. However, Article III-166(3) imposes a duty on the Commission to ensure the application of its provisions, adopting, where necessary, European regulations or decisions. The introduction of the principle of hierarchy of norms will solve the problem of overlapping of norms upon services of general economic interest in favour of the European law or framework law that regulates this matter

To conclude, the principle of hierarchy of norms, which introduces a clear division between primary law and secondary law, is not only a factor in the democratisation of the Union's normative system but also an element which simplifies the Union's everyday activities.

[113] This provision is the equivalent to Art 16 EC, but Art III-122 Constitutional Treaty contains a new legal basis.

2

Implications of a Binding European Charter of Fundamental Rights for the Individual Decisions Made by the European Public Administration

I. INTRODUCTION

The Economic Community founded by the Treaty of Rome has evolved into a Union of peoples and States in which citizens are much more concerned with European governance. The lack of legitimacy of the exercise of public powers by the European Union's institutions is still one of the more important subjects of the debates surrounding the Union.[1] The ECJ has drawn, from the legal traditions common to the Member States, general principles of law that strengthen the accountability of the Union and the Member States towards citizens, such as the principle of transparency or the principle of good administration.[2] These principles were part of the institutional analysis on European governance. The Inter-Institutional Declaration of 1993 and the institutional reports produced for the Intergovernmental Conference (IGC) of 1996 explicitly linked the concepts of democracy, transparency and subsidiarity with the aim of bringing the Union closer to its citizens.[3] According to the White Paper on European Governance, this should be based on five principles: openness, participation, accountability, effectiveness and coherence.[4] On 28 February 2002 the Convention on the future of the European Union held its inaugural session. One of its main concerns was to bring citizens closer to the European institutions.[5]

Provisions on administrative procedure are scarce and scattered throughout the Treaties and secondary legislation, whereas the powers of Community administration—and especially those fields where individuals have direct contact with

[1] On this debate see, *inter alia*, Weiler (1999), ch 8, 265–85. On the legitimisation of the Union through law see Cassese (2003d) 82–91; Della Cananea (2003c) 132.

[2] Lenaerts (2004).

[3] Inter-Institutional Declaration on Democracy, Transparency and Subsidiarity adopted by the Council, the Parliament and the Commission on 25 October 1993 [1993] OJ C329/132. See ch 1, section III of this book.

[4] *White Paper on European Governance*, COM (2001) 428 final [2001] OJ C287/1, 9.

[5] Laeken Declaration on the Future of the European Union, 15 December 2001, SN 273/01.

Community administration—are growing all the time. In this context the Charter of Fundamental Rights of the European Union is, on the one hand, a strong source of legitimacy for the EU as a community of law with a Constitutional treaty written on behalf of the citizens and States of Europe[6] and, on the other, an instrument for controlling the exercise of powers devolved by the Treaties to the Union's institutions and bodies.[7]

This chapter analyses the implications of the provisions of a binding Charter on the rights to good administration, access to documents and personal data protection in the individual decisions (administrative acts) made by the European public administration.

II. THE RIGHT TO GOOD ADMINISTRATION

On 22 February 2005, the judgment of the ECJ (Grand Chamber) in the *Max.Mobil* case recognised that the principle of sound administration was a general principle of Community law.[8] On this occasion, the ECJ recognised the principle of good administration as a principle of Community law in itself and not as a set of procedural rules. This judgment was an appeal by the European Commission against the judgment of the CFI of 30 January 2002[9] that declared admissible the application brought by the company Max.Mobil Telekommunikation Service GmbH for an annulment of the Commission's letter by which the latter refused to institute treaty infringement proceedings against the Republic of Austria.

The CFI has actively recognised various principles and rights under administrative law.[10] In the *Max.Mobil* case it went further, recognising not only the principle of good administration but also the right of individuals to good administration. According to the CFI, the right to good administration 'confirms that every person has the right to have his or her affairs handled impartially, fairly and within a reasonable time by the institutions and bodies of the Union'.[11]

The *Max.Mobil* case dealt with a complaint made by Max.Mobil, the second GSM operator to appear in Austria and which was later to become T-Mobile Austria. The company lodged a complaint with the Commission seeking, among other things, a finding that the Republic of Austria had infringed the combined provisions of Articles 82 and 86(1) of the EC. Essentially the complaint related to the lack of any distinction between the fee charged to Max.Mobil and that charged to Mobikom Austria AG (the first GSM mobile telephone network to appear on the Austrian market and whose shares are still held in part by the Austrian State through the

[6] Preamble.

[7] Commission Communication on the Charter of Fundamental Rights of the European Union, COM (2000) 559 final, 11.

[8] Case C-141/02, *Commission v Max.Mobil* [2005] ECR I-1283, para 72.

[9] Case T-54/99 *Max.Mobil v Commission* [2002] ECR II-313.

[10] For a recent example see Case T-211/02 *Tideland Signal v Commission* [2002] ECR II-3781.

[11] *Ibid*, 48. Arts 41(1) of the Charter and II-101 (1) of the Constitutional Treaty.

company Post und Telekom Austria AG) and to the preferential arrangements regarding fee payment and the allocation of frequencies enjoyed by Mobikom.

The Commission, by letter of 11 December 1998, rejected the complaint. Max.Mobil applied for the rejection measure to be annulled before the CFI.

The CFI's judgment comes in two parts, one on the admissibility of the application and another on its substance. The first part, on admissibility, is the more interesting because the Court develops its doctrine on a substantive right of individuals to good administration. The core of the reasoning relates, firstly, to whether a letter written by the Commission rejecting a company's complaint within the context of Article 86(3) of the EC is a decision or legal act within the meaning of Article 230(4) of the EC and therefore the subject of an action for annulment under that provision; and secondly, it questions the extent to which the Commission's discretion to initiate infringement proceedings under Article 86(3) of the EC is subject to judicial control. Regarding this particular aspect, the CFI held that the role of the Community judicature is limited in that case to a circumscribed review in which it merely checks, firstly, that the contested measure includes a statement of reasons which is *prima facie* consistent and reflects due consideration to the relevant aspects of the case; secondly, that the facts relied on are materially accurate; and, thirdly, that the *prima facie* assessment of those facts is not vitiated by any manifest error.[12]

With regard to the right to good administration, the CFI upheld its notion of good administration as a subjective right and not only a principle of EU law in which several procedural rules are included.[13] It held:

> Since the present action is directed against a measure rejecting a complaint, it must be emphasised at the outset that the diligent and impartial treatment of a complaint associated with the right to sound administration which is one of the general principles that are observed in a State governed by the rule of law and are common to the constitutional traditions of the Member States. Article 41(1) of the Charter of Fundamental Rights of the European Union proclaimed at Nice on 7 December 2000 . . . confirms that [e]very person has the right to have his or her affairs handled impartially, fairly and within a reasonable time by the institutions and bodies of the Union.[14]

The CFI also pointed out that it is for Community judges to monitor whether a Commission action was diligent and impartial, according to the right to good administration. In consequence, the CFI declared the action admissible, but the action was eventually dismissed because the Court held that the Commission undertook a diligent and impartial examination of the complaint, as required by the right to good administration.[15]

[12] Case T-54/99 (n 9), para 58.

[13] Months later the CFI referred to good administration as a principle of EU law in Case T-211/02, *Tideland Signal Ltd v Commission* (n 10), para 37.

[14] Case T-54/99 (n 9), para 48.

[15] With regard to the procedural rights of complainants conferred by the Commission in the absence of legislative provisions, see the Opinion of AG Pollares Maduro in Case C-141/02, delivered on 21 October 2004, para 55 and 56.

This CFI's decision of 30 January 2002 was appealed by the Commission before the ECJ, seeking its annulment because it considered that the letter refusing to institute Treaty infringement proceeding against the Republic of Austria fell outside the scope of judicial review.[16] The ECJ's decision of 22 February 2005 held that the CFI had erred in declaring the action brought by Max.Mobile against the Commission's letter admissible because it was not a decision subject to judicial review. According to the ECJ, the letter by which the Commission informed Max.Mobil that it was not intending to bring proceedings against the Republic of Austria could not be regarded as producing binding legal effects and therefore was not a challengeable measure. The ECJ's judgment on the *Max.Mobile* case made a minor reference to the right to good administration by saying that the decision upon Commission's letter not having binding legal effect 'is not at variance with the principle of sound administration or any other general principle of Community law'.[17] That was the only reference to the right to good administration made by the ECJ's decision on the *Max.Mobile* case, in contrast with the activism showed by the CFI in developing this right among the other principles of Community law.

1. Origin of the Right to Good Administration in Community Law

As happens with other rules of European administrative law, which have their origin in the Community Courts' case law,[18] the procedural rules included under the umbrella of good administration, such as the right to be heard before an administrative decision is taken which affects an interest, access to the relevant file, and the obligation on the Community administration to give reasons for decisions, are common to the legal traditions of Member States. Some of them were already in the Treaties (the right to a reasoned decision,[19] the right to write to the institutions in one of the Treaty languages and receive an answer in the same language,[20] the right to reparation for damage caused by the Community administration[21] and the right to a fair hearing although limited to the state aid field[22]), but most of them were developed by the ECJ in a comparative analysis of legal systems of the Member States.[23]

[16] The CFI later modified its position, declaring that 'legal or natural persons who request the Commission to take action under Art 86(3) EC do not, in principle, have the right to bring an action against a Commission decision nor to use the powers which it has under that article'. Case T-52/00 *Coe Clerici Logistics SpA v Commission* [2003] ECR II-2123, para 88.

[17] At n 8, para 72.

[18] Case 7/56 *Algera and others v Common Assembly* [1957] ECR 39 marked the beginning of the jurisprudence of the Community Courts in administrative law. In this case the Court had to deal with the revocation of administrative acts which was not provided for by the EEC. The solution was found by ECJ following the legal principles commonly accepted in the Member States. See Schwarze (1991) 4–5 and (1992) 1430.

[19] EC, Art 253.

[20] *Ibid*, Art 21(3).

[21] *Ibid*, Art 288.

[22] *Ibid*, Art 88(2).

[23] See, *inter alia*, Case 222/86 *Unectef v Heylens* [1987] ECR 4097, para 15, and the Opinion of AG Mancini of 18 June 1987, paras 5–6; Case 374/87 *Orkem v Commission* [1989] ECR 3283, paras 33 and

'Good administration' was conceived as a general term comprising a range of rules which require a certain standard of proper administrative practice. The Community Courts were more successful at harmonising procedural rules in fields of exclusive Community competence (eg competition, anti-dumping, customs and State aid policy implementation) than in other fields, in which national implementation plays a major role (fields of shared administration such as agricultural policy and structural funds). Nehl has highlighted this idea of horizontal convergence, which was easily achieved as compared with the much more problematic vertical convergence (the harmonising effect of fundamental procedural standards in the relationship between the Community and national administrations).[24]

Along with the development of these procedural rules by the Court, the contribution of the European Ombudsman to the expansion of those procedural rules within European public administration is also worth noting—namely for his reports on 'maladministration'.[25] These reports have contributed to a negative definition or delimitation of the concept of good administration, offering a wide concept of 'maladministration' by enumerating examples of acts that would fall within that concept.[26] According to the European Ombudsman, the following acts are included within the concept of 'maladministration': administrative omissions, abuse of power, negligence, unlawful procedures, unfairness, malfunction or incompetence, discrimination, avoidable delay, and lack of or refusal to provide information.[27] In 1998, a European Parliament Resolution adopted a definition of maladministration proposed by the European Ombudsman, according to which 'maladministration occurs when a public body fails to act in accordance with a rule or principle which is binding upon it'.[28] Among the initiatives of the European Ombudsman it is worth highlighting the proposal for a Code of Good Administrative Behaviour in the form of draft recommendations to the Commission, to the European Parliament and to the Council, which was made in 1999. Similar recommendations were made to other institutions and bodies in September 1999. However, it was not until 2001 that the European Parliament

41; Case C-269/90 *Technische Universität München v Hauptzollamt München-Mitte* [1991] ECR I-5469, paras 22 and 25; Case T-450/93 *Lisrestal and others v Commission* [1994] ECR II-1177, paras 42, 50, 51 and 52; Case T-167/94 *Nölle v Council and Commission* [1997] ECR II-2379, para 53.

[24] Nehl (1999) 7.

[25] Indeed, under the heading of 'The Ombudsman's mission', in his Annual Report of 1995, it was established that 'the first and most vital task of the European Ombudsman is to deal with specific instances of maladministration. He must provide an effective means of redress for citizens who are denied their legal rights, or who do not receive proper administrative treatment by Community institutions or bodies': available at http://www.euro-ombudsman.eu.int/report95/en/rep95_1.htm. See also Chiti (2000); Bonnor (2000).

[26] The First Annual Report of the European Ombudsman in 1995 included the broad concept of maladministration: 'there is maladministration if a Community institution or body fails to act in accordance with the Treaties and with the Community acts that are binding upon it, or if it fails to observe the rules and principles of law established by the ECJ and CFI'. Available at http://www.euro-ombudsman.eu.int/report95/en/rep95_1.htm

[27] *Ibid*.

[28] Resolution of 16 July 1998 [1998] OJ C292/168.

adopted a resolution approving a Code of Good Administrative Behaviour which European Union institutions and bodies, their administrations and their officials should respect in their relations with the public (hereinafter 'the Code').[29] A new version of the Code was produced in 2005, which intended to explain in more detail what the Charter's right to good administration should mean in practice.

With regard to the justification of procedural rules included under the umbrella of good administration, traditionally it refers, on the one hand, to the rationalisation, efficiency and effectiveness of administrative action which is better achieved through an administrative procedure in which there are clear rules on, for instance, the identification of the competent authority to adopt the decision, the time-limit within which a decision is to be adopted, the possibility of appealing it, etc. On the other hand, procedural rules find their justification in the process rights embodied in these rules, taking into account the impact of an administrative decision on the individual.[30] Finally, the evolution of the right to good administration in EC law and its increasing relevance is related to the birth and strengthening of European citizenship, although Article 41 of the European Charter of Fundamental Rights does not limit it to citizens but extends it to legal residents in the EU ('every person').[31]

2. Content of the Right to Good Administration

The European Charter of Fundamental Rights contains the first positive delimitation of the right to good administration. Prior to its proclamation in December 2000, there was a concept of maladministration, given by the European Ombudsman, and a set of procedural rules that, according to the jurisprudence of the Community Courts, constituted the principle of good administration. The limits to the right to good administration were set by the drafters of the European Charter of Fundamental Rights, taking into account the Community Courts' case law and the rights already recognised by the EC.[32] In the second meeting of the Convention,[33] the European Ombudsman, in a public hearing on the draft, suggested that citizens' right to good administration should be a principle of the Charter.[34] In that speech, the European Ombudsman recommended, in order to

[29] Resolution of 6 September 2001. The Code is available at http://www.euro-ombudsman.eu.int/code/en/default.htm

[30] Nehl (1999) 21–22.

[31] Kanska (2004) 302–3.

[32] Council of the EU, 'Explanation relating to the complete text of the Charter. December 2000': available at http://ue.eu.int/docCenter.asp?lang=en&cmsid=245.

[33] The European Council in Tampere, 15 and 16 October 1999, determined the precise composition of the body, called the Convention, to draw up the draft of the European Charter of Fundamental Rights: available at http://www.europarl.eu.int/summits/tam_en.htm. On the method used to draft the Charter see, *inter alia*, De Búrca (2001); Dutheil De La Rochère (2000) 223–7; Vitorino (2000) 499–508.

[34] European Ombudsman, 'Public Hearing on the draft Charter of Fundamental Rights of the European Union, Brussels, 2 February 2000. Preliminary Remarks', 4: available at http://www.euro-ombudsman.eu.int/speeches/en/charter1.htm. See also Söderman (2001) 8–14.

put the principle of good administration into practice, that a Regulation on good administrative behaviour and another on access to information and to documents be enacted.[35] That regulation on good administrative behaviour, when enacted, will be the first European law on administrative procedure to take into account the provisions of the Code that may possibly be introduced into EU Law.

The provision on the right to good administration[36] within the Charter contains three main rights, the first right accompanied by three subdivisions, whose interpretation is aided by the Code of Good Administrative Behaviour.[37] This is 'the right to have his or her affairs handled impartially, fairly and within a reasonable time by the institutions, bodies, offices and agencies of the Union'.[38] This provision re-words the principle of care or due diligence which, together with the duty to give reasons, was used by the Community Courts, generally, for judicial control of an administrative discretion.[39] According to the principle of care or due diligence, the administration must impartially and carefully collect and consider the relevant facts and legal points of any individual case before making a decision in relation to it.[40] Several provisions of the European Code of Good Administrative Behaviour explain the meaning of Article 41(1) of the Charter. These impose obligations on Community officials and other servants as regards their relations with the public, such as acting according to the principle of equality of treatment and avoiding any unjustified discrimination,[41] ensuring that measures taken are proportionate to the aim pursued,[42] ensuring that power is not abused,[43] and ensuring impartial treatment, such that officials are not biased when dealing with an issue and exercising their powers.[44] The right would also imply that officials must be objective when they make decisions, which means that they should only take relevant factors into account, giving each of those factors due weight in the decision-making process.[45] The meaning of fairness is established by the Code as acting impartially, fairly and reasonably.[46]

Allowing a reasonable time for the Community administration to handle affairs is related to the idea that a slow administration is a bad administration, as postulated by AG Jacobs.[47] It is also related to the idea of good administration of justice. Although there are no precise time-limits on administrative action in Community law, the ECJ established in the *Lorenz* case[48] a precise time-limit of two

[35] *Ibid.*
[36] European Charter of Fundamental Rights, Art 41; Constitutional Treaty, Art II-101.
[37] The references to the Code of Good Administrative Behaviour must be understood in the 2005 version, available at http://www.euro-ombudsman.eu.int.
[38] Charter of Fundamental Rights, Art 41(1); Constitutional Treaty, Art II-101(1).
[39] Nehl (1999) 119 and 163.
[40] *Ibid.*
[41] Art 5 of the Code.
[42] Art 6 of the Code.
[43] Art 7 of the Code.
[44] Art 8 of the Code.
[45] Art 9 of the Code.
[46] Art 11 of the Code.
[47] AG Jacobs' Opinion in Case C-270/99 *Z v Parliament* [2001] ECR I-9197, para 40.
[48] Case 120/73 *Gebrüder Lorenz GmbH v Federal Republic of Germany and Land de Rhénanie-Palatinat* [1973] ECR 1471, para 4.

months for the Commission to give its opinion with regard to a proposal of state aid notified by the Member State. And, since then, the idea of a reasonable time-limit for making decisions has been taken to be two months. That time-limit is foreseen in the Code of Good Administrative Behaviour[49] in general terms, although due to the complexity of the matters involved these may be solved after the time-limit of two months expires. In that case a definitive decision should be notified to the author as soon as possible.[50]

As mentioned above, the first provision of Article 41(1) of the Charter includes three more rights.[51] The first is the right of defence: 'the right of every person to be heard, before any individual measure which would affect him or her adversely is taken'. This right is commonly accepted in national legal orders as an essential administrative procedural rule and a central standard of administrative justice. It is linked to the rule of law and the right contained in Article 6 of the European Convention on Human Rights. The first domain in EC law in which it was recognised was competition law, where it was developed and introduced into a wide range of administrative procedures in which the applicant may be negatively affected by the outcome.[52] This right is developed by the Code as the core of the rights of defence, implying the submitting of written comments and, when needed, the presentation of oral observations before the decision is taken.[53]

The second right included in Article 41(2) of the Charter is 'the right of every person to have access to his or her file, while respecting the legitimate interests of confidentiality and of professional and business secrecy'. In the early days, the right of access to information was conceived as a necessary element in effectively exercising the right to be heard in the course of an administrative procedure. Its highest development by the Community Courts took place in EC competence cases, in which the Commission had an administrative legal framework for direct implementation.[54] In that area the Commission had—and still has—incisive supervisory and investigative powers over individuals, mostly legal persons, with the possibility of imposing pecuniary sanctions for anti-competitive behaviour.[55] The right of access to documents was included in primary law by the ToA and is still a prerequisite to the right to be heard, a fundamental element of the right to

[49] Art 17 of the Code reads: '*1.* The official shall ensure that a decision on every request or complaint to the Institution is taken within a reasonable time-limit, without delay, and in any case no later than two months from the date of receipt'.

[50] Art 17(2) of the Code.

[51] Charter of Fundamental Rights, Art 41(2).

[52] Initially the right to be heard was recognised in procedures in which a sanction or penalty was to be imposed, but later the Community Courts abandoned that formalistic interpretation in favour of a more liberal approach, accepting the spread of this right into areas of administrative decision-making which involve an individual interest liable to be adversely affected by its outcome. See Nehl (1999) 71.

[53] Art 16 of the Code.

[54] Case 64/1982 *Tradax Graanhandel BV v Commission* [1984] ECR 1359.

[55] Council Regulation (EC) No 1/2003 of 16 December 2002 on the implementation of the rules on competition laid down in Arts 81 and 82 of the Treaty [2004] OJ L1/1, which repealed Regulation No 17 of the Council of 6 February 1962. See Cassese (2003a) esp 35–38. See also Case C-94/00 *Roquette Frères SA v Directeur general de la concurrence and Commission* [2002] ECR I-9011.

defence.[56] Together with the right of access to documents, the Code includes the right to access information, which is currently a factor increasing transparency and participation and democratising the decision making-process within the EU's administration. The right of access to information establishes that the official who has responsibility for the matter concerned shall provide members of the public with the information that they request, taking care to ensure that this is clear and understandable. Furthermore, officials shall advise the person concerned to formulate his or her demand in writing and, if they are not competent in the matter, give advice as to which institution or agency is competent to deal with and attend to his or her request.[57]

The third clause in Article 41(2) of the Charter concerns 'the obligation of the administration to give reasons for its decisions'. The duty to give reasons was seen as the element that would allow judicial control of administrative discretion,[58] a way of testing whether the Community administration had fulfilled its duty of care[59] and an essential element for the defence of individuals affected by administrative decisions.[60] The importance of the duty is highlighted by the fact that the courts can detect a problem of inadequate reasoning on their own initiative and, therefore, annul the appealed decision on that ground.[61] Under this duty, the reasoning must disclose the essential elements explaining why the decision has been taken; in other words, it must express the *ratio decidendi* of the decision.[62] To fulfil this obligation, institutions do not need to refer to every legal or factual aspect relevant to the decision.[63] This obligation is currently included in primary law but it has a different scope. Article 253 of the EC imposes on the European Parliament, the Council and the Commission the obligation to state the reasons and the proposals or opinions on which regulations, directives and decisions are based. However, Article 41(2) of the Charter imposes an obligation on the Community administration, Commission, agencies and bodies to give reasons for every decision that is taken which may adversely affect the rights or interests of a private person.[64] On the one hand, the subjective scope of this obligation is narrower than that included in Article 253 of the EC, because it is addressed not at the European Parliament or the

[56] Art 23 of the Code.

[57] Art 22 of the Code.

[58] Shapiro (2002a).

[59] Nehl (1999) 119.

[60] Case C-269/90, *Technische Universität München v Hauptzollamt München-Mitte* [1991] ECR I-5469, para 22.

[61] Case T-95/94 *Sytraval and Brink's France v Commission* [1995] ECR II-2651, paras 52, 55 and 75. See also Case 350/88 *Delacre and others v Commission* [1990] ECR I-395, para 15.

[62] Lenaerts and Vanhamme (1997). According to them, there are two categories of administrative decision in which the statement of the grounds of the decision is more relaxed. First, decisions that are taken to comply with a judgment annulling a previous decision need not reiterate all the factual and legal elements on which they are based. Secondly, measures resulting from an administrative procedure in which the addressee has actively participated and during which he has acquired extensive knowledge of the facts is taken into account by the administration, especially in fields such as competition law and antidumping in which the concerned undertakings participate actively in the procedure: *ibid*, 565.

[63] Case 350/88 (n 61), para 16; Case T-3/89 *Atochem v Commission* [1991] ECR II-1177, para 222.

[64] Art 18(1) of the Code.

Council, but at the Community administration. On the other hand, its scope will better reflect the current situation in which not only the institutions are subject to the obligation to give reasons, but agencies and bodies must also express the grounds for their decisions.[65]

In conclusion, with respect to procedural rules contained in Article 41(1) of the Charter, their development by the Code constitutes *grosso modo* the guidelines for a future European law on administrative procedure. Among those rules the Code establishes, for instance, the obligation to personally notify private persons whose rights or interests may be adversely affected by individual acts of the institutions. The notification should be in writing and should contain the decision, indicating the options available to challenge the decision, and a statement of the grounds on which it is based by indicating clearly the relevant facts and the legal basis of the decision.[66] Only in the case of a large number of persons being affected by the same decision, where standard replies are made, is the statement on the grounds of the decision made available only on request.[67]

To continue with the analysis of Article 41 of the Charter, the second right included within this provision is the right to compensation for damage caused by the institutions and servants of the European Union in the performance of their duties. This clause is a reproduction of that contained in Article 288 of the EC regarding the non-contractual liability of the Community which, according to the general principles common to the laws of the Member States, 'shall make good any damage caused by its institutions or by its servants in the performance of their duties'.[68] The third paragraph of Article 288 extends this clause to the European Central Bank and its servants. The measure causing the damage may be of a legislative or administrative nature. To be recognised as non-contractual liability of the Community by the ECJ, the applicant must show that the act was illegal, that he or she suffered damage and that there was a causal link between that conduct and the damage suffered.[69] However, when the measure (legislative or not) is

[65] Regulations on so-called regulatory agencies, whose decisions have effect vis-à-vis third parties, impose on them a duty to give reasons. Examples include the European Agency for the Evaluation of Medicinal Products (Art 31(2) Council Regulation (EEC) No 2309/93 of 22 July 1993, laying down Community procedures for the authorisation and supervision of medicinal products for human and veterinary use and establishing a European Agency for the Evaluation of Medicinal Products [1993] OJ L214/1); OHIM (Art 73 Council Regulation (EC) No 40/94 of 20 December 1993 on the Community Trade Mark [1994] OJ L11/1); the Community Plant Variety Office (Art 75 Council Regulation (EC) No 2100/94 of 27 July 1994 on Community plant variety rights [1994] OJ L227/1); and the European Aviation Safety Agency (Art 44(1) Regulation (EC) No 1592/2002 of the European Parliament and of the Council of 15 July 2002 on common rules in the field of civil aviation and establishing a European Aviation Safety Agency [2002] OJ L240/1).

[66] Arts 18, 19 and 20 of the Code.

[67] Art 18(3) of the Code.

[68] Craig and De Búrca (2003).

[69] In one case the CFI admitted Community non-contractual liability although the damage was not a consequence of an illegal act. The Court held that 'when damage is caused by conduct of the Community institution not shown to be unlawful, the Community can incur non-contractual liability if the conditions as to sustaining actual damage, to the causal link between that damage and the conduct of the Community institution and to the unusual and special nature of the damage in question are all met' (Case C-237/98 *Dorsch Consult v Council and Commission* [2000] ECR I-4549, para 19). Case T-69/00

discretionary, the applicant must show that there has been a violation of a superior rule of law for the protection of individuals (it could be a treaty provision or a principle of law, such as proportionality, legal certainty or legitimate expectation) that was sufficiently manifest and grave to cause the damage.[70]

With regard to compensation for damage caused by a violation of the right to good administration as a superior rule of law, in Cases T-344/00 and T-345/00 the Commission's long period of inactivity was considered 'a clear and serious breach of the principle of sound administration giving rise, in principle, to liability on the Community's part'.[71] However, the ECJ overturned the CFI's decisions in those cases.[72] It held that the CFI had erred in law in holding, without having established the scope of the discretion enjoyed by the Commission, that the latter's inaction constituted a clear and serious breach of Community law giving rise to liability on the part of the Community.[73] Taking into account the extent of the discretion available to the Commission and all the factual circumstances, in particular the scale of divergence in the scientific data, it did not appear that the inaction on the part of the Commission, which made a decision after the date that the administration of progesterone was banned, was a clear violation of the limits of its discretion.[74]

The Code of Good Administrative Behaviour does not explain this clause relating to the Community's non-contractual liability in more detail, possibly because the ECJ's case law has delimitated its meaning and limits. There is no modification in its wording; it simply reproduces the provisions of Article 288 of the EC. There is no need to mention agencies and bodies because the case law on Article 288 has extended the term 'institutions' to cover all bodies and agencies. The ECJ has in the past ruled that the term 'institutions' used in the second paragraph of Article 288 must not be understood as referring only to the Community institutions listed in Article 7 of the EC. The term also covers, with regard to the system of non-contractual liability established by the Treaty, all other Community bodies established by the Treaty and intended to contribute to the achievement of the Community's objectives. Measures taken by those bodies, in the exercise of the powers assigned to them by Community law, are attributable to the Community, according to the general principles common to the Member States referred to in the second paragraph of Article 288.[75] Therefore, although agencies' regulations

FIAMM and FIAMM Technologies v Council and Commission [2005] ECR II-5393, para 160. However, the action was dismissed because it had not been established that the applicants suffered damage in excess of the limits of the risks inherent in their export operations.

[70] Case 5/71 *Zuckerfabrik Schoeppenstedt v Council* [1971] ECR 975, para 11; Case 20/88 *Roquette Frères v Commission* [1989] ECR 1553, para 23; Cases T-344/00 and T-345/00 *CEVA Santé Animale SA and Pharmacia Entreprises SA v Commission* [2003] ECR II-229, para 96.

[71] Cases T-344/00 and T-345/00 (n 70), para 103.

[72] Case C-198/03, *Commission v CEVA Santé Animale SA and Pfizer Enterprises Sàrl* [2005] ECR I-6357.

[73] *Ibid*, para 69.

[74] *Ibid*, para 89.

[75] Case T-209/00 *Lamberts v Médiateur* [2002] ECR II-2203, para 49; Case C-370/89, *Société Générale d'Entreprises Electro-Mécaniques SA (SGEEM) and Roland Etroy v European Investment Bank* [1992] ECR I-6211, paras 12–16.

include clauses on compensation for damages caused by them and their servants, they have only a declaratory effect.[76]

The last right recognised under the heading of the right to good administration (Article 41 of the Charter) is the right to receive official correspondence in one's own language.[77] This provision reproduces the right guaranteed by the third paragraph of Article 21 of the EC. In spite of its reference to 'every person', which was probably taken from the Code of Good Administrative Behaviour,[78] this right is to be applied under the conditions and within the limits defined by the Treaties (Article 52(2) of the Charter), and therefore it only applies to citizens of the Union, like the right included within Article 21(3) of the EC. Furthermore, this right relates only to correspondence maintained with the institutions, not with agencies or bodies. Agencies may limit their working languages without infringing the principle of non-discrimination. In the *Kik* case (in which a Dutch trade mark agent saw her application rejected because she refused to indicate one of the five languages of the OHIM (OHIM) as a secondary language for the opposition, revocation or invalidity proceedings (the five languages do not include Dutch)) the CFI ruled that the limitation did not involve an infringement of the principle of non-discrimination. According to the CFI, the provision imposing a duty on applicants to indicate a second language (from among French, English, German, Italian and Spanish) 'was adopted for the legitimate purpose of reaching a solution on languages in cases where opposition, revocation or invalidity proceedings ensue between parties who do not have the same language preference and cannot agree among themselves on the language of proceedings'.[79] The CFI held that the applicant was not entitled to rely on Article 21(3) of the EC, according to which every citizen of the Union may write to any of the institutions or bodies referred to in that provision or in Article 7 of the EC in one of the languages mentioned in Article 314 of the EC and have an answer in the same language, because the OHIM was not one of the institutions or bodies referred to in Article 7 or Article 21 of the EC.[80]

[76] For instance, Art 8 Regulation (EC) No 1406/2002 of the European Parliament and the Council of 27 June 2002 establishing a European Maritime Safety Agency [2002] OJ L208/1; Art 34 Regulation (EC) No 881/2004 of the European Parliament and the Council of 29 April 2004 establishing a European Railway Agency [2004] OJ L164/1.

[77] Charter of Fundamental Rights, Art 41(4).

[78] The Code refers to 'every citizen of the Union or any member of the public': Art 13. This provision extends it to legal persons such as associations (NGOs) and companies.

[79] Case T-120/99 *Kik v OHIM* [2001] ECR II-2235, para 62.

[80] *Ibid*, para 64. Worthy of note is Case C-160/03 *Kingdom of Spain v Eurojust* [2005] ECR I- 2077, in which the Kingdom of Spain sought the annulment of seven calls for applications for the recruitment of temporary staff issued by Eurojust, of the point concerning documents to be submitted in English by persons submitting their application form in another language, and of the various points concerning candidates' qualifications in respect of knowledge of languages. As AG Pollares Maduro's Opinion pointed out, the case was important because it provided the Court once again with an opportunity to examine the meaning and scope of the language regime of the institutions and bodies of the European Union. In the *Kik* case the Court gave a decision on the language regime applicable to the registration procedures in an agency of the European Community (OHIM), whereas in *Spain v Eurojust* it was called upon to give a decision concerning the language regime applicable to the recruitment procedures and internal proceedings of Eurojust, a European Union body. However, the Court declared the application

The rights established in Article 41 of the Charter, which this section has summarised, do not represent all the principles and rights developed by the Community Courts in this field, nor even those reproduced by the Code of Good Administrative Behaviour. For instance, Article 41 does not mention the principles of proportionality and legal certainty. Nonetheless, this provision makes the right to good administration more visible and, in doing so, contributes to the probability that it will be invoked by subjects within the EU's legal order.[81] The Community Courts will contribute to further development of this right which, together with the provisions of the Code of Good Administrative Behaviour, will form part of a future European law on administrative procedure, whose legal basis is Article III-398 of the Constitutional Treaty.[82]

3. Implications of a Binding Right to Good Administration for the Community Administration

Since the Charter was proclaimed in December 2000, several opinions of Advocates General in the ECJ have referred to it as an authoritative expression of the fundamental rights recognised in the EU.[83] The Charter makes such rights more visible and, in doing so, makes their invocation by individuals and private parties more possible.[84] However, not every provision of the Charter contains a fundamental right. The Preamble and Article 51(1) of the Charter declare that there are rights and principles within the Charter, but they do not explain how to distinguish rights from principles.[85] This distinction is essential if we are to determine the implications of its acquiring binding force. Therefore, it is worth asking whether the right to good administration is really a subjective right or only a Community law principle. The wording of Article 41 of the European Charter of Fundamental Rights suggests that it is a subjective right and not only a principle of Community law.[86] The Final Report of Working Group II on Incorporation of the Charter/Accession to the ECHR, after declaring that there are principles and rights

inadmissible because the acts contested were not included in the list of acts the legality of which the Court may review under Art 230 EC (paras 36–38).

[81] Lenaerts and de Smijter (2001).

[82] Page 9 of the Code. On this topic see ch 4.

[83] Opinions of AG Alber in C-340/99 *TNT Traco* [2001] ECR I-4109; of AG Tizzano in C-173/99 *BECTU* [2001] ECR I-4881; of AG Mischo in C-122 and 125/99 *D and Suède v Council* [2001] ECR I-4319, and in C-20/00 and 64/00 *Booker Aquaculture and Hydro Seafood* [2003] ECR I-7411; of AG Stix-Hackl in C-49/00 *Commission v Italy* [2001] ECR I-8575, in C-131/00 *Nilsson* [2001] ECR I-10165, and in C-459/99 *MRAX* [2002] ECR I-6591; of AG Jacobs in C-377/98 *Netherlands v Parliament and Council* [2001] ECR I-7079, in C-270/99 *Z v Parliament* [2001] ECR I-9097, and in C-50/00, *Unión de Pequeños Agricultores v Council* [2002] ECR I-6677; of AG Geelhoed in C-413/99 *Baumbast and R* [2002] ECR I-7091, and in C-313/99 *Mulligan and others* [2002] ECR I-5719. CONV 116/02, 4. See also Dutheil De La Rochère (2004).

[84] Lenaerts and de Smijter (2001) 281; Jacobs (2002). See also the Commission Communication on the Charter of Fundamental Rights of the European Union, COM (2000) 559 final, 1.

[85] Constitutional Treaty, Art II-111(1).

[86] Kanska (2004) 304.

within the Charter, confirms the idea of the Convention that produced the Charter that it should clearly express the nature of each provision in the wording of the respective articles.[87] In consequence, Article II-101 of the Constitutional Treaty is entitled 'Right to good administration'.

Taking into account the judicial activism that has been apparent as regards the right to good administration, especially from the CFI,[88] and the wording of Article 41 of the Charter, the judicial development of this provision into a subjective right can be predicted.[89] Furthermore, the Final Report points out that principles 'shall be observed and may call for implementation through legislative or executive acts; accordingly, they become significant for the Court when such acts are interpreted or reviewed'.[90] Whether the Charter becomes binding, the provision on the right to good administration will not need a legislative or executive act for its implementation.[91] It will not need legislative development that allows individuals to appeal breaches on the part of the Community administration. As a subjective right, the right to good administration may be invoked before the Community Courts against any administrative act that infringed it.

To sum up, if the Charter becomes legally binding, the right to good administration will have implications for individuals and private parties that may challenge any administrative measure that infringes their right to good administration. They can launch an appeal before the CFI requesting its annulment on the ground of an infringement of that right. The Community administration is currently obligated under the duties imposed by this principle, as the previous section shows us, but that does not mean that when the Charter becomes binding the transformation of the right to good administration into a subjective right does not have implications for the Community administration. According to Article II-112(1) of the Constitutional Treaty,

> Any limitation on the exercise of the rights and freedoms recognised by this Charter must be provided for by law and respect the essence of those rights and freedoms. Subject to the principle of proportionality, limitations may be made only if they are necessary and genuinely meet objectives of general interest recognised by the Union or the need to protect the rights and freedoms of others.

This provision imposes a condition that any limitation on the right to good administration that the Community's institutions wish to introduce should be provided for by a European law or framework law which must respect its essential content, namely the essence of those rights and freedoms. In addition, the limitation will be subject to the principle of proportionality and, therefore, it will

[87] CONV 354/02, Brussels, 22 October 2002, 8.

[88] Cases T-54/99, *Max.Mobil* (n 9) and T-177/2001, *Jégo-Quéré & Cie v Commission* [2002] ECR II-2365.

[89] Kanska (2004) 302–4.

[90] *Ibid.*

[91] It is submitted that Art II-112(5) of the Constitutional Treaty, regarding the application of principles through legislative or executive acts, will not be applicable to the right to good administration. On the aim of s 5 of Art II-112 see De Búrca (2003) 23.

subject to judicial review. The Community Courts will control whether those limitations are necessary to meet the objectives of general interest or to protect the rights and freedoms of others. Where a Court finds that those limitations are not justified in order to achieve an objective of general interest or are not proportional to it, the Court will annul them. In this situation the Community Court will act as a Constitutional Court, controlling legislative acts that impose any limitation on rights recognised by the Constitutional Treaty, such as the right to good administration.

III. THE RIGHT OF ACCESS TO DOCUMENTS

This section maps out the origins and evolution of the right of access to documents, analysing its features under the EC and focusing on the implications for the Community administration of its introduction into the Charter, as part of the rights of European citizens,[92] and into the second part of the Constitutional Treaty. Our target is to discover the extent to which the statement of the Final Report of Working Group II on Incorporation of the Charter/Accession to the ECHR—according to which the Charter simply reaffirms the rights currently recognised by the Treaties—is applicable to the right of access to documents.

1. Origin of the Right of Access to Documents

The right of access to documents was originally conceived as a procedural right linked to the right of the defence, as an inherent component of the right to be heard. This functional perspective of the principle was recognised by the ECJ in the early days and differs from the most recent vision of it, which we will call the constitutional perspective of access to documents.

Access to files was recognised by the ECJ early in the competition law cases as an essential element of a proper defence. Due to the far-reaching supervisory and investigative powers of the Commission in competition matters, the Court considered the right to be informed of the relevant evidence as an intrinsic element of an essential precondition to the effective exercise of the right to be heard or, in general, an essential precondition of the right of defence.[93] In those days, since no general principle of EC law could be said to exist with respect to access to documents, the Commission enjoyed an ample degree of discretion to choose which contents of its files were accessible to the parties.[94] Famous cases include the *Hercules*, *Cement* and *Soda-Ash* cases, in which the CFI developed the features of this right, holding that the Commission was under an obligation to make available to the undertakings involved all documents for and against the decision that it had

[92] CONV 354/02, Final Report of Working Group II on 'Incorporation of the Charter/Accession to the ECHR', 3.

[93] Nehl (1999) 43; Levitt (1997).

[94] See Lauwaars (1994).

obtained during the course of the investigation. That was because, according to the CFI, the Commission did not have an exclusive discretionary power to decide on the probative value of documents or, consequently, on the question of which parts of those documents were to be used in the proceedings and for what purpose.[95] It was suggested that in the *Soda-Ash* judgments, the Court was close to recognising that access to files was a basic procedural right.[96]

The right of access to documents was also recognised in anti-dumping proceedings, with less controversy than in competition matters, possibly because the regulation governing anti-dumping procedures expressly provided for such a right.[97] In the early case law the Court considered the right of access to information to be an essential part of the right to be heard and, also, that the Community institutions must act with all due diligence in performing their duties to provide the information necessary to the defence of the individual parties' interests. In doing so, the Community institutions would allow them to make known their views on the correctness and relevance of the facts and evidence presented by the Commission.[98]

In parallel to the development of the right of access to documents as a procedural right within the right of defence or, specifically, as an inherent part of the right to be heard, concerns over the democratic deficit of the institutions prompted the development of a constitutional-style right, adopting measures to improve public access to the information available to the institutions. To this end, the Final Act of the Treaty on European Union contained a Declaration on the right of access to information.[99] It stated:

> The Conference considers that transparency of the decision-making process strengthens the democratic nature of the institutions and the public's confidence in the administration. The Conference accordingly recommends that the Commission submit to the Council no later than 1993 a report on measures designed to improve public access to the information available to the institutions.

Since then, bringing the Community closer to its citizens has been a regular topic on the European agenda. For instance, at the Birmingham and Edinburgh European Councils of 16 October 1992 and 12 December 1992 respectively, the Heads of State and Governments stressed the need to make the Community more open and committed themselves to this objective.[100] After a comparative survey on

[95] Case T-7/89 *Hercules Chemicals v Commission* [1991] ECR II-1711, paras 53–54. See also Joined Cases T-10/92 and others, *SA Cimenteries CBR and Others v Commission* [1992] ECR II-2667; reiterated in Case T-65/89 *BPB Industries plc and British Gypsum Limited v Commission* [1993] ECR II-389, para 30. *Soda-Ash* judgments are referred to in the cases T-30/91, T-31/91, T-32/91 *Solvay v Commission*, T-36/91 and T-37/91 *ICI v Commission* [1995] ECR II-1775, II-1821, II-1825, II-1847 and II-1901.

[96] Levitt (1997) 1415–16 and Nehl (1999) 52.

[97] Art 7(1)(a) of Council Regulation (EEC) No 3017/79 of 20 December 1979 on protection against dumped or subsidised imports from countries not members of the European Economic Community [1979] OJ L339/1, as amended by [1980] OJ L62/40.

[98] Case C-49/88 *Al-Jubail Fertilizer and others v Council* [1991] ECR I-3187, para 17.

[99] Declaration No 17, TEU signed at Maastricht, 7 February 1992.

[100] The European Council in Birmingham, 16 October 1992, adopted a Declaration entitled 'A Community close to its citizens', in which it stressed the need to make the Community more open to its citizens (Bulletin EC 12-1992, 7).

public access to documents in the Member States and some non-member countries, the Commission adopted a Communication to the Council, the European Parliament and the Economic and Social Committee on openness in the Community, setting out the basic principles governing access to documents.[101] On 6 December 1993, the Council and the Commission approved a Code of Conduct concerning public access to Council and Commission documents, establishing the principles that were to govern that access and, therefore, implementing the principle of transparency.[102] According to the Code, the Commission and the Council would take steps to implement the principles before January 1994. To that end, the Council adopted a Decision on public access to Council documents in 1993[103] and the Commission followed suit in 1994.[104] The Decisions were very similar in substance, because their rules came from the Code of Conduct concerning public access mentioned above, although they differed with respect to their structure.[105]

The Code was published as an annex to the Commission's Decision and contains simple rules on access to documents in a general principle. The aim was that the public would have the widest possible access to documents held by the Commission and the Council. That general principle has informed the ECJ's doctrine since then.[106] The Code contained basic rules on access to documents—such as the definition of 'document', defined as any written text whatever its medium which contains existing data held by these institutions[107]. However, the Code did not give any indication as to who could ask for access to a document, how to make an application and whether an applicant could access documents held by bodies other than the Council and the Commission. The list of exceptions to the general principle was also very limited. Hence, access could be denied where disclosure

[101] Commission Communication to the Council, the Parliament and the Economic and Social Committee: Openness in the Community, COM (1993) 258 final, 2 June 1993 [1993] C/166/4. The comparative survey on public access to documents was included as an annex to the Commission Communication on public access to the institutions' documents, adopted on 5 May 1993 [1993] OJ C156/5.

[102] The principles relating to public access to documents were as follows: the public would have the widest possible access to documents held by the Commission and the Council; a document was defined as any written text that contained existing data and was held by the Commission and the Council; and the exceptions to that access were listed in the Code of Conduct ([1994] OJ L46/59).

[103] Decision 93/731/EC of 20 December on public access to Council documents [1993] OJ L340/43.

[104] Decision 94/90/ECSC, EC, Euratom, of 8 February on public access to Commission documents [1994] OJ L46/58.

[105] The Commission's decision made reference to the rules contained within the Code, which was published as an annex, whereas the Council's decision incorporated those rules into its text.

[106] For instance, in the Community case law it is easy to find statements to the effect that 'public access to documents of the institutions is an approach to be adopted in principle, whereas the power to refuse access is the exception': Case T-2/03 *Verein für Konsumenteninformation v Commission* [2005] ECR II-1121, para 105. See also Case T-211/00 *Aldo Kuijer v Council* [2002] ECR II-485, para 55.

[107] Years later, the CFI clarified the term 'documents' by saying that its meaning is not formal, does not refer to a formal document, but refers to the information. Therefore, access should relate to the information contained in the document. In the *Hautala* case, the CFI held that the contested decision of the Council, by which the principle of access to documents was applied only to documents as such and not to the information contained in them, was vitiated by an error of law and must therefore be annulled. Case T-14/98 *Heidi Hautala v Council* [1999] ECR II-2489, paras 87–88.

might undermine the protection of public interest, protection of the individual, considerations of privacy, or protection of commercial and industrial secrecy, or due to a request for confidentiality by the supplier of information,[108] etc. Years later these exceptions were delimited by the Community Courts. In consequence, the list of the exceptions established by Regulation No 1049/2001 is larger, in accordance with the development of case law in this matter. In fact, the majority of the Community case law on access to documents concerns the interpretation of these exceptions in accordance with the proportionality principle.[109]

Let us return to the Commission and Council's Decisions in the 1990s: both were criticised because 'the philosophy followed was that access to documents and transparency were simply an extension of the requirements of good administration rather than the outcome of any belief in the value of participatory democracy'.[110] In fact, as we saw in the previous section, the right of access to documents forms part of the right to good administration (the right of every person to have access to his or her file);[111] for instance, the Code of Good Administrative Behaviour establishes the right of access to documents among its provisions.[112] The right to good administration has been used to highlight the need for a concrete and individual examination of the exception before denying access to documents applied for.[113]

Since the 1990s, the openness of the actions of public authorities has been considered closely and linked with the democratic nature of the institutions. The fact that citizens are aware of what the administration is doing is seen as a guarantee that it will operate properly. As AG Tesauro observed in his Opinion in *Netherlands v Council*, the openness of the public authorities' action tends to secure better knowledge of acts and measures on the part of citizens, and is directly linked to the democratic nature of the institutions. AG Tesauro stated:

> Only where there is appropriate publicity of the activities of the legislature, the executive and the public administration in general, is it possible for there to be effective, efficient supervision, *inter alia* at the level of public opinion, of the operations of the governing

[108] For instance, in the *Mattila* case the exception of protection of public interest (in particular international relations) used by the Council and the Commission to deny public access to some documents to the applicants was rejected by the ECJ. This annulled the CFI's decision, saying that, in accordance with the principle of proportionality, the case law of the Court and Decisions 93/731 and 94/90, the Council and the Commission must examine whether partial access should be granted to the information covered by the exceptions, in the absence of which a decision refusing access to a document must be annulled. Case C-353/01 *Oil Mattila v Council and Commission* [2004] ECR I-1073, paras 30–32.

On the exceptions, it must also be kept in mind that access to documents has a limit when the documents are of a confidential nature according to primary Community law, since Art 214 EC states that information 'of the kind covered by the obligation of professional secrecy' must not be disclosed by members and servants of the Community institutions. See Lenaerts and Vanhamme (1997) 541.

[109] Eg the *Hautala* and *Mattila* cases (nn 107 and 108). Regulation (EC) No 1049/2001 of the European Parliament and of the Council of 30 May 2001 regarding public access to European Parliament, Council and Commission documents [2001] OJ L145/43.

[110] Curtin and Meijers (1995) 91.

[111] Art 41(1) of the Charter.

[112] Art 23 of the Code. On 15 April 1997 the European Ombudsman launched an initiative stressing the need for the Commission to increase the development of procedural rights for private complainants under the Art 169 procedure as a matter of good administrative behaviour. See Söderman (1998) 75–76.

[113] Case T-2/03 *Verein für Konsumenteninformation v Commission* (n 106), para 107.

organization and also for genuinely participatory organizational models to evolve as regards relations between the administration and the administered.[114]

The introduction of openness and transparency as principles within the decision-making process, with the aim of increasing the democratic nature of the Community and bringing it closer to citizens, prompted the introduction of a new provision into the EC (Article 255). The extension of those principles has determined the introduction of a Title within the first part of the Constitutional Treaty on the democratic life of the Union, which establishes, among other things, the right of access to documents.[115]

2. The Current Meaning of the Right of Access to Documents

The ToA introduced Article 255 into the EC; this provision governs the right of public access to European Parliament, Council and Commission documents.[116] After the ToA came into force (1 May 1999), the scope, limits and arrangements for exercising the right of access to documents were established in Regulation (EC) No 1049/2001 of the European Parliament and the Council of 30 May 2001. Besides pre-existing rules and principles of EC law on this matter (see section III.1), this Regulation introduced some innovations that, on the one hand, highlight the constitutional perspective of the right to access to documents as related to the democratic nature of the European public administration and, on the other, reflect the current state of the case law on access to documents with a long list of exceptions to the general principle of ensuring the widest possible access.[117]

Whilst Regulation No 1049/2001 departs from the general principles on access to documents established by the Code of Conduct, it is much more ambitious.[118] Its

[114] Opinion of AG Tesauro, Case C-58/94 *Netherlands v Council* [1996] ECR I-2169, para 14. A recent example of this tendency is Regulation (EC) No 1367/2006 of the European Parliament and of the Council of 6 September 2006 on the application of the provisions of the Aarhus Convention on Access to Information, Public Participation in Decision-making and Access to Justice in Environmental Matters to Community institutions and bodies [2006] OJ L264/13.

[115] Art I-50(3)(4) of the Constitutional Treaty.

[116] Art 255 EC reads: '*1.* Any citizen of the Union, and any natural or legal person residing or having its registered office in a Member State, shall have a right of access to European Parliament, Council and Commission documents, subject to the principles and the conditions to be defined in accordance with paragraphs 2 and 3. *2.* General principles and limits on grounds of public and private interest governing the right to access to documents shall be determined by the Council, acting in accordance with the procedure referred to in Art 251 within two years of the entry into force of the Treaty of Amsterdam. *3.* Each institution referred to above shall elaborate in its own Rules of Procedure specific provisions regarding access to its documents.'

[117] Hence, the European Ombudsman said in his speech presented to the Public Hearing on the draft Charter of Fundamental Rights of the European Union, in Brussels on 2 February 2000, that 'this document [Regulation No 1049/2001] seems to consist mainly of a long and obscure list of possible reasons to deny access to documents. This cannot be what was intended when the Treaty of Amsterdam was drafted'. Speech available at http://www.euro-ombudsman.eu.int/speeches/en/charter.1.htm.

[118] General principles established by the Code of Conduct such as guaranteeing the widest possible access to documents not covered by an exception (ie when disclosure would infringe a specific public or private interest); applicants, whether natural or legal persons, do not have to justify their applications;

purpose is not only to ensure the widest possible access to documents, but also to establish rules ensuring the easiest possible exercise of this right and to promote good administrative practice with respect to access to documents.[119] Furthermore, in order to ensure the full application of its provisions to all activities of the Union, the Regulation establishes that all agencies of the Union should apply these principles.[120] Among the new features introduced by the Regulation, the abolition of the author rule is worthy of note;[121] also the obligation on the institution concerned to balance interests;[122] the obligation to give partial access to those parts of the documents not covered by an exception;[123] and the

documents containing all information kept in any form whatsoever referred to areas within the competence of the institution concerned; refusal to disclose a document must be based on an analysis of the harm that would be caused by disclosure to either public or private interests. To that end, in response to a request the institution has to undertake an individual examination of the documents referred to, applying the principle of proportionality, before refusing access to the documents applied for (Case T-2/03 (n 106), para 107); and, finally, all decisions refusing even partial access may be the subject of an administrative appeal to the institution concerned, which must give reasons for its refusal. All these principles were established by the Code of Conduct and, currently, are part of Regulation No 1049/2001.

[119] Regulation No 1049/2001 (n 109), Art 1.

[120] *Ibid*, Preamble.

[121] Therefore, an applicant could apply for access to a document elaborated by a third party (eg a Member State, an undertaking, etc) but held by the institution concerned. A Member State may request the Commission or the Council not to communicate to third parties a document originating from that State without its prior agreement (Art 4(5) of Regulation No 1049/2001). In the *Mesina* case, Italy refused to allow access to its correspondence with the Commission on State aid (Case T-76/02 *Messina v Commission* [2003] ECR II-3203). In the *Co-Frutta* case, the CFI held that when there is doubt as to the authorship of a document it is important to construe and apply the authorship rule strictly (confirmed in Case C-41/00 *Interporc v Commission* [2003] ECT I-2125, para 70), but not in cases where there is no doubt, since the Member States alone are the authors of the documents in question, as in this case (Case T-47/01 *Co-Frutta Soc Coop rl v Commission* [2003] ECR II-4441, para 61). The abolition of the author rule occurred when Regulation No 1049/2001 entered into force on 3 June 2001 and applied only from then.

[122] The protection of certain interests must be balanced with the public interest in disclosure and, if the latter is preponderant, the exception to the right of access would not be applicable. The principle of proportionality is the key factor. In the *Verein für konsumenteninformation* case, the CFI held that the Commission's refusal to examine concrete and individual documents was a breach of the principle of proportionality (Case T-2/03 *Verein für Konsumenteninformation v Commission* (n 106), para 100).

[123] This innovation comes from the case law. In Case T-14/98 (n 107), Ms Hautala, a Member of the European Parliament, wrote to the Council seeking clarification on the eight criteria for arms exports defined by the European Council of Luxembourg in 1991 and Lisbon in 1992. In its answer, the Council referred to a report of the Working Group on Conventional Arms Exports to explain the adoption of the eight criteria. Ms Hautala asked to be sent the report mentioned in the Council's answer. Access to the contested report was refused under Art 4(1) of Decision 93/731, because it contained highly sensitive information and the disclosure would undermine public security. Ms Hautala sought the annulment of the decision for infringement of Art 4(1) of Decision 93/731, Art 190 EC (current Art 253) and a fundamental principle of Community law according to which citizens of the European Union must be given the widest and fullest possible access to documents of the Community institutions. Taking into account this principle and the fact that the exceptions to it should be construed and applied strictly, the CFI annulled the contested decision. According to the CFI, Art 4(1) of Decision 93/731 must be interpreted in the light of the principle of the right to access to information and the principle of proportionality. Therefore, the Council had to balance the interest of public access to certain parts of the documents against the extra labour involved, thus safeguarding the interests of good administration. The CFI concluded that the Council was obliged to examine whether partial access should be granted to information not covered by the exceptions laid down by the Decision. The contested decision was void because the Council considered that the principle of access to documents applies only to documents as

introduction of some exceptions, such as defence and military matters and legal opinions.[124]

In order to establish rules ensuring the easiest possible exercise of the right of access to documents and, therefore, promoting the constitutional nature of this right, it is worth noting that Regulation No 1049/2001 obliges each institution to keep a register of documents open to the public and to give direct access to it in electronic form.[125] Furthermore, the institutions shall provide information and assistance to citizens on how and where applications for access to documents can be made.[126] This rule is connected to the development of good practices to facilitate the exercise of this right by the Community administration,[127] such as informing the public of the rights they enjoy under this Regulation[128] and establishing an inter-institutional committee to examine best practice, analyse possible conflicts and discuss future developments of the right.[129]

Substantive rules ensuring the easiest possible exercise of this right are accompanied by detailed procedural rules on how to gain access to documents, promoting good administrative practice. For instance, the Administration now has a shorter time-limit to give an answer (15 days and not a month as before), and, another 15 days for the processing of a successful application. Failure by the institution to reply within that period is considered a negative reply, entitling the applicant to institute court proceedings against the institution and/or make a complaint to the European Ombudsman.[130]

Having described the new features introduced by Regulation No 1049/2001, the next step in obtaining a fuller picture of the right of access to documents within the current EU legal system is to assess the scope of the right. This will be done first by considering the reach of Regulation No 1049/2001 (ie which institutions are covered by the Regulation? Who can rely upon it?). Secondly, we will consider judicial protection of the right in the case law of the Community Courts.

(a) Which Bodies are under an Obligation to Provide Access to their Documents?

According to Regulation 1049/2001, the Council, the Commission and the European Parliament are obliged to provide access to any document held by them. Furthermore, the three institutions adopted a joint declaration in relation to the

such and not to the information contained in them, which was declared an error in law by the CFI in Case T-14/98 *Heidi Hautala v Council* (n 107). This judgment was confirmed by the ECJ in Case C-353/99 *Council v Heidi Hautala* [2001] ECR I-9565. With respect to partial access to documents see, *inter alia*, Case T-204/99 *Mattila v Council and Commission* [2001] ECR II-2265 and C-353/01 *Oil Mattila v Council and Commission*, (n 108).

124 Defence and military matters were expressly excluded from the right of access to documents by Decision 2000/527 of the Council, which amended Decision 93/731. On access to legal opinions see Case T-610/97 *Carlsen and others v Council* [1998] ECR II-485.

125 Regulation No 1049/2001 (n 109), Arts 11 and 12.

126 *Ibid*, Art 6(4).

127 *Ibid*, Art 15.

128 *Ibid*, Art 14(1).

129 *Ibid*, Art 15(2).

130 *Ibid*, Arts 6, 7 and 8.

Regulation in which they committed themselves to extending the scope of this right to any agency or body of the European Union.[131] Indeed, the regulations governing each agency were amended in order to guarantee the right of access to their documents and that an agency decision denying access can be the subject of a complaint before the Ombudsman or the subject of an action before the ECJ of the European Community under Articles 195 to 230 of the EC.[132]

To sum up, the right of access to documents currently applies to agencies and bodies of the Union, and therefore the provision contained within the Constitutional Treaty does not make any modification regarding who (institutions, bodies, agencies) must guarantee access to its documents. Article II-102 ensures the right of access to documents held by the institutions, bodies, offices and agencies of the Union, whatever their relationship with any citizen of the Union and any natural or legal person residing or having its registered office in a Member State. Therefore, there is no innovation in this respect except for the explicit acknowledgement of something that is current practice.

(b) Who Can Access Institutions' and Bodies' Documents?

Article 255 of the EC mentions a minimum group of beneficiaries, which has been augmented by the institutions. Article 255 and Regulation 1049/2001 guarantee

[131] [2001] OJ L173/5.

[132] European Environment Agency (Regulation No 1641/2003 of the European Parliament and of the Council of 22 July 2003 [2003] OJ L245/1); European Food Safety Authority (Regulation No 1642/2003 of the European Parliament and of the Council of 22 July 2003 [2003] OJ L245/4); European Aviation Safety Agency (Regulation No 1643/2003 of the European Parliament and of the Council of 22 July 2003 [2003] OJ L245/7); European Maritime Safety Agency (Regulation No 1644/2003 of the European Parliament and of the Council of 22 July 2003 [2003] OJ L245/10); Translation Centre for the bodies of the European Union (Regulation No 1645/2003 of the European Parliament and of the Council of 22 July 2003 [2003] OJ L245/13); European Agency for Reconstruction (Regulation No 1646/2003 of the European Parliament and of the Council of 22 July 2003 [2003] OJ L245/16); European Agency for the Evaluation of Medicinal Products (Regulation No 1647/2003 of the European Parliament and of the Council of 22 July 2003 [2003] OJ L245/19); European Training Foundation (Regulation No 1648/2003 of the European Parliament and of the Council of 22 July 2003 [2003] OJ L245/22); European Foundation for the Improvement of Living and Working Conditions (Regulation No 1649/2003 of the European Parliament and of the Council of 22 July 2003 [2003] OJ L245/25); Community Plant Variety Office (Regulation No 1650/2003 of the European Parliament and of the Council of 22 July 2003 [2003] OJ L245/28); European Monitoring Centre for Drugs and Drug Addiction (Regulation No 1651/2003 of the European Parliament and of the Council of 22 July 2003 [2003] OJ L245/30); European Monitoring Centre on Racism and Xenophobia (Regulation No 1652/2003 of the European Parliament and of the Council of 22 July 2003 [2003] OJ L245/33); OHIM (Regulation No 1653/2003 of the European Parliament and of the Council of 22 July 2003 [2003] OJ L245/36); European Agency for Safety and Health at Work (Regulation No 1654/2003 of the European Parliament and of the Council of 22 July 2003 [2003] OJ L245/38); European Centre for the Development of Vocational Training (Regulation No 1655/2003 of the European Parliament and of the Council of 22 July 2003 [2003] OJ L245/41).

Besides these bodies and agencies, the Committee of the Regions and the Economic and Social Committee also responded to the call by the institutions and adopted a system for accessing their documents in line with the provisions in Regulation No 1049/2001 (n 109): Decision No 64/2003 of 11 February on public access to Committee of the Regions documents [2003] OJ L160/96, and Decision No 603/2003 of 1 July on public access to European Economic and Social Committee documents [2003] OJ L205/19.

access to documents for citizens and residents of the European Union and to all legal persons whose registered offices are located in a Member State. The Council, Commission and Parliament's implementing decisions extended this right to all natural and legal persons, even those who are not citizens of the European Union or who do not have their registered offices in a Member State.[133]

(c) Judicial Protection of the Right of Access to Documents

As was mentioned in the introduction to this chapter, the right of access to documents has two perspectives: a functional one, as an essential element of the right of defence, and a constitutional one, as a right linked to the principle of transparency and the democratic character of the institutions. This latter right has brought it within the democratic life of the Union (Article I-50 Constitutional Treaty). Depending on which perspective of the right is being used, the ECJ may apply varying levels of control. Whereas in the earliest case law on access to documents it was conceived as a procedural right linked to the right of defence, given the functional perspective at stake, recent case law on access to documents relates to its constitutional perspective, linked to the principle of transparency and the democratic character of the institutions. In these later cases the discretionary power of the institutions is wider (although under strict judicial control) than in cases where the functional perspective of the right of access to documents, that is, as an essential element of the right of the defence, is at stake.

A paradigmatic example of the later case law adopted from a constitutional perspective is the *Hautala* case, in which the main idea is that although the right of access to documents is not absolute and its exercise may imply some restrictions, these should correspond to objectives of general interest of the European Union and respect the principle of proportionality.[134] In the *Hautala* case, AG Léger held that it is necessary to assess whether the exceptions contained at that time in Decision 93/731 were applied in a proportionate manner, respecting the right of access to documents introduced into the European Charter of Fundamental Rights.[135] The Council's appeal against the CFI's judgment of 19 July 1999, in which the Court recognised Ms Hautala's right to gain partial access to the documents she had applied for, was dismissed by the ECJ, following the Opinion of AG Léger.

[133] Council Decision 2001/840/EC of 29 November 2001 amending the Council's rules of procedure, Art 1, annex III [2001] OJ L313/40; Commission Decision 2001/937/EC, ECSC, Euratom, of 5 December 2001, amending its rules of procedure, Art 1.2, annex II [2001] OJ L345/94; Amendment of 13 November 2001 to the Rules of Procedure: Access to European Parliament documents (A5-0349/2001), Amendment 5, Rule 172(1), available at http://www.europarl.europa.eu/registre/recherche/info_en.cfm.

[134] See n 123.

[135] Opinion of AG Léger, Case C-353/99 *Council v Heidi Hautala* (n 123), para 112.

3. Implications of a Binding European Charter of Fundamental Rights for the Right of Access to Documents

The previous section shows that under the current provisions—that is, Article 255 of the EC and Regulation 1049/2001—the right of access to documents covers the documents and information of the institutions as well as those kept by the institutions and agencies or bodies of the European Union. As we have seen, agencies and bodies have adapted their regulations in order to guarantee the effectiveness of this principle. From the point of view of beneficiaries, the institutions have modified their procedural rules in order to open up access to their documents not only to citizens of the European Union and legal persons registered in a Member State, as Article 255 states, but also to citizens and legal persons of third countries.

Article 42 of the Charter is identical to the wording of Article 255 of the EC and it is stated in the explanatory notes to the Charter that the scope and meaning of the right introduced into the Charter is the same as that recognised by Article 255 of the EC.

Nonetheless, this does not mean that the introduction of the right of access to documents within the Charter and the Constitutional Treaty (Articles I-50(3)(4) and II-102) does not have implications for the Community administration. On the contrary, it will have three main implications. Firstly, its classification as a fundamental right constitutes a further stage in the process of its recognition and the establishment of its ranking within the Community legal order.[136] Unlike the decision to place the right outside the section dealing with citizenship of the Union under the ToA, the decision to introduce the right of access to documents within the Charter of Fundamental Rights reinforces its fundamental status, making it more visible and promoting its use.

Secondly, Article 52 of the Charter is applicable to Article 42 requiring that any limitation on the right of access to documents must be made by a European law or framework law, therefore giving a more active role to the European Parliament, respecting the essence of this right. Moreover, limitations may be made only if they are necessary and genuinely meet objectives of general interest recognised by the Union or the need to protect the rights and freedom of others, subject to the principle of proportionality.[137] As we saw with respect to the right to good administration, any limitation will be subject to the principle of proportionality and will therefore be under judicial control. Community Courts will control whether those limitations are necessary to meet objectives of general interest or to protect the rights and freedom of others. When the Court reaches the finding that those limitations are not justified in order to obtain an objective of general interest or are not proportional to it, the Court will annul them. The Community Court will act as a Constitutional Court controlling legislative acts that impose limitations on

[136] Opinion of AG Léger, Case C-353/99, 79.
[137] Charter of Fundamental Rights, Art 52; Constitutional Treaty, Art II-112 (1).

rights recognised by the Constitutional Treaty, such as the right of access to documents.

Thirdly and finally, the right of access to documents within the Constitutional Treaty is not only a fundamental right, but also an essential element for the effectiveness of the democratic life of the Union, to which Title VI of the first part of the Constitutional Treaty is dedicated. Title VI highlights the constitutional nature of the right of access to documents, which, as mentioned above, has been given more relevance than the functional perspective of this right since the 1990s. Title VI establishes, among the principles relating to the democratic life of the Union, the principle of transparency of proceedings of the Union administration, which is based in part on citizens' right of access to documents held by the Union's institutions, bodies, etc.[138] Access to their documents is related to the effective participation of citizens in the Union's activities.[139]

IV. THE RIGHT TO PROTECTION OF PERSONAL DATA

Some features of the right to the protection of personal data in EU law distinguish it from the right to good administration and right of access to documents. On the one hand, personal data protection was introduced as an autonomous right by Directive 95/46/EC of the European Parliament and the Council of 24 October 1995 on the protection of individuals with regard to the processing of personal data and on the free movement of such data,[140] whereas the rights to good administration and of access to documents have their origin in the Community Courts' case law. On the other hand, norms of personal data protection are applicable to Community institutions, agencies and bodies but also to Member States when implementing EU law, whereas the rights to good administration and access to documents are, in principle, only applicable to Community institutions, agencies and bodies. Indeed, Directive 95/46/EC was aimed at harmonising national legislation on data protection, where its diversity could have been an obstacle to the attainment of the internal market.

The Constitutional Treaty constitutionalises this right, firstly among citizenship rights, within the title 'The Democratic Life of the Union' in Part I (Article I-51), and secondly as a fundamental right, under the heading 'Freedoms' in Part II, within the European Charter of Fundamental Rights (Article II-68).

This section analyses the implications of that constitutionalisation because, as we will see below, it is far from being a 'photographic restatement of the existing law', as someone has described the European Charter of Fundamental Rights.[141] Nonetheless, before that, some discussion of the current regulation on this right is needed.

[138] Constitutional Treaty, Art I-50(3)(4).
[139] The principle of participatory democracy is established by Art I-47 of the Constitutional Treaty.
[140] [1995] OJ L281/31.
[141] WD N 4 and WD N 16 by Baroness Scotland of Asthal.

1. Its Origins in EU Law

Whereas most of the rights contained in the Charter of Fundamental Rights were recognised by the European Community Courts' case law, personal data protection was not recognised expressly as an autonomous right until the mid-1990s, when Directive 95/46/CE was approved. Before that, the ECJ dealt with cases in which personal data protection was at stake but considered it a breach of the right to respect of privacy (Article 8 ECHR) as the applicant alleged.[142]

Regarding its origins, it is sufficient for our purposes to say that, in Europe, personal data protection was conceived as a necessity due to technological progress in the computer sector. It was conceived as an element of the right to privacy.[143] In response to growing concerns throughout Europe in 1968, a Consultative Committee of the Council of Europe approved Recommendation No 509 of the Council of Europe Parliamentary Assembly on 'Human rights and the modern scientific and technological developments'. In 1979 the European Parliament approved a Resolution on 'The safeguarding of the rights of the individual against growing technical progress in the computing sector'.[144] Also during that period, several countries enacted norms on personal data protection.[145] In 1981, the Council of Europe approved the Convention for the Protection of Individuals with regard to Automatic Processing of Personal Data, by which Member States pledged to respect individuals' right to privacy, whatever their nationality or residence status, with regard to the automatic processing of personal data.[146] This Convention and the norms of that period tried to reconcile the growth of computers and the transmission of data with people's right to a private life.[147] The European Court of Human Rights' case law has contributed to this conception on data protection as an essential element of the right to privacy.[148]

Directive 95/46/EC on the protection of individuals with regard to the processing of personal data and on the free movement of such data was an important turning point for the recognition of the right to data protection as an autonomous right, not only as an element of the right to privacy. The Directive's legal basis is Article 95 of the EC because its aims are to harmonise national legislation, taking into account the increment of cross-border flows of personal data resulting from the

[142] For instance, Case C-404/92 *X v Commission* [1994] ECR I-4737.

[143] On the origins of this right in Europe, see Piñar Mañas (2006) 3–4.

[144] On 8 May 1979.

[145] In Germany (Law of 1977), France (Law of 1978, modified to incorporate into French law Directive 95/46/CE), in Denmark (1978), etc. See Piñar Mañas (2006) 3.

[146] Strasbourg, 28 January 1981, art 1. This Convention entered into force on 1 October 1985 after its ratification. On 8 November 2001 an additional Protocol was added, on the creation of an independent supervisory body to monitor the respect of rights recognised by the Convention and the addition of some norms on the flow of data across national borders.

[147] Piñar Mañas (2006) 4.

[148] *Gaskin v United Kingdom*, 7 July 1989, Series A no 160; *Z v Finland*, 25 February 1997 EHRR 1997-I; *MS v Sweden*, 25 August 1997 EHRR 1997-IV; *Amann v Switzerland* [GC] 16 February 2000, ECHR 2000-II; *Rotaru v Romania* [GC] 4 May 2000, , ECHR 2000-V; *Segerstedt-Wiberg and Others v Sweden*, 7 June 2006, ECHR 2006.

establishment and functioning of the internal market, and to ensure the free movement of personal data by harmonising the level of protection of the rights and freedoms of individuals with regard to the processing of their personal data in Member States.[149] The European Parliament and the Council adopted Directive 95/46/CE in order to address differences in the level of protection of the right to privacy in Member States, which would have constituted an obstacle to the pursuit of a number of economic activities at the Community level.

The provisions of Directive 95/46/EC give substance to and develop the principles of personal data protection contained in the Convention of the Council of Europe of 1981, also adopting its structure in defining some concepts, such as the processing of personal data, personal data filing systems, processors, third parties, recipients and the data subject, followed by some principles applying to data processing and their exceptions, and concluding with sanctions and remedies for infringement. The principles of Directive 95/46/EC have been translated into specific rules for the telecommunications sector through Directive 97/66/EC of the European Parliament and of the Council of 12 July 2002 concerning the processing of personal data and the protection of privacy in the telecommunications sector.[150] This has been adapted to developments in the markets and technologies for electronic communications services by Directive 2002/58/EC.[151]

Among the principles legitimating the processing of personal data, Directive 95/46/EC establishes that it must be done fairly and lawfully. The collection of data must be for specified, explicit and legitimate purposes and must be done in a way that is not excessive in relation to the purposes for which it is collected. Data must be accurate and kept up to date and should be stored for the shortest time possible depending on the purpose for which it was collected. Member States must respect these principles when determining precisely the conditions under which the processing of personal data is lawful, but it must be taken into account that personal data may be processed only if the data subject has unambiguously given his consent or when the processing is necessary for the performance of a contract to which the data subject is party, or processing that is necessary for compliance with a legal obligation to which the controller is subject, or where it is necessary to protect the vital interests of the data subject, etc.[152]

The obligations and rights established by Directive 95/46/EC may be restricted by Member States for reasons of national security, defence or public security or for the prevention, investigation and prosecution of criminal offences.[153] Nonetheless, the Directive establishes the right of the data subject to object at any time, on

[149] Directive 95/46/EC (n 140), Preamble, paras 5 and 8.

[150] [1998] OJ L24/1.

[151] Directive 2002/58/EC of the European Parliament and of the Council of 12 July 2002 concerning the processing of personal data and the protection of privacy in the electronic communication sector [2002] OJ L201/37.

[152] Directive 95/46/EC, Arts 6 and 7.

[153] Art 13 of Directive 95/46/EC envisages the restriction of rights and obligations when it is necessary to safeguard an important economic and financial interest of a Member State or of the European Union and when the protection of the data subject or of the rights and freedoms of others are involved.

compelling legitimate grounds relating to his particular situation, to the processing of data relating to him, except where otherwise provided by national legislation,.[154] When the use of the data is for direct marketing, the data subject may object to the processing and has the right to be informed before personal data is disclosed for the first time to third parties.[155] In all Member States a public authority must be responsible for monitoring the application of national legislation pursuant to the Directive with investigative powers, effective powers to intervene imposing sanctions, banning the processing of personal data, etc. The public authority created by each Member State has powers to engage in legal proceedings where the national norms adopted pursuant to the Directive have been violated.[156]

These rules imposed on Member States by Directive 95/46/EC were not applicable to the Community administration until Regulation No 45/2001 was approved. This anomalous situation, generated by Directive 95/46/EC, in which Member States had to respect the Directive's provisions on personal data protection when implementing Community law whereas Community institutions and bodies were not subject to those rules, was righted by Article 286 of the EC, introduced by the ToA. This provision establishes the application of Community acts to the protection of individuals regarding the processing of their personal data and the free movement of such data to the Community institutions and bodies. Its second paragraph contains the legal basis used to enact Regulation No 45/2001 on the protection of individuals with regard to the processing of personal data by the Community institutions and bodies and on the free movement of such data, which was approved.[157] This Regulation is inspired by the same principles as Directive 95/46/EC and establishes an independent supervisory authority, called the European Data Protection Supervisor, to ensure that the fundamental rights and freedoms of natural persons, in particular their right to privacy, are respected by Community institutions and bodies.[158] Furthermore, a Data Protection Officer, who will report to the European Data Protection Supervisor, must be appointed in each Community institution and body to ensure compliance with Regulation No 45/2001.[159] Nonetheless, in spite of these normative instruments, personal data protection is far from being a right with a uniform guarantee in EU law. As the following section will show, normative instruments in this field have limited scope.

2. Scope of the Right to Protection of Personal Data

On reading the Preamble to Directive 95/46/EC and certain provisions of Regulation No 45/2001, the first impression is that their scope is limited with

[154] Directive 95/46/EC, Art 14(a).

[155] *Ibid*, Art 14(b).

[156] *Ibid*, Art 28.

[157] Regulation (EC) No 45/2001 of the European Parliament and of the Council of 18 December 2000 on the protection of individuals with regard to the processing of personal data by the Community institutions and bodies and on the free movement of such data [2001] OJ L8/1.

[158] Arts 41–48.

[159] Arts 24–25.

respect to Community acts, even in the first pillar of the European Union. Directive 95/46/EC declares that the principles that it contains are applicable to all processing of personal data by any person whose activities are governed by Community law.[160] The activities referred to in Titles V and VI of the Treaty on European Union regarding public safety, defence, State security and activities of the State in the area of criminal law fall outside the scope of Community law, and therefore the Directive's provisions cannot be applied to those activities.[161] To eliminate any doubt regarding this limitation, the Directive declares in the same paragraph that the processing of personal data relating to State security matters remains outside the scope of the Directive.

With regard to the processing of personal data by the Community administration, Regulation No 45/2001 also limits its scope to the first pillar of the European Union.[162] In consequence, the European Data Protection Supervisor does not have competence to monitor the collection, storage and processing of personal data carried out by Europol or any other body outside the first pillar.

The ECJ's decisions have contributed decisively to the delimitation of the scope of personal data protection within the current Treaties. Case law on this matter is based on two premises. Firstly, the limitations in both Directive 95/46/EC and Regulation 45/2001 apply to Community acts (first pillar). And, secondly, the legal basis of the Directive on harmonisation of national legislation for the completion of the common market (Article 95 EC). The *Rundfunk* and *Lindqvist* cases are the leading cases in relation to personal data protection: here, the ECJ adopted a broad interpretation of the scope of Directive 95/46/EC.[163] However, this broad interpretation became subject to a serious restriction in the recent *PNR* case[164] (see (c) below).

(a) The Rundfunk Case

In the *Rundfunk* case, an Austrian national judge applied to the ECJ for a preliminary ruling asking, firstly, whether the provisions of Community law on data protection (Directive 95/46/EC) should be interpreted as precluding national legislation which requires a public broadcasting organisation, as a legal body, to communicate, and a State body to collect and transmit data on income for the purpose of publishing the names and income of employees of a broadcasting organisation governed by public law. In the case of an affirmative answer, the question arose as to whether those provisions precluding national legislation of the

[160] Preamble to Directive 95/46/EC (n 140), para 12.

[161] *Ibid*, para 13.

[162] 'This Regulation shall apply to the processing of personal data by all Community institutions and bodies insofar as such processing is carried out in the exercise of activities all or part of which fall within the scope of Community law': Art 3 of Regulation No 45/2001 (n 157).

[163] Joined Cases C-465/00, C-138/01 and C-139/01 *Österreichischer Rundfunk and Others* [2003] ECR I-4989 and Case C-101/01 *Lindqvist* [2003] ECR I 12971.

[164] Joined Cases C-317/04 *European Parliament v Council of the European Union* [2005] ECR I-2457, and C-318/04 *European Parliament v Commission* [2005] ECR I-2467.

kind described above are directly applicable, in the sense that an organisation obliged to make any disclosure may rely on them to prevent the application of contrary national legislation, and may not therefore rely on an obligation under national law against the employees concerned by the disclosure. These questions were raised in proceedings between, firstly, the Rechnungshof (Court of Audit) and a large number of bodies subject to its control and, secondly, Ms Neukomm and Mr Lauermann and their employer Österreichischer Rundfunk (ORF), a broadcasting organisation governed by public law, concerning the obligation on public bodies subject to control by the Rechnungshof to disclose details of salaries and pensions exceeding a certain level paid to their employees and pensioned employees, together with the names of the recipients, for the purpose of drawing up an annual report to be transmitted to the Nationalrat, the Bundesrat and the Landtage (the lower and upper chambers of the Federal Parliament and the provincial assemblies), a copy of which would be made available to the general public.

Before answering those questions, the ECJ declared Directive 95/46/EC to be applicable to the case despite its legal basis. In this sense, the ECJ held that recourse to Article 100A (current 95) of the EC as a legal basis does not presuppose the existence of an actual link with free movement between Member States in every situation referred to by the measure founded on that basis.[165] Therefore, the applicability of Directive 95/46 cannot depend on whether the specific situation at issue in the main proceedings has a sufficient link with the exercise of the fundamental freedoms guaranteed by the Treaty, specifically, the free movement of workers. According to the ECJ:

> A contrary interpretation could make the limits of the field of application of the directive particularly unsure and uncertain, which would be contrary to its essential objective of approximating the laws, regulations and administrative provisions of the Member States in order to eliminate obstacles to the functioning of the internal market deriving precisely from disparities between national legislations.[166]

Moreover, this interpretation is confirmed by the wording of Article 3(1) of the Directive, which defines its scope in broad terms without making the application of the rules on protection dependent on whether the processing has an actual connection with freedom of movement between Member States.[167] As we saw above, this broad interpretation on the applicability of Directive 95/46/EC was restricted in the *PNR* case (see below).

With regard to the questions referred to the ECJ for a preliminary ruling in the *Rundfunk* case, the Court answered them by saying that the data at issue in the main proceedings (monies paid by certain bodies and the recipients) constituted personal data within the meaning of Article 2(a) of Directive 95/46/EC, and that their transmission to the Rechnungshof and inclusion by the latter in a report intended to be communicated to various political institutions and widely diffused

[165] *Rundfunk* case (n 163), para 41.
[166] *Ibid*, para 42.
[167] *Ibid*, para 43.

constituted the processing of personal data within the meaning of Article 2(b) of the Directive.[168] However, the provisions of Directive 95/46, insofar as they govern the processing of personal data liable to infringe fundamental freedoms, in particular the right to privacy, must necessarily be interpreted in the light of fundamental rights, which, according to settled case law,[169] formed an integral part of the general principles of law whose observance the Court ensured.[170] Therefore, any interference with this right by the application of national legislation could be justified under Article 8(2) of the ECHR, and it was a matter for the national courts to examine whether the wide disclosure not merely of the amounts of annual income above a certain threshold of persons employed by the bodies subject to control by the Rechnungshof and also the names of the recipients of that income, was both necessary for and appropriate and proportional to the aim of keeping salaries within reasonable limits.[171]

The second question referred to the ECJ for a preliminary ruling in the *Rundfunk* case was the direct applicability of the provisions of Directive 95/46/EC (Articles 6(1) and 7) by national courts in the absence of national legislation or in instances of incorrect transposition in the national legal system. The ECJ answered that those provisions are sufficiently precise to be relied on by individuals and applied by the national courts. Moreover, the ECJ held that, 'While Directive 95/46 undoubtedly confers on the Member States a greater or lesser discretion in the implementation of some of its provisions, Articles 6(1)(c) and 7(c) or (e) for their part state unconditional obligations'.[172]

Whereas in the *Rundfunk* case the ECJ clarified the scope of Directive 95/46/EC by stating that it was not limited to cases in which the common market's freedoms are at stake, and it found that any application of its provisions must respect fundamental rights (especially Article 8(2) ECHR), in the *Lindqvist* case the contribution by the ECJ to the clarification of the scope of personal data protection in EU law related to the frontiers of the first pillar. If a charitable or religious is included within the first pillar and if a network is created from a personal computer using the personal data of colleagues, it falls within the provisions of Directive 95/46/EC.

(b) The Lindqvist *Case*

In the *Lindqvist* case the Göta hovrätt (Göta Court of Appeal) of Sweden applied to the ECJ for a preliminary ruling on the interpretation of Directive 95/46/EC. Mrs Lindqvist was charged with an infraction under Swedish legislation on the protection of personal data, for publishing personal data concerning a number of people working with her on a voluntary basis in a parish of the Swedish Protestant

[168] *Ibid*, para 64.
[169] Case-274/99 *Connolly v Commission* [2001] ECR I-1611, para 37.
[170] *Rundfunk* case (n 163), para 68.
[171] *Ibid*, para 90.
[172] *Ibid*, para 100.

Church on her website. In 1998, Mrs Lindqvist set up web pages at home on her personal computer in order to allow parishioners preparing for confirmation to obtain any information they may need. The pages contained information on Mrs Lindqvist and 18 colleagues in the parish, sometimes including their full names and in other cases only their first names. She also described the positions held by her colleagues and their hobbies, including in many cases their family circumstances and telephone numbers and other matters, for example that one of them had injured her foot and worked part-time on medical grounds. Her colleagues did not know of the existence of those pages, although once they did, they disapproved of them and she then removed the pages.

Among the questions referred by the Göta Court of Appeal to the ECJ on the scope of Directive 95/46/EC, it is worth highlighting the first: whether the act of referring, on a web page, to data concerning Mrs Lindqvist's colleagues constituted the processing of personal data wholly or partly within the scope of Directive 95/46/EC?[173] To answer this question, the starting point of the ECJ's judgment was the definition of 'personal data' (any information relating to an identified or identifiable natural person), of 'processing of such data' (as any operation or set of operations which is performed upon personal data, whether or not by automatic means, which includes the operation of loading personal data onto a web page), and of 'wholly or partly . . . automatic' (such as placing information on a web page that entails, under technical and computer procedures, the operation of loading that page onto a server and the operations necessary to make that page accessible to people who are connected to the Internet). Once it had outlined the meaning of these terms, the ECJ concluded that the act of referring to various persons on a web page, and identifying them by name or by other means (giving their telephone number or information regarding their working conditions and hobbies), constitutes the processing of personal data wholly or partly by automatic means within Article 3(1) of Directive 46/95/EC.

More interesting is the question referred to the ECJ on whether Mrs Lindqvist's acts were covered by one of the exceptions contained in Article 3(2) of Directive 95/46/EC. These exceptions are, firstly, the processing of personal data in the course of an activity which falls outside the scope of Community law, such as those provided for by Titles V and VI of the TEU, and in any case processing operations concerning public security, defence, State security and the activities of the State in the area of criminal law; and secondly, whether those activities were carried out in the course of the private or family life of individuals.[174]

With regard to the first exception, the ECJ rejected the contention that Mrs Lindqvist's activities were outside the scope of Community law, even though they were not economic but charitable and religious. The Court recalled its doctrine on the recourse to Article 100A of the EC as a legal basis on which Directive 95/46/EC

[173] Art 3(1) of Directive 95/46/EC reads: 'Scope. *1.* This Directive shall apply to the processing of personal data wholly or partly by automatic means, and to the processing otherwise than by automatic means of personal data which form part of a filing system or are intended to form part of a filing system.'

[174] Directive 95/46/EC (n 140), Art 3(2), second indent.

was based, which does not presuppose the existence of an actual link with free movement between Member States in every situation referred to by the measure founded on that basis.[175] A contrary interpretation would introduce legal uncertainty as to the limits of the field of application of the Directive.[176] Hence, the exception contained in the first indent of Article 3(2) of Directive 95/46/EC—in other words, activities provided for by Titles V and VI of the TEU and processing operations concerning public security, defence, State security and activities in the area of criminal law—are 'activities of the State or of State authorities and unrelated to the fields of activity of individuals'.[177] Therefore, the ECJ concluded that the exception in the first indent of Article 3(2) of Directive 95/46/EC applied only to the activities that are expressly listed therein or which can be classified in the same category (*ejusdem generis*).[178]

With regard to the second exception contained in the second indent of Article 3(2) of Directive 95/46/EC, it applies 'only to activities which are carried out in the course of private or family life of individuals, which is clearly not the case with the processing of personal data consisting in publication on the internet so that those data are made accessible to an indefinite number of people'.[179]

The last question concerning the scope of Directive 95/46/EC that was referred to the ECJ was whether it is permissible for the Member States to provide for greater protection of personal data or a wider scope than is required under Directive 95/46/EC. The ECJ recalled the fact that the Directive is intended to ensure that the level of protection of the rights and freedoms of individuals regarding the processing of their personal data is equivalent in all Member States and that the harmonisation of those national laws is therefore not limited to minimal harmonisation but amounts to harmonisation which is generally complete. However, nothing prevents a Member State from extending the scope of the national legislation implementing the provisions of Directive 95/46/EC to areas not included within the scope thereof, provided that no other provision of Community law precludes it.[180]

(c) The PNR *Case*

The above cases show how, through a preliminary ruling, the ECJ contributes to delimiting the scope of Directive 95/46/EC as extending as far as possible within the first pillar, but covering acts not directly related to the common market freedoms. However, the case law also reveals the limits of personal data protection established by current legislation. The decision adopted by the ECJ in Cases C-317/04 and C-318/04 (*Passenger Name Record* cases, hereafter '*PNR* case') constituted a restrictive

[175] Joined Cases C-465/00, C-138/01 and C-139/01 *Österreichischer Rundfunk and Others* (n 163), para 41 and the case law cited therein.

[176] *Ibid.*

[177] Case C-101/01 *Lindqvist* (n 163), para 43.

[178] *Ibid*, para 44.

[179] *Ibid*, para 47.

[180] *Ibid*, paras 95, 96 and 98.

interpretation of Directive 95/46/EC's scope, in which the ECJ annulled two decisions on the processing and transfer of PNR data by air carriers to the US Department of Homeland Security and on the adequate protection of PNR personal data transferred to that Department.[181]

Following the terrorist attacks of 11 September 2001, the United States passed legislation in November 2001 providing that air carriers operating flights to or from the United States or across US territory had to provide the US customs authorities with electronic access to the data contained in their automated reservation and departure control systems (Passenger Name Record or PNR data). The Commission entered into negotiations with the United States authorities in order to adopt a decision on the adequacy of such data transfer according to Article 25(6) of Directive 95/46/EC on the transfer of personal data to third countries. In spite of reservations of a legal nature expressed by the European Parliament regarding the proposal that had been submitted to it and due to the urgency of the situation given that a large number of airlines in the EU granted the US authorities access to their PNR data, mainly to avoid penalties, both the Commission and Council adopted decisions subject to actions for annulment by the Parliament.

The Commission's decision was at issue in Case C-318/04, where the Parliament submitted an action for annulment based on four grounds, alleging that the decision was *ultra vires* and breached the fundamental principles of the Directive, fundamental rights and the principle of proportionality. The ECJ decided to annul this decision based on the first ground (*ultra vires*), without examining the other grounds.

The allegation of *ultra vires* was well-founded according to the ECJ, because the Decision based on Article 25 of Directive 95/46/CE infringed Article 3(2) of the Directive, relating to the exclusion of activities which fall outside the scope of Community law. According to that provision, the Directive shall not apply to the processing of personal data 'in the course of an activity which falls outside the scope of Community law, such as those provided for by Titles V and VI of the Treaty on European Union and in any case to processing operations concerning public security, defence, State security (including the economic well-being of the State when the processing operation relates to State security matters) and the activities of the State in areas of criminal law'.

However, the Commission considered that the air carriers' activities clearly fell within the scope of Community law. The Commission held that activities of private parties were at issue, not the activities of the Member States in which the carriers concerned operated. The aim pursued by the air carriers in processing PNR data was compliance with the requirements of Community law. That activity was not included in the exception to Article 3(2) of the Directive, which refers to the activities of public authorities—which fall outside the scope of Community law.

Although the ECJ admitted that PNR data are initially collected by airlines in the course of an activity which falls within the scope of Community law (the sale of an

[181] Joined Cases C-317/04 and C-318/04, *PNR* case (n 164).

aeroplane ticket constitutes the supply of services), the transfer of PNR data to the Bureau of Customs and Border Protection of the Department of Homeland Security of United States constitutes processing operations concerning public security and the activities of the State in the area of criminal law. In consequence, the ECJ declared that the decision on adequacy concerning the processing of personal data was included in the first indent of Article 3(2) of the Directive, and was therefore void because it did not fall within the scope of the Directive.[182]

Decision 2004/496/EC of the Council, on the conclusion of an Agreement between the European Community and the United States of America on the processing and transfer of PNR data by Air Carriers to the United States Department of Homeland Security, was the issue at stake in Case C-317/04. The Parliament formulated six grounds for its annulment based on the incorrect choice of Article 95 EC as a legal basis, breach of Article 300(3) EC, Article 8 of the ECHR, the principle of proportionality, the requirement to state reasons, and the principle of co-operation in good faith. As happened in Case C-318/04, the ECJ examined the first ground (on the adequacy of the legal basis) and annulled the agreement.

With regard to the legal basis used, the Parliament submitted that Article 95 of the EC did not constitute an appropriate legal basis for Decision 2004/496, because the Decision did not have as its objective and subject-matter the establishment and functioning of the internal market, by contributing to the removal of obstacles to the freedom to provide services, and did not contain provisions designed to achieve such an objective. Its purpose was to make lawful the processing of personal data that was required by US legislation.[183] On the other hand, the Council considered Article 95 of the EC to be a correct legal basis because the conditions of competition between Member States' airlines operating international passenger flights to and from the US could have been distorted if only some of them granted the US authorities access to their databases.[184] The Commission considered that Article 95 was 'the natural legal basis' for the decision, because the Agreement concerned the external dimension of the protection of personal data when transferred within the Community.[185]

Taking into account that the Agreement related to the same transfer of data as the Decision on adequacy and that such data processing operations were excluded from the scope of the Directive, the ECJ concluded that Article 95 of the EC, read in conjunction with Article 25 of the Directive, could not justify Community competence to conclude the Agreement.[186] Consequently, the Court declared Decision 2004/496 to be annulled.

Whereas in the *Rundfunk* and *Linqvist* cases the ECJ held that the applicability of Directive 95/46/EC cannot depend on whether the specific situation has a sufficient link with the exercise of the fundamental freedoms guaranteed by the Treaty and

[182] *Ibid*, paras 56–61.
[183] *Ibid*, para 63.
[184] *Ibid*, para 64.
[185] *Ibid*, para 65.
[186] *Ibid*, paras 67–68.

that 'a contrary interpretation could make the limits of the field of application of the Directive particularly unsure and uncertain and therefore contrary to its essential objective of approximating the laws, regulations and administrative provisions of the Member States in order to eliminate obstacles to the functioning of the internal market deriving precisely from disparities between national legislations',[187] in the *PNR* case the ECJ seemed to have forgotten its own doctrine, leaving the institutions without a legal basis to act in similar cases in which the personal data protection right is involved.

As we will see in the next section, problems such as those arising from the transfer of PNR data to the United States would be solved under the Constitutional Treaty, which introduces a new legal basis on data protection not limited to Community acts, resulting from the elimination of the pillar structure.

3. Personal Data Protection in the Charter and in the Constitutional Treaty

(a) Introduction

Within the Constitutional Treaty the right to data protection is duplicated, which also occurs with respect to rights accruing from EU citizenship, such as the right of access to documents. The personal data protection right is included, firstly, within the title on the Democratic life of the Union (Article I-51), which is based on the principles of transparency of proceedings and participation of citizens in Union action. In the context of openness and access to documents guaranteed by this title, the protection of personal data is a logical consequence of enhanced participation. The Praesidium refused to remove rights included not only in the Charter but also in Part I of the Constitutional Treaty because it considered that the notion of EU citizenship was so fundamental to the Union that it should figure early on.[188] Furthermore, the right to the protection of personal data, which was included in the Charter of Fundamental Rights (Article 8), remains in Article II-68 of the Constitutional Treaty as it was conceived by the Charter. The provision on regulation of the right in Article II-68 refers to some principles of data processing such as the necessity to process data fairly, for specified purposes and on the basis of consent of the person concerned or some other legitimate basis laid down by law, and that the person concerned has the right of access to the data and the right to have it rectified.[189] Although this provision does not mention all the principles under which the processing of personal data must be subject, according to the Final Report of Working Group II[190] and the Explanations of the Charter, the current principles developed by secondary norms and the case law must be understood as

[187] At n 163.
[188] Ladenburger (2006) 30.
[189] Constitutional Treaty, Art II-68(2).
[190] CONV 354/02 (n 92), 6.

implicit.[191] Indeed, according to the explanation in Article 8 of the Charter, this right must be exercised under the conditions established by Directive 95/46/EC and its limitation must respect the conditions established by Article 52 of the Charter. Therefore, the data protection right may be limited only by European law, in that it should respect the essence of this right and the principle of proportionality. Hence, with the Constitutional Treaty in force, Community Courts will control whatever limitation is imposed on this right, for instance, by a European law which, updating the Europol Convention or falling within the scope of the current third pillar, does not respect the essence of this right or the principle of proportionality which imposes limits on it.

(b) Implications

Two innovations were added to the right to personal data protection in the Constitutional Treaty. Firstly, the Constitutional Treaty establishes a new legal basis relating to the right to data protection (Article I-51(2)), complementing the statement of a fundamental right to data protection (Articles I-51(1) and II-68). This legal basis covers data processing both by the Union's institutions, bodies and agencies and by Member States acting within the scope of Union law. In the future, Union legislation on data protection by Member States will not be considered as an 'annex' to the internal market as is the case currently, due to the fact that it is based on Article 95 of the EC.[192] Secondly, the new legal basis covers all data processing within the scope of Union law, including the current second and third pillars (see below).[193] Indeed, the Constitutional Treaty will have a great impact on this right, due to the elimination of the pillar structure, because its regulation will be extended to third and second pillar policies.[194] It will be applicable to all fields of EU law with the limitations imposed only by a European law or framework law.[195] Nonetheless, it will be in the Area of Freedom, Security and Justice that the right of data protection will play a major role. Within this area, it is worth noticing the impact that the Constitutional Treaty will have on the activities of Europol as the main data collector and storer.

Europol was created by Council Act of 26 July 1995, which drew up a Convention based on Article K.3 of the TEU,[196] on the establishment of a European Police Office (Europol Convention) to improve the effectiveness and co-operation of the

[191] Art 52(2) of the Charter reads: 'The Charter does not alter the system of rights conferred by the Treaties.' Explanations in Document CHARTE 4473/00 CONVENT 49, of 11 October 2000.

[192] Ladenburger (2005a) 171.

[193] Art I-51, in accordance with the elimination of the pillar structure, proclaims that 'European laws or framework laws shall lay down the rules relating to the protection of individuals with regards to the processing of personal data by Union institutions, bodies, offices and agencies, and by the Member States when carrying out activities which fall within the scope of Union law'.

[194] The second pillar will be brought under the heading 'Union External Action': Title V, third part of the Constitutional Treaty. The third pillar will be brought under the heading 'Area of Freedom, Security and Justice', also in the third part of the Constitutional Treaty, Title III, Chapter IV.

[195] Charter of Fundamental Rights, Art 52(1); Constitutional Treaty, Art II-112(1).

[196] [1995] OJ C316/2.

competent authorities in the Member States in preventing and combating terrorism, unlawful drug trafficking and other serious forms of international crime where there are factual indications that an organised criminal structure is involved within two or more Member States. The Convention entered into force in 1999, and since then Europol activities have focused on the collection, transmission and processing of information related to unlawful drug trafficking, illegal immigration networks and other serious forms of international crime.

During the Convention on the Future of Europe period, (2002–2003), concern was expressed in several documents on Justice and Home Affairs with respect to Europol's activities, which are subject neither to democratic control by the European Parliament[197] nor to judicial control by the ECJ.[198] Under the current arrangements, the data subject has the right to ask Europol to delete his or her data when proceedings against that person are dropped or if he or she is acquitted.[199] But, if the enquirer is not satisfied with Europol's reply or if there is no reply within three months, the only option that remains is to refer the matter to a Joint Supervisory Body.[200] This body is established under Article 24 of the Europol Convention, with the function of reviewing the activities of Europol in order to ensure that the rights of individuals are not violated by the storage, processing and illegal utilisation of data held by Europol. It is composed of members or representatives of each of the national supervisory bodies (not more than two for each Member State).[201] The decision of the Joint Supervisory Body is final and binding on Europol.

The same situation is applied to Eurojust's processed data.[202] Every person has the right to access his or her own personal data processed by Eurojust and to ask for correction and deletion if they are incorrect or incomplete.[203] If access is denied or if the applicant is not satisfied with the reply given to his or her request, or if there is no answer, an appeal may be made against that decision before a Joint Supervisory Body.[204] As with the Europol Convention, the decision of the Joint Supervisory Body is final and binding on Eurojust.

[197] The adoption of a common position by the Council does not require consultation with the European Parliament (Art 32 TEU) in spite of a Protocol that amended the Europol Convention with the aim of introducing Parliamentary control over the actions of Europol (a Council Act of 27 November 2003 drew up a Protocol amending the Europol Convention on the basis of Art 43(1) of that Convention [2004] OJ C2/1). This Protocol imposed a duty on the President of the Council, assisted by the Director of Europol, to inform the European Parliament or discuss general questions relating to Europol (Art 34(2) Europol Convention). Prior to this Protocol, Europol's Convention established that the President of the Council had to forward a special report to the European Parliament each year (Art 34) (n 196).

[198] *Justice and Home Affairs—Progress Report and General Problems*, CONV 69/02, 31 May 2002, 10–11; *Note of the Plenary Meeting*, Brussels, 6 and 7 June 2002, CONV 97/02, 19 June 2002, 4–6.

[199] Europol Convention (n 196), Art 8(5).

[200] *Ibid*, Art 20(4).

[201] *Ibid.*

[202] Eurojust was set up by Council Decision 2002/187/JHA of 28 February 2002, on the basis provided for by Arts 31 and 34(2)(c) of the TEU[2002] OJ L63/1. This was amended by Council Decision 2003/659/JHA of 18 June 2003 [2003] OJ L245/44.

[203] Council Decision on Eurojust (*ibid*), Arts 19 and 20.

[204] The Joint Supervisory Body monitors Eurojust's activities collectively to ensure that the processing of personal data is carried out correctly. It is composed of one judge from each Member State. The judges should not be members of Eurojust: Council Decision on Eurojust (*ibid*).

Chapter five analyses the provisions of the Constitutional Treaty (Articles III-365 and III-367) that authorise the ECJ to review Europol and Eurojust's actions. It is sufficient for our purposes in this chapter to underline that under the Constitutional Treaty, both bodies (Europol and Eurojust) may be under the supervision of the European Data Protection Supervisor. The European Data Protection Supervisor is an independent supervisory authority responsible for ensuring that the fundamental rights and freedoms of natural persons, and in particular their right to privacy, are respected by the Community institutions and bodies.[205] To that end, European law on Europol and on Eurojust should make these bodies subject to the supervision of the European Data Protection Supervisor. In that case, European law would have to determine the fate of the Joint Supervisory Bodies of Europol and Eurojust, whose role would be redundant. The European Data Protection Supervisor's decisions may be challenged before the ECJ.[206]

The Constitutional Treaty will have less impact upon other systems of information and data collection, such as the Schengen Information System (SIS), the Customs Information System (CIS) and Eurodac.

Although the SIS was created within the third pillar, using a legal basis under Title VI of the Treaty on European Union, under the heading of 'Provisions on Police and Judicial Cooperation in Criminal Matters', it is currently included within the Community pillar and is therefore under the supervision of the Community Courts.[207]

The CIS was established by Council Regulation (EC) No 515/97 of 13 March 1997 on mutual assistance between the administrative authorities of the Member States and co-operation between the latter and the Commission to ensure the correct application of the law on customs and agricultural matters, and therefore falls within the institutional and legal framework of the Community pillar.[208] The CIS consists of a database accessible via terminals in each Member State and at the

[205] Regulation (EC) No 45/2001 (n 157), Arts 41–48.

[206] *Ibid*, Art 32.

[207] The Schengen *acquis* was integrated into the framework of the European Union by the Schegen Protocol or Schegen Acquis, Protocol No 2, 1997, annexed to the TEU and to the EC by the ToA. Art 1 of the Protocol states that closer co-operation within the scope of the Schengen agreements must be conducted within the legal and institutional framework of the European Union with respect for the Treaties. A recent decision of the ECJ, in Case C-503/2003 *Commission v Spain* [2006] ECR I-1097, declared that the Kingdom of Spain had failed to fulfil its obligations under Arts 1 to 3 of Council Directive 64/221/EEC of 25 February 1964 on the co-ordination of special measures concerning the movement and residence of foreign nationals which are justified on grounds of public policy, public security or public health, by refusing entry into the territory of States party to the Schengen Agreement to two third country nationals who were married to Member State nationals, on the sole ground that they were persons for whom alerts were entered in the Schengen Information System for the purposes of refusing them entry, without first verifying whether their presence constituted a genuine, present and sufficiently serious threat affecting one of the fundamental interests of society. This judgment is an example of how the ECJ supervises the integration of the Schengen *acquis* within the Community *acquis*: Alcoceba Gallego (2006).

[208] [1997] OJ L82/1. The aim of the CIS is to assist in preventing, investigating and prosecuting operations which are in breach of customs or agricultural legislation, by increasing, through more rapid dissemination of information, the effectiveness of the co-operation and control procedures of Member States' competent authorities (Art 23(2) of Regulation No 515/1997).

Commission. The rights of persons with regard to their personal data in the CIS, in particular their right to access such data, are governed by the national law of the State in which such rights are invoked. Indeed, someone who wants to bring an action or complaint relating to the processing of his or her data by the CIS must do so before the national court or authority designated for this purpose.[209] When in any Member State a court or other authority designated for that purpose makes a final decision to amend, supplement, correct or delete data in the CIS, the CIS must be amended accordingly. This provision is also applicable to the Commission when its decision on data contained in the CIS is declared void by the ECJ.[210]

Council Regulation (EC) No 2725/2000 of 11 December 2000[211] established Eurodac for the comparison of fingerprints for the effective application of the Dublin Convention, which determines the State responsible for examining applications for asylum lodged in one of the Member States of the European Communities.[212] Eurodac consists of a Central Unit established within the Commission, which operates a central computerised database of fingerprint data which is transmitted between the Member States and the central database. The Preamble to Regulation No 2725/2000 establishes the application of Directive 95/46/EC to Member States when processing personal data within the framework of the Eurodac system.[213] The Preamble also refers to the application of that Directive to the Commission, by virtue of Article 286 of the EC. This reference must be understood with respect to Regulation No 45/2001, which developed the provision contained in Article 286 after the Regulation on Eurodac was approved. The Eurodac Regulation provides for data protection rules and for a joint supervisory authority, endowed with the task of monitoring the activities of the central unit to ensure that the rights of data subjects are not violated by the processing or use of the data. It also monitors the lawfulness of the transmission of personal data to the Member States by the central unit. Under the Constitutional Treaty these duties these duties will be assumed by the European Data Supervisor, which will replace the joint supervisory authority envisaged in the Eurodac Regulation (Article 20(11)) and will exercise all the powers conferred on it.

209 Regulation No 515/1997, Art 36(5).

210 *Ibid*, Art 32(5).

211 [2000] OJ L316/1. The implementation of that Regulation was approved in Council Regulation (EC) No 407/2002 of 28 February 2002 [2002] OJ L62/1.

212 [1997] OJ C254/1.

213 Council Regulation No 2725/2000 (n 212), Preamble, para 15.

3

The Impact of the Charter of Fundamental Rights on Decisions Adopted by Member States

I. FUNDAMENTAL RIGHTS OF THE UNION AND MEMBER STATES: WHAT DOES 'IMPLEMENT' MEAN?

1. General Considerations: The Relevance of the Topic

The incorporation of the European Charter of Fundamental Rights into the Constitutional Treaty—Part II—has the immediate consequence of transforming the rights contained in the Treaty into valid legal norms which apply not only to the acts of the EU, but also to acts of the Member States when they apply EU law. Clearly, in principle, fundamental rights form part of the *aquis communautaire*—also as general principles of Community Law—[1] which controls the acts of the Community institutions; however, at the same time, Member States cannot avoid their application in specific circumstances.[2] According to the Presidency Conclusions of the Brussels European Council (21/22 June 2007), the TEU reform will include in the article on fundamental rights—Article 6 a cross reference to the Charter on fundamental rights, in order to give it legally binding value.

[1] Fundamental rights, as general principles of Community Law and, if incorporated to the Treaties, as 'legal' rights, have to do with the rule of law and protection of individuals, and they are means of controlling the acts of the Community institutions and national authorities when applying Union Law. As affirmed by Advocate General Mengozzi in Joined Cases C-354/04 and C-355/04, 'unfounded is the suspicion often voiced that the jurisdiction of the Court with regard to respect for fundamental rights as general principles of Community law is inspired not so much by genuine concern for the protection of such rights as by a desire to defend the primacy of Community law and of the Community court in relation to the law and authorities of the Member States' (para 180). More clearly, in Case C-229/05 *PKK and KNK v Council* (not yet published), the Court of Justice affirmed that 'the European Community is a community based on the rule of law in which its institutions are subject to judicial review of the compatibility of their acts with the EC Treaty and with the general principles of law which include fundamental rights' (para 109).

[2] The main aim of the European Union Agency for Fundamental Rights is, in fact, 'to provide the relevant institutions, bodies, offices and agencies of the Community and its Member States when implementing Community law with assistance and expertise relating to fundamental rights in order to support them when they take measures or formulate courses of action within their respective spheres of competence to fully respect fundamental rights', Article 1 Regulation (EC) No 168/2007 of the Council of 15 February 2007 [2007] OJ L53/1.

For this reason, having analysed the implications of the Charter of Fundamental Rights on acts of the European administration, it is interesting to focus on its consequences for the acts of authorities within the Member States. Specifically, this chapter attempts to build a general thesis regarding the significance and meaning of the formula contained in Article 51 of the Charter in order to demarcate the scope of application of the fundamental rights of the EU to Member States, and examine the consequences of the recognition of the right to good administration, access to documents and the protection of personal data to them. To this end, an analysis of the jurisprudence of the ECJ in this area will be undertaken, and the chapter will also examine the extent to which the ECJ's case law has been incorporated into this provision. It is, however, necessary to clarify that the limited reach of this book tends to restrict the study of the meaning of implementation to the scope of the fundamental rights to the Charter.

The application of the Charter of Fundamental Rights to national administrations is important for two reasons: on the one hand, the ECJ would be the competent organ to interpret and apply the rights to the acts of national administrations—without prejudice, of course, to the competences of national jurisdictions—[3]; on the other hand, the rights would be binding—and, therefore, could be directly invoked before national courts—even if they are not recognised or are not recognised to the same extent in national systems, thereby expanding the sphere of protection of citizens of the EU (and even, where appropriate, nationals of third countries).

[3] With the consequent risk of collision with the constitutional jurisdiction of some of the Member States, an issue that will not be considered here as it is outside the scope of this book. At this point it is sufficient to point out that the Council of State, the highest consultative organ of the government in the Spanish legal system, stated in its Opinion 2544/2004 of 21 October relating to the Treaty Establishing a Constitution for Europe, that 'apart from the difficulties arising in practice, it seems that there are sufficient guarantees that the provisions of the Charter will not cause collisions or discrepancies with the protection of those rights and freedoms contained in the Spanish Constitution'. According to the Council, the only legal problems arising from the Constitution will be the existence of three regimes—the Spanish Constitution, the regime within the Council of Europe and the Charter—for the protection of fundamental rights, and they will have to be resolved case by case. This was done by the Spanish Constitutional Court in its Opinion 1/2004 of 13 December: it found that there is no contradiction between the Spanish Constitution and Art II-111 of the Constitutional Treaty, given that Art 10(2) of the Spanish Constitution (which provides that 'Provisions relating to the fundamental rights and liberties recognized by the Constitution shall be construed in conformity with the Universal Declaration of Human Rights and international treaties and agreements thereon ratified by Spain'), meaning that the rights contained in the Charter will have to be taken into account as an interpretative criterion of the rights recognised by the Spanish Constitution, as is the current practice with respect to the rights contained in the European Convention on Human Rights.

With respect to indications of the future attitude of the Constitutional Court to EU law, two factors are relevant: first of all, in the decision above, the Court found that in the hypothetical case where EU law is found to be incompatible with the Spanish Constitution and none of the ordinary mechanisms established to avoid such incompatibility proves effective, it will be up to the Court itself it to deal with any problems that arise (point 4); secondly, since its judgment 64/1991 of 22 March (point 4), the Court has confirmed that 'to the extent that an act of public power is challenged which was taken pursuant to European Community law, and violates a fundamental right, this Court will be competent to hear the case independently of whether the act is valid or not from the point of view of the Community legal order, without prejudice to the effects of the act under Art 10(2) of the Constitution', an opinion which was recently repeated in judgment 58/2002 of 19 April (point 11).

2. Subjecting National Administration to the Fundamental Rights of the Union

Article 51(1) of the Charter contains one of the most confusing and obscure clauses to be found in the entire Charter of Fundamental Rights. Under the heading 'Field of Application', it establishes that 'The provisions of this Charter are addressed to . . . the Member States only when they are implementing Union law'.

Thus, it is clear that the fundamental rights protected by the EU apply to the Member States. What is not evident is when the Member State can be said to be involved in the 'application' or 'implementation'—the terms are synonyms—of EU law.

To 'apply' or 'implement', according to a standard dictionary, means 'to put a particular measure into practice to achieve a determined result, to carry something out'. Thus, application or implementation of the law of the EU would mean the adoption of a measure—either legal or administrative—for the achievement of some of the specific objectives of the EU. In short, it means 'to put into practice'. In fact, according to the *Oxford Dictionary of Law*, implementation is the process of bringing any piece of legislation into force.

This seemingly simple definition is complicated by the fact that the case law varies with respect to the application of the fundamental rights protected by Community law to Member States. Can a Member State be said to implement EU law by the mere fact that the administrative act in question is financed by the EU? Should this concept be limited to the strict implementation of an EU law? Is it sufficient, in order to determine the scope of application of fundamental rights, that there is a connection between the national act and EU law?

(a) Case Law on the Application of Fundamental Rights of the EU to Member States

The ECJ has had an opportunity to deal with this issue on many occasions since the 1980s, the most important of which will be examined subsequently. On examining the case law, one thing becomes clear: the concept of 'implementation' is open and can only be understood in general terms, based on a series of general criteria using the specific elements occurring in each individual case as a reference.

In any attempt to anchor the concept, it must be accepted that there are two different branches of case law regarding the development and the reach of the requirement that Member States respect fundamental Community rights. The first of these—and the oldest—can be characterized as a strict interpretation and relates to the ability to invoke the fundamental rights against the acts of national authorities when they apply Community law, and means that Member States cannot introduce disproportionate or unnecessary restrictions on such rights. The second can be characterised as a broad interpretation and relates to the duty on Member States to respect fundamental rights when their acts fall within the field of application of Community and involves the requirement to interpret the substance of the situation in conformity with the fundamental right applicable to the case.

It is clear that limiting the binding effect of fundamental rights to national authorities only when their acts can be said to be an application of EU law is not the same as asserting that such rights are binding when the acts are included in the field of application of EU law. Both of these perspectives will now be considered in more depth.

The branch of case law associated with the strict interpretation begins with the judgment of the ECJ in Case 5/88 *Wachauf v Bundesamt für Ernährung und Forstwirtschaft*,[4] which asserted that 'those requirements [the requirements stemming from the protection of fundamental rights in the Community legal order] are also binding on the Member States when they implement Community rules, [and] the Member States must, as far as possible, apply those rules in accordance with those requirements' (para 19), except for possible restrictions to such requirements which 'in fact correspond to objectives of general interest pursued by the Community and do not constitute, with regard to the aim pursued, a disproportionate and intolerable interference, impairing the very substance of those rights' (para 18). This branch of case law was followed by Case C-2/92[5]; Case C-292/97[6]; Joined Cases C-20/00 and 64/00[7]; and Joined Cases C-387/02, 391/02 and 403/02.[8] In this sense, Case C-540/03[9] deserves special mention for being the first in which the Court applied the Charter of Fundamental Rights to decide a case brought before it.[10]

Basically, this branch supports the proposition that fundamental rights of the EU legal order negatively bind Member States (negatively in the sense that they are obliged not to impair the effects of those rights) when they apply Community law. This implies a strict interpretation of the term: implementation means applying EU law, that is, taking legal or administrative measures pursuant to a Community rule.

4 [1989] ECR 2609. In this case there was doubt as to the compatibility of a national decision with Community law relating to a refusal to compensate a leaseholder of a farm for improvements carried out under the milk quota scheme. Thus, it related to the correct application of a rule of Community law—two regulations on the supplementary charges on milk—which left a certain margin of appreciation to Member States. A similar case had already been decided in this way: Joined Cases 201 and 202/85 *Klensch v Secrétaire d'État* [1986] ECR 3477 (para 8).

5 *The Queen v Ministry of Agriculture, Fisheries and Food, ex parte Dennis Clifford Bostock* [1994] ECR I-955 (para 16)

6 *Karlsson and others* [2000] ECR I-2737 (paras 37, 45 and 58).

7 *Booker Aquaculture and Hydro Seafood* [2003] ECR I-7411 (paras 68 and 88).

8 *Berlusconi and others* [2005] ECR I-3565 (para 69).

9 *Parliament v Council* [2006] ECR I-5769 (paras 104 and 105).

10 This judgment concerned an action for annulment brought by the European Parliament against various provisions of Directive 2003/86/EC of the Council, of 22 September 2003, on the right to family reunification [2003] OJ L251/12. In the action, it was argued that the Directive allowed Member States to make national laws within the framework of this directive which could violate fundamental rights. The Court rejected the challenge, finding that 'while the Directive leaves the Member States a margin of appreciation, it is sufficiently wide to enable them to apply the Directive's rules in a manner consistent with the requirements following from the protection of fundamental rights', concluding that 'the requirements flowing from the protection of general principles recognised in the Community legal order, which include fundamental rights, are also binding on Member States when they implement Community rules, and that consequently they are bound, as far as possible, to apply the rules in accordance with those requirements' (paras 104 and 105).

The second branch, identified as a broad interpretation, originated in Case C-260/89.[11] In this case, the Court clearly broadened the field of application of Community law fundamental rights to the acts of national administrations, finding that 'where such rules [national rules] do fall within the scope of Community law, and reference is made to the Court for a preliminary ruling, it must provide all the criteria of interpretation needed by the national court to determine whether those rules are compatible with the fundamental rights the observance of which the Court ensures' (para 42),[12] in such a way that those rules 'must be interpreted in the light of the general principles of law and in particular of fundamental rights' (para 43). In other words, when an internal act carried out by national authorities falls within the scope of Community law, this act must be interpreted in the light of Community fundamental rights, and in accordance with the criteria provided by the ECJ. This branch of case law has been supported by Case 2/92 cited above (in relation to the statement that it is for the ECJ to provide the interpretative criteria of such rights, para 16) and Case C-177/94[13]; Case C-299/95[14]; Case C-368/95[15]; Case C-309/96[16]; Case C-85/97[17]; Case C-274/96[18]; Case C-112/00[19]; Case C-36/02[20]; and Case 13/05. [21] Finally, in Case C-432/05—the second time that the European Court of Justice has invoked the Charter of Fundamental Rights—the Court mentions the right to effective judicial protection (Article 47 of the Charter) in a case in which, in a narrow sense, community rules were not at stake.[22]

The fundamental question thus asks when exactly a particular act or situation falls within the scope of Community law.[23] Some of the judgments state that this

[11] *ERT v DEP* [1991] ECR I-2925. In this judgment the ECJ responded to various questions raised in a preliminary reference from a Greek court regarding compatibility with the Treaty provisions on the free movement of goods and services and rules regarding competences of a national law which granted a single entity exclusive broadcasting rights for the entire country territory and whose consent was required to carry out any activity over which it enjoyed exclusive rights. For present purposes the interesting question in this case was whether Community fundamental rights created obligations for Member States and, that being so, if the Greek provision violated the freedom of expression contained as a fundamental right in Art 10 of the ECHR.

[12] Precedents for this branch of case law can be found in the following judgments: Joined Cases 60 and 62/84 *Cinéthèque v Fédération nationale des cinémas français* [1985] ECR 2605 (para 26) and Case 12/86 *Demirel v Stadt Schwäbisch Gmünd* [1987] ECR 3719 (para 28).

[13] *Criminal proceedings against Perfili* [1996] ECR I-161 (para 20).

[14] *Kremzow v Republik Österreich* [1997] ECR I-2629 (para 15).

[15] *Vereinigte Familiapress Zeitungsverlags- und vertriebs GmbH v Bauer Verlag* [1997] ECR I-3689 (para 24).

[16] *Annibaldi v Sindaco del Comune di Guidonia and Presidente Regione Lazio* [1997] ECR I-7493 (para 13).

[17] *Société financière d'investissements v Belgian State* [1998] ECR I-7447 (para 29).

[18] *Bickel and Franz* [1998] ECR I-7637.

[19] Para 75.

[20] *Omega* [2004] ECR I-9609 (para 33).

[21] *Chacón Navas/Eurest* [2006] ECR I-6467 (para 56).

[22] Case *Unibet*, not yet published. The Court of Justice had to resolve a preliminary ruling about whether the principle of effective judicial protection of an individual's rights under Community law must be interpreted as requiring it to be possible in the legal order of a Member State to bring a free-standing action for an examination as to whether national provisions are compatible with Article 49 EC if other legal remedies permit the question of compatibility to be determined as a preliminary issue.

[23] The terms 'national situation', 'measure', 'rule' and 'act' will be used interchangeably throughout this chapter to characterise acts of the authorities of the Member States subject to the fundamental rights of the Union.

occurs when such an act can hinder one of the fundamental freedoms contained in the Treaty (free movement of services in Case C-260/89 or Case C-36/02; free movement of goods in Cases C-368/95 and C-112/00). Others employ a broader formula, requiring that the situation be in some way connected to 'any of the situations contemplated by the Treaty', as in Case C-299/95 (para 16).[24] Indeed, some equate this expression to those national situations 'governed by Community law', such as Case C-274/96 (para 14)[25] or Case C-309/96 (para 24). Finally, as is obvious, a national measure will fall within the scope of Community law if it has as its object 'the implementation of a provision of Community law' regardless of the specific area involved, as confirmed again by Case C-309/96 (para 21).[26] This occurs when the national provision constitutes the clear execution of a provision of Community law (Case 12/86, para 28).

In sum, in accordance with this branch of case law characterising a broad interpretation, so long as there is a connection between the national situation and Community law, Community law fundamental rights will apply, establishing a canon of interpretation for the legality of national measures.

It can be appreciated that, even if the judgments cited here attempt to list the cases in which a situation or a national measure could be subject to the application of Community law or fall under its scope, the concept of application or implementation is still too vague, and thus an analysis of the concrete circumstances of each case is required and a solution can only be found on a case-by-case basis with respect to the application of the fundamental rights of the EU to Member States.

[24] In this judgment, the ECJ ruled out any connection with Community law and thus avoided ruling on a national act that condemned a citizen to life imprisonment after a trial which had been found to be contrary to Art 6 of the ECHR. With respect to the applicant's argument that his imprisonment was a violation of his right to free movement of persons, the Court found that this situation had no connection whatsoever with any of the situations envisaged in the Treaty provisions relating to free movement of persons given that there was an insufficient link between his imprisonment and the right and that the legislation which led to his imprisonment was not aimed at giving effect to Community law; therefore 'the national legislation applicable in the main proceedings relates to a situation which does not fall within the field of application of Community law' (para 18).

[25] In this case the Court decided on the compatibility of Art 12 EC (non-discrimination) of an Italian rule which granted the German-speaking inhabitants of the province of Bolzano the right to have a criminal trial in a language other than the national language (Italian) but did not extend this right to other citizens of the Union of the same linguistic group (in this case, an Austrian national). The ECJ concluded that this was a situation governed by Community law in the sense that when any person exercises their right to move to or reside in another Member State, they are entitled not to be discriminated against with respect to nationals of the State in respect of the use of a language already used in the State; thus, this law was in contravention of the principle of equal treatment enshrined in EC Treaty.

[26] In this judgment, the ECJ ruled out that the national measure in question—an Italian regional law which created a natural and archaeological park—constituted a situation governed by Community law, given that there was no specific provision of Community law which covered this matter nor did the Community have the competence in this area; in consequence, it could not be considered a measure implementing Community law.

(b) The Formula in Article 51(1) of the Charter: Subjecting Member States to Community Fundamental Rights 'only when they are implementing Union law'

An attempt was made by the Convention that promulgated the Charter of Fundamental Rights to codify the case law of the Court analysed above.[27] The formula put forward by the Convention whereby Member States are bound by EU fundamental rights does not, however, completely resolve the divergences in the case law; in fact it has the opposite effect—it introduces more confusion, if it were possible—in asserting that such an application occurs 'only when they are implementing Union law'.

The explanations from the Praesidium that accompanied the Charter, subsequently adopted by the Praesidium of the Constitutional Treaty in the Constitutional Treaty itself,[28] do not shed any light on whether they refer to the first or the second branch of case law, given that they refer to both branches. Moreover, they erroneously state that the two braches are equivalent: according to the Convention, 'it follows unambiguously from the case law of the ECJ that the requirement to respect fundamental rights defined in an EU context is only binding on the Member States when they act in the context of Community law', and it refers to Case C-5/88 and Case C-260/89 in support of this contention. However, the expression used does not correspond at all to that used by the ECJ; as explained above, the first line states that such rights are binding when the national authority 'is applying a Community rule', while the second line uses the expression 'falls within the scope of Community law'. Moreover, Case C-292/97, which also features in the explanations as confirming the two previous judgments, supports only the first branch of case law in providing for a connection between national acts and Community law in cases on the application of Community law, and not other cases which do not strictly relate to application, but where a connection between national law and Community law does exist.

All things considered, if the first part of the explanations that accompany the provision opts for a broad interpretation, the second part tends towards a strict interpretation. This is why the Convention's explanations do not settle the issue.

Moreover, the literature on the Charter published by members of the European Convention is contradictory with respect to specifying the extent of application of

[27] This is evidenced by the explanations of the Praesidium attached to the Charter and the preparatory works of the Convention of the Charter.

[28] By virtue of Art II-112(7) Constitutional Treaty, these explanations shall be given due regard by the Courts of the Union and of the Member States. Of course, by including the courts of the Member States, this provision is in accordance with the idea of the application of fundamental rights to Member States when they apply EU law. The explanations are contained in Declaration No 12 appended to the Constitutional Treaty.

the formula used in the Charter. Thus, while Braibant defends a strict interpretation,[29] Rodríguez Bereijo argues for a broad interpretation.[30]

The confusion is exacerbated by the two Commission Communications on the Charter. In the first of these, *Communication from the Commission on the Charter of Fundamental Rights of the European Union*, the Commission states that the Charter applies 'to the Member States solely where they implement Union law' specifying that 'this solution is in line with the consistent case law of the ECJ, which has pointed out on numerous occasions that Member States are required to respect fundamental rights when implementing Community law.'[31] In the second, *Communication on the Legal Nature of the Charter of Fundamental Rights of the European Union*, the Commission asserts that the Charter would apply to 'Member States when they act within the field of European law', and continues: 'This is made clear by Article 51(1), which provides that the Charter is addressed to . . . the Member States, when they give effect to Union law.'[32] Thus, for the European Commission, applying EU law and acting within the field of EU law are the same thing.[33]

The disagreement in the legal literature focusing on this article revolves around its scope. Whereas for some, implementing EU law is the same as acting in the field of Community law—understood as transposing directives or implementing Community rules[34]—others maintain that it is sufficient that the relevant case has a nexus with Community law in order to invoke the fundamental rights of the EU against national bodies.[35]

[29] This proposal was made in his capacity as a member of a Convention, arguing that the expression 'field of application of Community law' be replaced by 'in applying Community law', considering that the first expression was too broad and imprecise (CHARTE 4372/00 CONVENT 39, 16 June 2000). This author, however, prefers the expression 'put into practice' rather than 'apply'; Braibant (2001) 251.

[30] He interprets the expression 'are implementing' in Art 51(1) of the Charter as the equivalent of an act within the Community legal system: Rodríguez Bereijo (2002) 208. In fact, in his proposals as a member of the Convention, he proposed retaining the expression 'in the field of application of Community law' (CHARTE 4372/00 CONVENT 39, 16 June 2000).

[31] COM (2000) 559 final of 13 September 2000, 4 and 9 respectively.

[32] COM (2000) 644 final of 11 October 2000, 5.

[33] For its part, the Economic and Social Committee, in its Opinion Towards an EU Charter of Fundamental Rights [2000] OJ C367/8, uses the expression 'apply, implement or transpose Community law', while the European Parliament asserts that the Charter 'should have binding force on Member States in implementing and transposing Community law': Resolution of 16 March 2000 (CHARTE 4199/00 CONTRIB 90, 5 April 2000).

[34] Fernández Tomás (2001) 67 and 68.

[35] This is the position of Jacqué (2002) 75 and 76, for whom the expression 'does not simply cover the application of a regulation or the transposition of a directive but must be understood as an integral part of every act or omission relative to Community law' (p 76). Also Craig (2006) 502 considers that the narrow interpretation is regrettable in normative terms and that the Praesidium intended to reflect the existing corpus of the ECJ jurisprudence.

In the same sense see Requejo Isidro (2004) 216, 234 and 235. Also Rubio Llorente (2002) 41–42, who affirms that the expression contains an elastic criterion which will allow the scope of the internal acts under ECJ control to be extended. Koukoulis-Spiliotopoulos (2002) 73 and 75–76 also argues in favour of a broad interpretation. In his opinion, the rights must be binding when the national act falls within the scope of EU law; otherwise a retreat in the level of protection of fundamental rights would occur. Saiz Arnáiz (2001), analysing the case law on the matter, points out that the ECJ has gradually extended its field of activity on the protection of fundamental rights against national acts wherever there is a

Ultimately, the provision contains a broad, open-ended formula whose precise meaning will be determined by the ECJ in the exercise of its jurisdictional function in each specific case.

3. A Theory of the Concept of Implementing EU Law from the Perspective of the Protection of Fundamental Rights against the Acts of Member States

The basic issue—which forms the substantive subject matter of this chapter—is the control exercised by the ECJ over the activities of the authorities of the Member States from the viewpoint of EU fundamental rights and the extent to which national courts can be made to respect those rights.

sufficient connection or link between Community law and the national measure. In this way he identifies four types of measures that can be subject to control: national acts executing Community rules; the transposition of directives; derogations or exceptions permitted by Community law; and acts which affect the general principles of Community law. Thus, he concludes that '*the theoretical impact of the Charter on the activity of national public power* and therefore national legal systems is notable' (emphasis in original). However, he does not rule out a possible change in the attitude of the Court as a result of Art 51 of the Charter. For his part, Alonso García (2002) 155–8, responding to a question posed by himself relating to whether the literal reading of Art 51 of the Charter could be interpreted as a restriction on the binding effect of fundamental rights only in cases of the strict execution of EU law, and after having examined the case law of the ECJ on this matter, finds that it is sufficient that an element of connection exists between the national measure and the Community rule; and so the implementation or execution of Community law is not necessarily required. Moreover, in support of this assertion, he states that a different interpretation would go against the philosophy that seems to have inspired the Charter. In concluding his argument he makes the following statement, reproduced here in full because of its clarity and relevance for the current object of inquiry: 'in other words, accepting that on the one hand, a constantly increasing fan of sectoral competences assumed by the Communities and the Union within which the *in genere* protection of fundamental rights doesn't feature, and which moreover the Charter itself and the recently mentioned Art 51(2) doesn't change, while on the other hand another distinct role which fundamental rights are called upon to perform in the Communities and the Union, that is to apply to each and every of the sectoral competences mentioned, what is certain is that the expansive list of rights, freedoms and principles incorporated in the Charter appear to foster a climate of co-existence "based in common values" which would entail a more rigorous study of these values as essential elements the free movement provisions upon which the internal market hinges, or even, in the longer term, as the essential elements of an increasingly fortified European citizenship in the context of an area of freedom, security and justice which, as can be found in the Preamble of the Charter, "places the individual at the heart of its activities"; which would translate, in the final analysis, in a slow and progressive expansion of the current range of judicial control from Luxembourg of Member States which, all things considered, would be ill-suited to a restrictive interpretation, in the terms provided of the notion of "application of Union law" contained in Article 51(1).'

Another equally interesting opinion—and an original one among those offered by commentators on this topic—is that of Biglino Campos (2003) 393–4, who sees in the case law of the ECJ and the Constitutional Treaty a difference in degree between fundamental rights. From this perspective, she points out that when the Court is faced with a potential violation by a State of a fundamental right contained in the Treaties—basically, any of the fundamental freedoms—the solution should be based on the supremacy of Community law; on the other hand, when the unwritten rights integrated into the legal system as general principles are violated, a Member State measure must presuppose the application of Community law and there must be some sort of connection between Community law and the measure. This difference, according to the author, can also be seen in the provisions of the Charter: the fundamental rights contained in other parts of the Constitutional Treaty (freedoms, non-discrimination, protection of personal data, citizenship rights) bind States in a negative sense—they cannot violate them in any case—while those that appear in Part II of the Treaty only bind States when they apply EU law (an expression that will support the existence of a Community connection). All in all, there is 'a hierarchy between fundamental rights' whose 'value is determined by its connection to European integration'.

The principles of subsidiarity and conferral should act as important parameters when determining the relationship between the fundamental rights and national authorities and setting the limits of judicial control. Therefore, EU law and the mechanism of establishing fundamental rights and ensuring their respect, guaranteeing their protection, should come into play only when a situation arises which is of interest for the Community legal order, and not simply any case that arises.

For this reason there are limits, contained in the formula 'only when they are implementing Union law' in Article 51 of the Charter. What merits attention, in consequence, is when the application or implementation of EU law is at stake.

First of all, it is necessary to frame the question properly, given that opting for a broad or narrow interpretation is no small matter and has important consequences.

Effectively, a broad interpretation implies that, once rights are established, even where EU law is not being applied but there simply exists a connection between the national situation and a Community rule, such rights would be binding on Member States and, therefore, the sphere of protection of EU citizens would be widened. Moreover, the ECJ would assume a more important role, through the preliminary reference procedure or infringement proceedings under Article 226 EC.[36] However, with respect to preliminary rulings, the number of cases brought before the ECJ under this procedure involving possible breaches of EU fundamental rights would increase, causing such actions to move from their natural base, namely the internal jurisdictions of Member States. Moreover, this would create more work for the European Commission in exercising its functions as guardian of the Treaties and in its capacity as the body in charge of monitoring compliance with EU law in cases of non-fulfilment due to violations of fundamental rights. Finally, but probably most importantly, this would run the risk of exaggerating the differences between the two systems for the protection of rights—Community and national—affecting the equilibrium of the system[37] and potentially causing serious conflicts (competence claims on behalf of some of the Constitutional Courts of the Member States; diverging interpretations of rights which are substantially the same due to the Community relevance of a national measure; the possible effects on the principles of conferral, subsidiarity and the autonomy of the Member States, etc).

For its part, a strict interpretation could be a retrograde step with respect to the protection of fundamental rights from the perspective of citizenship of the EU in relation to the current state of a large proportion of the case law of the ECJ, and could seriously hamper the search for uniformity in the standards of the protection of the rights of EU citizens.

In developing a theory of the meaning and scope of the term 'implement', it is also useful to mention some of the antecedents to Article 51(1) of the Charter. In one of

[36] It must be borne in mind that the analysis at hand relates to the implications of the Constitutional Treaty for the decisions of the national authorities of Member States, which is why we restrict the role of the ECJ to infringement proceedings and preliminary references. Generally, the ECJ also decides cases regarding the violation of fundamental rights by the European administration through actions for annulment and omission, which has been covered in ch 2.

[37] As Biglino Campos points out at (2003) 391.

the provisional versions of this provision (then Article 46), the expression used made no mention of applying EU law, but spoke of acting 'within the scope of Union law'.[38]

[38] CONVENT 34 CHARTE 4316/00, 16 May 2000. Initially, the Convention considered the broad expression and not the expression used in the final draft of the Charter. In the information note presented by the Secretary of the Convention to the members regarding horizontal questions (CHARTE 4111/00 BODY 3, 20 January 2000) it had already asserted that 'The Charter is intended to apply to the Union's institutions and not to activities of Member States which fall outside the scope of EC or EU legislation. This would be consistent with ECJ case law, whereby Member States are bound to respect fundamental rights whenever they act within the scope of the Treaties for the purposes either of implementing Community (or EU) legislation or derogating from it', specifically citing Case 260/89, which contains the broad interpretation. In the first proposals of Articles (CHARTE 4123/1/00 REV 1 CONVENT 5, 15 February 2000), an approximation of a possible draft of the provisions relative to horizontal clauses was contemplated—which was proposed as a possible solution to problems relating to specific rights and not general ones. In this way, it was asserted (as part of the Preamble or Art 1) that the provisions of the Charter 'are binding on Member States only where the latter transpose or apply the law of the Union', thereby adopting the strict interpretation. The objective, as highlighted by the note to the Praesidium, was 'to indicate clearly that the Charter's scope is restricted to the European Union and to avoid any application to the Member States when they are acting within their own jurisdiction'. However, it cites in support of this assertion Joined Cases C-60 and 62/84 as well as Case C-299/95 , both of which support the broad interpretation. In the new proposals of some of the Articles of the Charter (CHARTE 4149/00 CONVENT 13, 8 March 2000), the integration of the clause relating to the field of protection in Art 1 was proposed, with a different but equally restrictive wording: 'The provisions of this Charter shall be applicable to the institutions and organs of the Union in the framework of the powers and tasks conferred on them by the Treaties, and to the Member States when implementing Community law.' In drafting the horizontal clauses presented by the Praesidium to the members of the Convention of 18 April 2000 (CHARTE 4235/00 CONVENT 27), the expression used is 'exclusively within the framework of implementing Community law'. The explanatory note accompanying the proposal maintains that 'It follows from the case law of the ECJ that the requirement to respect fundamental rights is also binding on the Member States when they act in the context of Community law', mentioning Case C-5/88 , which, as has been stated, does not used this expression but 'when they implement Community rules', which is not the same. Finally, as just mentioned, the new proposals for horizontal clauses presented on 16 May 2000 (in CHARTE 4316/00 CONVENT 34) contain the expression 'exclusively within the scope of Union law', adding to the explanations a reference to Case C-292/97 , which is in line with the strict interpretation of the term 'implement Community law'.

There were amendments to these drafts, both expanding the field of application of the Charter when Member States act in the field of application of Community law as well as restricting its application to the application and execution of Community law (amendment presented by Jürgen Gnauck aimed at avoiding binding Member States too much), to the direct application of Community law (amendment presented by Ingo Friedrich and Peter Mombaur), and even only to the institutions and organs of the Union. The amendments can be found in CHARTE 4372/00 CONVENT 39, 16 June 2000; a summary of amendments can be found in CHARTE 4360/00 CONVENT 37, 14 June and CHARTE 4383/00 CONVENT 41, 3 July.

With respect to these amendments the Praesidium presented an agreed formula for the then Art 46(2) which preserved the broad interpretation: 'The institutions and bodies of the Union, the Member States, exclusively within the scope of Community law, and the social partners at Community level, acting within the framework of their respective powers and in accordance with the principle of subsidiarity, shall observe the social rights and implement the social principles set out in this Charter' (CHARTE 4373/00 CONVENT 40, 23 June).

However, in the draft Charter presented at the end of September 2000 (CHARTE 4487/00 CONVENT 50, 28 September) a different and more strict draft was proposed, which in the end was to become the final draft: 'The provisions of this Charter are addressed to the institutions and bodies of the Union with due regard for the principle of subsidiarity and to the Member States only when they are implementing Union law.'

In the explanations to the various provisions (presented after CHARTE 4473/00 CONVENT 49, 11 October), the Praesidium got rid of the references to judgments favouring the broad interpretation and simply cited two judgments: Case C-5/88 and C-292/97, both of which favour a strict interpretation.

Thus we can conclude that the final draft of Art 51 would seem to attempt to restrict the broad

However, bearing in mind that the explanation of the Praesidium specifically mentioned this expression, the final version of the text of the Charter restricts the application of the Charter to the Member States only when they implement EU law.

Therefore, in keeping with this literal meaning and contrary to some of the earlier versions of the Article, the binding legal status of the Charter would bring about a change in the field of application of the fundamental rights of the EU to the Member States, given that the connection between the rights and Member States acts, involving the intervention of the ECJ, would only occur in cases of strict application of Community law, that is, execution of a provision of the Treaty, transposition of directives, and execution of EU policy by national authorities. Moreover, the use of the term 'only' in Article 51 of the Charter seems effectively to signal an intention that the Member States would be bound by the fundamental rights only with respect to acts that could be considered to be a strict application of EU law. Such a strict interpretation seems to be confirmed by the fact that the aforementioned article can be distinguished from expressions used in other provisions of the Treaty—such as Article 10 or 226 which, when referring to the acts of the Member States with respect to EU law, use a much broader formula: ensure compliance with the obligations emanating from the Treaty or the acts of the institutions of the EU or breach one of the obligations imposed by the Treaty. In other words, the fact that, as opposed to other parts of the Treaty, the formula used in Article 51 links the applicability of EU fundamental rights to Member States only with respect to legal and administrative measures purely applying EU law, distinguishing itself in this way from the other broader formulas contained in the Treaty, could lead us to the conclusion that this provision is amending the case law of the ECJ on this issue.[39]

However, this interpretation of Article 51(1) of the Charter cannot hold, as it goes against the logic of the Community legal system. This is not only because the explanations given by the Convention, by referring to the two branches of case law, show that there was no intention to restrict the application of the rights, but also precisely because of the interpretation given to the correct understanding of Articles 10 and 226 of the European Community Treaty.

Effectively, the EU emerged and operates pursuant to the achievement of a series of common objectives (now contained in Article 2 EC), in the framework of the competences ceded to it by the Member States (Article 5). To this end, certain powers have been conferred on the EU in specific sectors, which vary according to their exclusivity and their reach, establishing certain principles that make the functioning of the system possible. Among them is the principle of loyal co-

interpretation contained in some of the judgments of the ECJ, but it can be said to be more the product of confusion rather than a reasoned decision based on a specific objective. Although both the expansive and restrictive amendments of the scope of application of the Charter can be objectively justified, the Praesidium did not contain such justifications in its explanations to the Charter.

[39] A more obvious intention to restrict and contain the activity of the ECJ was Art 46(d) of the TEU, according to which competence is attributed to the ECJ to hear possible infringements of fundamental rights caused by the Community institutions. However, it did not produce the desired effect.

operation (Article 10), according to which the EU and Member States 'shall facilitate the achievement of the Community tasks', but also that they 'shall take all appropriate measures, whether general or particular, to ensure fulfilment of the obligations arising out of this Treaty or resulting from action taken by the institutions of the Community', refraining from 'any measure which could jeopardise the attainment of this Treaty', On the other hand, monitoring compliance with the obligations contained in EU law, carried out by the ECJ on the initiative of the Commission, is achieved through the infringement procedure—complemented by an enforcement procedure set out in Article 228 EC[40]—which is not limited to cases where the Member State in question applies a Treaty provision or an act of a Community institution; it applies to any act of a Member State (regardless of the type of organ)[41] that contravenes an obligation arising out of EU law.

Restricting the application and control of compliance of fundamental rights to cases where an infringement or violation arises due to the non-application or incorrect application of a rule of Community Law is contrary to the logic of the functioning of the system. Moreover, it would run the risk of making ineffective some of the rights enshrined in the Charter because only rarely would a Member State apply EU law in relation to them.[42] If, along with this, we take into account that EU law is characterised by the principle of indirect implementation and that the European administration is increasingly ceding tasks to national administrations, it is clear that the exercise of such functions—which may or may not involve strict implementation—should be governed by fundamental rights protected by the EU and be applied according to their parameters.

In this sense, the Constitutional Treaty uses the term 'implement Union Law' as the equivalent of putting EU law into practice: Article III-285 provides for the 'effective implementation of Union law' as a 'matter of common interest' and 'essential for the proper functioning of the Union'.

Furthermore, it is also clear that the existence of a catalogue of binding fundamental rights which are legally applicable and enforceable by the Courts contributes to the legitimacy of the system.[43] Moreover, given that the Charter envisages the rights that it contains as instruments for the protection of citizens against the exercise of public powers, an overly strict interpretation would entail a reduction of the private sphere of the citizen, meaning that decisions which negatively affect individuals would not be capable of being subjected to the scrutiny of a court, especially in relation to rights which are not recognised—at least to the same extent—in national legal orders, such as the right to good administration. In other words, if the Charter implies, in itself, an increase in the protection of the rights of Member State nationals, which they can invoke against the acts of the national

[40] For a more in-depth analysis of this matter see Martín Delgado (2004).

[41] This includes judicial bodies, as the ECJ found in Case C-224/01 *Köbler* [2003] ECR I-10239, and which was confirmed in Case C-173/03 *Traghetti del Mediterraneo* [2006] ECR I-5177.

[42] De Witte (2001) notes this risk when affirming that 'The Charter would, therefore, promise more than it could deliver'.

[43] This idea is Ladenburger's (2005b). In the same vein, see Rubio Llorente (2002) 28. For a general overview on fundamental rights as a system, see Díez Picazo (2005).

administrations in national courts, a strict interpretation of the field of application of those provisions would imply that such decisions, taken within the framework of the application of EU law, would be outside judicial control in cases where the internal legal order did not recognise such rights to the same extent.

For this reason, Article 51(1) should not be interpreted in a literal sense.

However, neither does this mean that a radically flexible interpretation should be adopted, in such a way that the fundamental rights contained in the Charter bind Member States independently of their nature and field of application. Some link between the national act and EU law is required so that it can be assessed, interpreted and guided according to the fundamental right applicable to the act. This link would be established when the national act falls within the competence of the EU (either exclusive, shared or complementary), when the act affects some Community obligation relating to this field, or when the national act impedes, hinders or negatively affects one of the objectives of the EU.

Indeed, the formula outlined above should be interpreted not as a restriction on the expansionist tendencies of the ECJ,[44] but as a consolidation and formalisation of the case law (even if, perhaps, it advises prudence by using the adverb 'only'), and as a safeguard of the State's ability to introduce exceptions to the fundamental rights enshrined in the pursuit of national interests, provided of course that they are proportionate.[45]

Moreover, the second subsection, first paragraph of Article 51 of the Charter should be borne in mind, according to which, 'They [the institutions and organs of the EU and the Member States] shall therefore respect the rights, observe the principles and promote the application thereof in accordance with their respective powers'. This means that the fundamental rights do not bestow competences in themselves, except where a transfer of sovereignty occurred in a specific case, in such a way that only in situations involving the application of an EU rule in areas of exclusive EU competence, in areas of shared competence, areas of co-ordination of economic and employment policies, areas relating to common foreign and security policy, in the areas affected by EU supporting, complementary or co-ordinating action, and, finally, in areas which make use of the flexibility clause, national authorities will be obliged to respect fundamental rights and promote the principles contained in the Charter. Thus, where the act falls within one of these areas, even if it does not constitute an application or execution of EU law in a strict sense, provided that the national measure is connected to EU law, the public powers of the Member State—including national courts[46]—will be obliged to respect the fundamental rights of the EU and the situation should be interpreted in the light

[44] In the sense that the provision mentioned was not intended to modify the case law of the ECJ. See Ladenburger (2002) 827–8.

[45] This is how one of the members of the Convention—Lord Goldsmith—put it in his proposal, which is the closest to the final text (CHARTE 4372/00 CONVENT 39, 16 June 2000).

[46] As Craig maintains (2006), this is really important because it means that the Charter has horizontal effects: it must be applied not only where the case involves a public authority, but also to conflicts between individuals (p 501).

of these rights. We will now consider the situations in which this connection can occur.

In the manner outlined above, EU fundamental rights bind Member States, but only in the sphere of competences transferred to the EU,[47] where EU law takes precedence over national law. From this perspective, in the areas where EU law takes precedence over national law, it is utterly logical and coherent that the fundamental rights recognised by EU law should apply.

The implementation or application of EU law is, from a positive perspective, the same as taking legal or administrative measures in the field of EU law, or, more clearly, to put into practice or carry out EU law; in other words, to contribute to making a European law practically effective, having a real influence on the situation regulated and doing so in the manner envisaged by the regulation.

In such cases, the State in question acts in the pursuit of the objectives of the EU, which would occur in the following cases:[48]

— when the national act applies Union law, but also when is aimed at applying a provision of EU law (Case C-309/96, para 21), in the sense of both an administrative measure and legal measures, which occurs normally in the fields of the EU's exclusive competence;
— when the matter is governed by EU law, that is, when it falls within the scope of a particular EU law (Treaty article, regulation, directive or decision);[49] when its aim is to guarantee the fulfilment of a law of the EU legal order;[50] when it pursues one of the objectives of a Community policy;[51] or, generally, when Member States are exercising competences conferred on them by the Treaty or EU law, which are all those situations principally within the shared competences of the Union.

However, from a negative perspective, implementation also requires respect for the freedoms contained in EU law, in such a way that if a national measure affects a fundamental freedom recognised in Community law (Case C-274/96, para 18), inhibiting its full application, even if it involves a situation governed by national law, the Member State will be bound by fundamental rights.[52]

[47] Note that what is being referred to is the field of competences of EU law and not the exercise of competences conferred within the framework of EU law, a term which was contained in the previous draft but is more strict.

[48] The case law of the ECJ has been taken as a reference for these cases; it will be indicated as appropriate.

[49] Cases C-274/96, para 14; C-309/96, para 24; Case C-81/05 *Cordero Alonso* [2006] ECR I-7569, para 35.

[50] Case C-299/95, para 17.

[51] Case C-309/96, para 22.

[52] This was confirmed by the ECJ in some of its decisions, all preliminary references from Spanish courts in relation to Directive 80/987/EEC of the Council, of 20 October 1980, on the approximation of the laws of the Member States relating to the protection of employees in the event of the insolvency of their employer [1980] OJ L283/23. Spanish law established a Guaranteed Salary Fund to administer the debts of insolvent companies of the nature covered by the Directive but not other companies contracted by virtue of an act of conciliation (through an agreement between the company of the worker confirmed by a court, which in Spain has the same effect as a legally binding judgment). The courts' questions

Therefore, implementation of EU law occurs when there is a European law which should be brought into force by the Member States (through the application of those laws, the achievement of particular aims, or the compliance with obligations), as well as when the national measure affects some of the fundamental freedoms of the EU[53]. In other words, the term implementation covers each of the ways in which Member States act within the scope of Union Law, where they are required to respect the Charter of Fundamental Rights.

Thus, implementation connects sectoral competences of the EU with the exercise of those competences—exclusive, shared, co-ordinating and supporting—in the framework of EU law.

Effectively, national administrations act as a European administration when they act within the framework of EU law: the circumstances of the specific case are such that a national situation is transformed into a situation with Community relevance, thereby setting aside compliance with and respect for the requirements of the fundamental rights of the European Union. Control over the legality of these acts is exercised by the ECJ,[54] through an action of fulfilment by the Commission in cases

related to the question whether this differentiation constituted unjustified discrimination and therefore violated the principle of equality enshrined in Community law as a fundamental right. The ECJ left to the national courts the question whether the payments claimed fell within the scope of the Directive, but not without first stating that 'The right reserved to national law to specify the benefits payable by the guarantee institution is conditional upon observance of fundamental rights, which include *inter alia* the general principle of equality and non-discrimination' (Case C-520/03 *Olaso Valero* [2004] ECR I-12065, para 34; in the same sense see Case C-177/05 *Guerrero Pecino* [2005] ECR I-10887, para 26, and Case C-81/05 *Cordero Alonso*, para 37). Therefore, while the national courts are left to determine whether a particular activity fell within the scope of a Community law, they must, in any case, respect the principle of equality. Thus, when the issue related to discrimination contrary to Community law, 'a national court must set aside any discriminatory provision of national law, without having to request or await its prior removal by the legislature, and to apply to members of the disadvantaged group the same arrangements as those enjoyed by other workers' (Case C-442/00 *Rodriguez Caballero* [2002] ECR I-11915, para 43; the same principle was contained in Case C-81/05 cited above, para 45, which contains the requirement to respect the principle of equality, even if it does not relate to the strict application of Community law).

Moreover, it should also be taken into account that the ECJ confirmed in Case C-34/02 *Pasquini* [2003] ECR I-6515 that 'National law must, however, observe the Community principle of equivalence, in accordance with which the detailed procedural rules governing the treatment of situations arising out of the exercise of a Community freedom must be no less favourable than those governing purely internal situations, and the Community principle of effectiveness, in accordance with which those procedural rules must not render virtually impossible or excessively difficult the exercise of rights arising out of the situation of Community origin' (para 73).

[53] This type of distinction is drawn by Besselink (2001). The recent judgment of the ECJ in Case C-300/04 *Eman and Sevinger* [2006] I-8055 clearly shows this idea. A national from The Netherlands, residing in Aruba (which is a Dutch territory) was not allowed to exercise his right to vote in the election of members of the European Parliament; the ECJ held that 'in the current state of Community law, there is nothing which precludes the Member States from defining, in compliance with Community law, the conditions of the right to vote and to stand as a candidate in elections to the European Parliament by reference to the criterion of residence in the territory in which the elections are held; the principle of equal treatment prevents, however, the criteria chosen from resulting in different treatment of nationals who are in comparable situations, unless that difference in treatment is objectively justified' (para 61). In conclusion, although the question of determining who is entitled to vote in elections to the European Parliament is a national matter, a breach of the principle of equality transforms the national act into an act of European relevance and fundamental rights and freedoms granted in the EU apply.

[54] Under the Constitutional Treaty, the legal basis for this control is Art I-4, which recognises the basic liberties of the Union and the principle of non-discrimination, and Art I-29, which gives the Court

of a direct breach of the mandatory provisions of a fundamental right;[55] through the preliminary reference procedure where there is doubt as to interpretation or validity with respect to a national measure and an EU law, as the only organ qualified to interpret the fundamental rights enshrined in the Community legal system; or by national judges, with due deference to the supremacy of EU law in all other cases.[56] In fact, the effective application of the Charter to national measures will depend on the national courts.[57]

competence to guarantee respect for Union law in relation to its interpretation and application. In any case, it would be necessary to explicitly acknowledge this competence, which is not acknowledged in the current Treaties (Art 46(d) of the TEU restricts the role of the Court as a defender of fundamental rights to acts of the Community institutions) nor in the Constitutional Treaty (the Court is not even mentioned in Part II with the exception of the Preamble, the article relating to the Ombudsman and the provision regarding the juridical value of the explanations drawn up by the Convention).

[55] The work of the Commission in the framework of breaches of Community law due to violations of fundamental rights by Member State authorities is extremely important. Therefore, it is necessary to take into account their acts in relation to their interpretation in the field of application of the Charter and the term 'implement Union law'. Thus, their activities relating to the interpretation of the sphere of application of the Charter and the term 'apply European law' must be taken into account. For an example, see the reply of the Commission to the questions from the European Parliament of 3 June 2000 (E-2200/00) and 25 October 2000 (E-3337/00). The first of these dealt with the prosecution of a Greek woman by the authorities of Monte Athos, for providing services involving practical psychological philosophy without authorisation from the Greek Minister for Education and Religious Affairs, which in turn requires the approval of the hierarchy of the orthodox church. The compatibility of this system with freedom of religion was questioned. The Commission opined that the matter dealt with was a question which did not fall under the scope of Community law and therefore found that it was not competent to initiate an action for infringement against Greece. The second case related to a series of measures that obstructed journalists working for a particular television channel by members of the Austrian Liberal Party. When the Commission considered whether these measures restricted the freedom of the press and violated the principle of democracy and whether they should be explicitly condemned, it found that the situation did not fulfil the criteria for the application of the Treaty in the area of violation of fundamental rights. For a lucid analysis of the practical application of the Charter by the Commission with numerous references to specific cases, see Ladenburger (2002).

[56] In this sense, national judges also have a part to play; the real effect of the rights provided by the Charter in national systems depends largely on them, independently of the provisions relating to their sphere of application. Thus, as Martin-Retortillo (2002) points out, 'the door is open to unexpected protagonists, with steps and consequences which are not easy to predict' (p 185). Interestingly—and something that could help to determine the possible interpretation of Art 51 of the Charter given by the Spanish jurisdictional organs—it should be noted that the Spanish Constitutional Court, in its Opinion 1/2004 of 13 December, considered that the application of EU law was equivalent to acting within EU law or the existence of some sort of connection with its legal system (point 6).

[57] Recent Spanish cases applying the Charter in situations unconnected to EU law are very relevant in this sense. Many judgments refer to the provisions of the Charter to support their arguments, independently of the sphere of application of the particular article and the connection with EU law. For example, the judgment of the Supreme Court of 8 February 2001 (RJ 2001/544), which, confirming the judgment of a lower court that found against an association of fishermen which refused membership to a woman despite the fact that the rules of customary law did not permit it, referred among other texts to Chapter III of the Charter when it was still only a draft. Furthermore, the judgment of the Supreme Court of 26 March 2005 (Case 1469/2002) invoked Art II-101(2)(c) to decide a case in which a refusal to grant a licence for arms was deemed to have been based on wrong reasons. The judgment of the Supreme Court of 22 February 2005 (Case 3055/2001) referred to the same provision to decide a case involving a refusal to grant a licence to open a roadside service station on a national motorway. The judgment of 9 December 2003 (Case 3932/1998) mentions Art 11 of the Charter along with Art 10(1) and (2) of the ECHR in a matter relating to the plurality of the media. An example of the application of the Charter to situations relating to EU law can be found in the judgment of the Supreme Court of 26 April 2005 (Case 7321/2002), involving a challenge to the findings of the Competition Tribunal regarding its competence

In conclusion it can be said that Article 51 (1) of the Charter of Fundamental Rights of the European Union does not introduce anything new in relation to the jurisprudence of the ECJ as regards the application of fundamental rights to

to impose a sanction in a case of alleged restrictive practices contrary to national competition law and the EC Treaty, where the Court invoked Art 47 of the Charter, which enshrines the right to a presumption of innocence, along with Art 6(2) of the ECHR and Art 24(2) of the Spanish Constitution, considering them 'wholly applicable in procedures relative to the violation of competition laws where sanctions can be applied to undertakings' (point 4). The same was done in a similar case before the Supreme Court on the same date (Case 5853/2002). This is also occurring at the lower levels of jurisdiction. Thus, for example, the judgment of the Superior Court of Justice of Castilla y León of 21 March 2005 (Case 372/2005) invoked Arts 20, 21 and 30 of the Charter in order to settle a case of unfair dismissal.

We can also consider the judgments of the Supreme Court of 26 March 2002 (RJ 2002/3341), 27 March 2002 (RJ 2002/3341), 2 April 2002 (RJ 2002/3343), and many others on the same matter, which dealt with the legality of a forced expropriation of a series of businesses valued at 0, that is, without any compensation. Although most of the judges found the act to be legal, there was one dissent that referred to Art 17(1) of the Charter—which proclaimed the right to just compensation in situations of expropriation—to justify his opinion that all expropriation must be appropriately compensated to ensure the balance between the protection of property and the requirements of the general interest.

Finally, and although more judgments will be referred to when analysing the rights to good administration, protection of information and access to documents individually in the second part of this chapter, it is worth mentioning the judgment of the Supreme Court of 13 December 2005 (Case 120/2004), a case challenging a Regulation for lack of reasons, which transferred the ownership of certain archival documents to an autonomous administration—and therefore constituted a purely internal situation—where the Court refered to Art 101(2)(c) of the Constitutional Treaty (also citing Art 41 of the Charter) as a basis for the decision. Another case where the Charter was relied upon in a purely internal situation involved a challenge to an agreement of the National Securities Commission regarding the exclusion of the listing of companies of a specific commercial entity (judgment of the Supreme Court of 23 May 2005 (Case 2414/2002)). In the same vein see the judgment of the Supreme Court of 22 February 2002 (Case 3055/2001). Moreover, there are cases where the parties to the case invoked the Charter in defence of their interests, as happened in the judgment of 29 March 2004 (Case 48/2002), where Art 33 of the Charter was invoked to challenge a Regulation regarding the fate of professional military personnel.

This phenomenon has also been observed with respect to the decisions of the Spanish Constitutional Court. Thus in its judgment 290/2000 of 30 November, a dissenting opinion expressed by one of the Judges of the Court cited Art 8 of the Charter as an important factor for the protection of personal information even if it was not in force. On the same day, judgment 292/2000 of 30 November (therefore also given before the entry into force of the Charter) also invoked Art 8—along with other international texts—to justify the unconstitutionality of a series of provisions of the Organic law on the protection of personal information by infringing the provisions of the fundamental right to the protection of personal data (point 8). Moreover, judgment 53/2002 of 27 February, which dealt with an appeal on grounds of unconstitutionality—*recurso de inconstitucionalidad*—against a particular provision of the law on the right to asylum invoked Arts 18 and 19 of the Charter on the basis that the right to asylum was a matter for EU law. More recently, in judgment 273/2005 of 27 October, the Constitutional Court invoked Art 23 of the Charter, albeit recognising that it did not have legally binding force, among the various measures for the protection of the rights of children in support of its argument (point 6). In judgment 17/2006 of 30 January, the Court referred to Art 24(1) of the Charter to base its finding of a violation of the Attorney General's right to defence for not being able to participate in a judicial procedure involving the legal recognition of minors (point 5). Judgment 41/2006 of 13 February, cites Art 21(1) of the Charter in an action challenging a dismissal on the grounds of discrimination. Even the applicants rely on the Charter to support their claims; an example of this is the Order of the Constitutional Court No 235/2002 of 26 November, which rejected a claim for protection where the claiming party alleged a violation of the right to private property and to this end did not invoke Art 33 of the Spanish Constitution but Art 17 of the Charter.

Basically, the use of Art 10(2) of the Spanish Constitution has the effect that the Spanish Courts, including the Constitutional Court itself, act as a bridge between the rights contained in the Charter and the parties who can benefit from them.

Member States, so that it can be asserted that the Court will continue to rely on its main case law where the application of EU fundamental rights will apply to Member States when they act within the scope of EU law.[58] One innovation, however, is the second part of this provision, which creates an obligation—also on Member States when implementing EU law—to respect the rights and observe the principles and promote the application thereof in accordance with their respective powers, such that the fundamental rights not only operate negatively as a criterion for the validity, interpretation and limit of the acts of public powers (Article 52 of the Charter), but also so that they can be invoked to demand positive action from public powers in the sphere of European law.

Thus, an interpretation of the term 'implement' such as that given in this chapter would assume the competence of national courts to ensure respect for EU fundamental rights by national authorities when they act as part of the European administration, or, which amounts to the same thing, citizens of the EU will be able to invoke the rights contained in the Charter before national judges and national courts against acts of the public authorities of their country when they fall under the scope of EU law.[59] A consequence of this will be an increase in indirect control exercised by the ECJ through the preliminary reference procedure, gradually transforming it into a 'Constitutional Court', and therefore becoming less like an administrative Court—at least with respect to fundamental rights—with the result that the rights of individuals will have an increased relevance in terms of the interests of the EU.[60]

The Charter will become an instrument by which individuals can limit the powers of the Community institutions and the Member States when they exercise the functions conferred on them by EU law or their acts affect its sphere of application, and the essential core of the European Treaties.

II. THE RIGHTS TO GOOD ADMINISTRATION, ACCESS TO DOCUMENTS AND PROTECTION OF PERSONAL DATA: EFFECTS OF RECOGNITION IN NATIONAL LEGAL SYSTEMS

1. A Preliminary Question

As we have seen, the Charter of Fundamental Rights is binding on Member States when they apply EU law. However, some of the rights contained in the Charter do

[58] In this sense, De Witte (2001) states, however, that 'the ECJ may feel under pressure to refrain from pursuing this line of judicial review',—referring to the broad interpretation—(p 86).

[59] An important decision in this sense is that of the Spanish Council of State in its Opinion on the Constitutional Treaty. Pronouncing on the field of application of Part II, it stated that 'the rights and freedoms of the Charter constitute the parameters of legality of any act or disposition *within the field of application of European Union law* appreciable by whichever court of the Member States. The incorporation of the Charter into the Treaty thus has important consequences for national courts which in the application of Community law will be bound both by the Charter and the Spanish Constitution' (emphasis added).

[60] This is how Rossi (2002) sees it (pp 275–7).

not relate in any way to the Member States as agents of the Union. The rationale for including such rights in a catalogue addressed to the institutions, organs and bodies of the EU and national authorities when they act in the field of application of EU law relates to the need to reinforce the identity of European citizens with the Union to which they belong, increasing their protection against the increasingly powerful Community institutions, and to consolidate the nucleus of the identity of the EU in the face of future enlargement.[61]

Some of the articles of the Charter determine the scope of the right contained in them, , without relying on the general limiting effects of Article 51. Problems arise when the specific provisions relative to the sphere of application are not the same and their application is restricted only to the institutions, organs and bodies of the EU, without mentioning the Member States.[62]

Thus, doubts arise as to which prevails: the general provision of Article 51 or, on the contrary, the specific provisions.

An argument in favour of applying the general article is based on the fact that the Convention that drafted the Charter ultimately opted to locate in the last part of the text the provisions on the sphere of application of the Charter and the details of its limits and conditions for the exercise of the rights contained in the Charter, rather than specifying the limits in each particular case (as was proposed at one stage[63] and was done in relation to the addressees of particular rights). Thus, it seems that this general clause, precisely due to its general nature, would refer to all the rights, independently of the content of individual provisions.

Against this solution is the *lex specialis* argument, which would argue for the prevalence of the content of the provision that regulates the right in question. Moreover, the Charter does state that it does not add any competences to the EU or modify the competences defined in the Treaties. However, accepting this interpretation, many of the rights enshrined—for example, the right to good administration or the right of access to documents—would not be applicable to the activities of the national administrations even if they apply (in the most literal sense of the term) the law of the EU.[64]

A third solution is possible: independently of the general and particular provisions regarding the field of application of the Charter, the specificity and diversity of the rights contained in the Charter, and the special nature of the EU

[61] The conclusions of the Cologne European Council (3–4 June 1999) highlighted the relationship between the Charter of Fundamental Rights and the legitimacy of the Union and citizens' identification with the Union.

[62] Such is the case with the right to good administration and access to documents; the provision that regulates the right to the protection of personal data, on the other hand, expressly provides for its application to Member States when carrying out activities that fall within the scope of EU law.

[63] This has been proposed by some of the literature on the subject. In this sense see Curtin and van Ooik (2001) 108–9 and 112–13.

[64] And others, such as the right to not to be sentenced to death or executed (Art 2(2)) would not be applicable in any situation, because the field of activity of the European institutions have little or nothing to do with these rights. In other words, the content of the Charter overlooks Union competences: Rubio Llorente (2002) 34. That is why some authors maintain that, in these cases, the Charter 'speaks directly to national legislators and judges': Carreti (2006) 169.

itself—a supranational organisation created with the aim of achieving a series of concrete objectives—the sphere of application of the fundamental rights contained in the EU's legal system could be specified in relation to each of those rights, obviously paying attention to the provision or provisions that contains it, but also taking into account the jurisprudence of the ECJ, including the nature and the field of protection of the right in relation to the provisions of the European Convention on Human Rights and the common constitutional traditions of the Member States (Articles 52 and 53). This is the preferred solution in this chapter and is the one adopted when considering the applicability of the rights with which this chapter is concerned to the Member States, taking as a reference point the material discussed in the first section of this chapter in relation to the concept of implementation.

2. The Field of Application of the Right to Protection of Personal Data, Access to Documents and Good Administration

Given that the analysis in this second section of the chapter will focus on the right to good administration, access to documents and the protection of personal data (being, perhaps, the most 'administrative', ie the most relevant for the relationship between the administration and the citizen), it is important, along with what has just been outlined, to take into account the content of Article 52(2), according to which, 'Rights recognised by this Charter which are based on the Community Treaties or the Treaty on European Union shall be exercised under the conditions and within the limits defined by those Treaties'. The meaning of this is clear: wherever a provision exists which regulates any of the rights contained in the Treaties, it is this provision that will prevail and that must be adhered to. Its aim is also clear: maintain the status quo,[65] and at the same time avoid the incoherence and contradictions that could result from the duplication of regulation. And the consequences of these provisions are also clear: there are certain rights that are more important from the EU's perspective because they relate more to the achievement of the aims pursued by the EU and, for this reason, along with the Charter, are contained in the Treaties.[66]

Thus, from the point at which both the right of access to documents and the right to the protection of personal data are based on the Treaties, those provisions should be referred to when analysing their field of application. The same applies to one of

[65] The Convention was clear that this should not affect the legal status of the fundamental rights recognised by the EC Treaty as evidenced by the explanatory documents to the Charter, with respect to the provision just referred to. However, the main effect of the recognition of the binding effect of the provisions of the Charter will be its broad and transformative application.

[66] Perhaps it would have been easier to have reproduced the regulation on these provisions instead of establishing general clauses as exceptions to other general clauses. However, given its particular origins, the Charter did not attempt to modify the existing Treaties. Moreover, even if such a modification could have been introduced during the drafting of the Treaty establishing a Constitution for Europe, the members of the Convention were unanimous in their desire not to tamper with the essential content of the Charter, only making urgent amendments.

the rights contained in the general right to good administration, as we will see shortly.

Given that the origins and the content of these three rights were studied in detail in chapter 2, the analysis here will be limited to their application to the activities of Member States, in keeping with the general emphasis in this chapter.

(a) The Right to Good Administration

As has already been outlined, the right to good administration was created by the ECJ. However, until its formalisation in the Charter, it was considered more of a principle rather than a right in itself. As Kanska points out, 'the novelty of Article 41 of the Charter is that it transforms some elements of the objective principle of legality into a subjective right to good administration'.[67]

Despite the importance of these new provisions, the Convention did not wish to extend their application to the Member States when they apply EU law, but rather aimed to restrict them to the 'institutions, bodies, offices and agencies of the Union'. There is no doubt as to the literal meaning of the provision and the preliminary work of the Convention.

However, if one analyses the content of this general right—or, rather, package of rights—more closely, it can be seen that the apparent inapplicability of this provision to the Member States is not as it appears, or at least, that such inapplicability should be qualified.

In the first place, one of the three rights expressly mentioned in Article III-101(2)—the right emanating from the obligation on the administration to give reasons for its decisions (para (c))—does apply to Member States by virtue of the provisions of Article I-38 of the Constitutional Treaty (with respect to the application of which Article II-112(2) must be referred to). This provision (Article I-38) states in paragraph 2 that '[l]egal acts shall state the reasons on which they are based and shall refer to any proposals, initiatives, recommendations, requests or opinions required by the Constitution'; it includes, thus, the legal acts mentioned in Article I-37 of the Treaty, that is, the implementing acts, whose adoption is reserved for Member States.[68]

[67] (2004) 300. This author, moreover, affirms that 'the Charter is also the first official attempt at a *positive* definition of the meaning of "good administration"' (p 303).

[68] The final text of Art I-38(2) relates to a modification made by the IGC that adopted the Draft Treaty presented by the Convention. The draft that was adopted mentioned, just like the current Art 253 EC Treaty, the different measures and acts which the institutions of the Union can adopt (adjusting the names thereof to their new titles in the Treaty). The substitution of this detailed provision for the more general 'legal acts' means that measures which require reasons for their adoption will include not only European laws, European framework laws, European regulations and European decisions, but also 'implementing acts' of Member States, which are defined as those acts 'necessary to implement legally binding Union acts'.

This is not a completely new provision; the current jurisprudence of the ECJ extends the duty to provide reasons to national administrative acts connected to Community law. See eg Case C-222/86 *Unectef v Heylens* [1987] ECR 4097, which established the obligation to give reasons for decisions taken by national authorities when they affect a fundamental right protected under the Treaty (paras 14–17). For

Secondly, the jurisprudence of the ECJ has applied the principle of good administration to Member States in cases of composite administration and it is unlikely that this will change,[69] especially if one takes into account that the execution of EU law is, first and foremost, decentralised and that the result of many of the decision-making procedures in which the European institutions participate—mainly the Commission—in the final instance, depends on the activities of national administrations (for example, with respect to state aid or competition). In these instances, a case of maladministration involving a national authority could influence the activities of the European institutions, resulting in maladministration at the European level. Moreover, when a Member State applies EU law in a way that violates the rights implicit in the right to good administration, it could jeopardise the achievement of the objectives pursued by the European measure and, therefore, violate the principle of institutional loyalty and even, in certain cases, breach the obligations assumed under Community law. Furthermore, there are examples of mixed procedures where the decision adopted by a national authority has an effect on the legal order of a different Member State. On the other hand, the open-ended nature of the right to good administration (which entails or could entail many rights for the citizen and obligations for the administration applicable in their mutual relations) makes this right a source of progress in the field of EU law which should be sustained and even extended to the Member States.[70] Finally, it must not be forgotten that there may be cases where the internal order does not have the resources—legal or judicial—to guarantee the protection of subjective rights that apply to the citizen by virtue of EU law. In such cases it is clear that the obligations

its part, the judgment in Case C-70/95 *Sodemare and others v Regione Lombardia* [1997] ECR I-3395 provided that this obligation could not be extended to national provisions of a general character.

With the drafting of the Constitutional Treaty, the obligation to give reasons is not only extended to implementing acts, thy also become an integral part of a fundamental right in itself, as is the case with the right to good administration.

[69] Kanska (2004) is also of this opinion, finding that 'it is arguable that the ECJ might interpret the scope of Art 41 as applying to cases of composite administration (when the national administration acts as an agent for the Community)'. The author criticises the restrictions in the field of application of the right to good administration because it can result in differential treatment of Union citizens with respect to the country in which the citizen is invoking their rights and it presupposes the loss of the opportunity of establishing common standards to the activities of Member States in the application of the law of the Union (p 309).

[70] The general idea of good administration found in the jurisprudence of the ECJ consists in the establishment of a series of guarantees which should be effective in administrative procedure, and which take shape when administrations are under a duty to closely and impartially examine all the elements relevant to the matter with which it is dealing, in the rights of the interested parties to express their point of view and the duty to give sufficient reasons for the decision (see Case C-269/90 *Criminal Proceedings against Bonfait* [1990] ECR I-4169, para 14 and the judgment of the CFI in Case T-167/94 *Nölle v Council and Commission* [1995] ECR II-2589, para 73). Thus, this general idea should also be present in the procedures followed and the decisions adopted by the Member States when they apply EU law, without being subordinated to the provisions of national law. A similar idea relative to the openness of the right to good administration is expressed by Ladenburger (2005a) in finding that Art 41 of the Charter 'will no doubt evolve as a fundamental base for a case law on standards of general administrative law complementary to legislation under Article III-304' (current Art III-398 Constitutional Treaty) (p 170). In the same vein, Tomás Mallén (2004) describes the right to good administration as a 'right under dynamism' (p 93).

under EU law relating to EU fundamental rights should be applied to Member States.[71] Ultimately, this consists of a specially created right to regulate the relationship between the administration and the citizen, in such a way that in a system of indirect execution in which, moreover, the majority of decisions that directly affect citizens are adopted by national administrations independently of the European institutions and individuals, the EU cannot remain on the sidelines and refrain from requiring good administration from national bodies when they apply EU law.[72] Thus, the connection between national acts and European acts becomes an

[71] An example of this can be seen in Case T-167/94 , already cited. In this case, a German company used Art 288 of the EC Treaty to claim compensation for damage caused as a result of the application of a Community Regulation containing anti-dumping measures against certain products originating in China, which was subsequently declared invalid by the ECJ. Among other sums, the company was claiming the payment of interest on credit received by the company, which was procured in order to comply with the anti-dumping law. The Council and the Commission—the defendants in the case—argued that the claim should be rejected on the grounds that the applicant had not exhausted domestic procedures. However, the Court found that 'Since public authorities in the Federal Republic of Germany can incur liability only if fault is established on the part of the authority responsible, and since the declaration of the invalidity of Regulation No 725/89 by the ECJ was attributable to the unlawful conduct of the Community institutions and not that of the public authorities in Germany, prior exhaustion of domestic remedies could not, in the present case, ensure effective protection for the subjective rights which the applicant derives from Community law' (para 41). In this case, the original act was a national measure (it was an internal German body that had demanded the payment in the application of the Community Regulation), contested before a national body, which was finally referred to the ECJ through the preliminary reference procedure. Although ultimately the claim for compensation was rejected on the grounds that the violation was insufficient from the point of view of the criteria for establishing a violation characterised by Community law (the violation of the principle of good administration and the duty to act with due diligence was not so disproportionate as to reach the requisite levels), the judgment highlights the fact that Community law should offer ways to protect the rights that it recognises in cases where national systems cannot protect such rights.

[72] It is from this that one of the greatest paradoxes of the indirect execution of EU law stems. As is known, the indirect execution of Community law implies that national administrations are in charge of the execution of Community laws; the execution of Community laws by Community institutions is reserved to very specific cases. Thus, the relationship between public power and the individual takes place between citizens, the EU and national administrations. However, with respect to much of Community procedure, although measures are ultimately processed by national administrations, they lack autonomous decision-making power, in such a way that they are obliged to refer to the Community institutions—usually the Commission—to provide a solution to a case. Moreover, the obligations occurring under the principle of good administration usually apply to the Community administration rather than national administrations. With respect to the current issue, that is, guarantees in administrative procedure and their enforcement against national administrations, the judgment of the CFI in Case T-450/93 *Lisrestal and others v Commission* [1994] ECR II-1177 provides an example. The European Social Fund granted aid to a Portuguese enterprise in order to finance certain training and career guidance courses for young people, which constituted 50% of the total aid received by the enterprise for such activities (the other 50% came from the Portuguese authorities). Staff from the Social Fund carried out an inspection of the project and discovered that the enterprise had sub-contracted part of the courses to five companies which lacked the necessary infrastructure and personnel to carry out these functions, and the courses provided did not correspond with those outlined under the project. The Portuguese authorities issued various certificates addressed to the companies informing them that an inspection had been carried out by the Community and that no decision had yet been taken pursuant to this inspection. As a result of the visit by the inspectors, the European Social Fund decided to reduce the sum granted to the project and reclaim some of the funds provided from the companies involved, a decision which was communicated to the national authorities which, in turn proceeded to notify the Commission's decision to the companies. In fact, the national authorities simply informed the companies that the European Social Fund had decided, as a result of the inspection, that certain activities did not qualify for funding as they were not in accordance with the courses outlined in the project and

argument in favour of defending the application of the guarantees implicit in the right to good administration to national measures.

Thirdly, the expansive force of all declarations of rights[73] could result in internal courts referring to the right to good administration recognised in the Charter as a source of interpretation and a source of inspiration in the exercise of its judicial function in national law.[74] They are the two sides of the same coin: on one side,

that, therefore, they should return the corresponding sums within a fixed period. The companies brought an action for annulment, alleging a breach of their right to a defence. In the administrative procedure in question, the companies did not have any relationship with the European Social Fund, given that the exclusive contact with the Fund was the Member State, to whom one usually has the right to submit observations. In the case, the Portuguese authorities simply informed the Social Fund of their willingness to accept the decision which the Commission adopted, but did not give the companies involved the opportunity to put forward their case. As a consequence of all of this, the CFI found that, given the direct and individual effect of the Commission's decision on the respondent companies, it could not adopt such a decision without first giving the companies a chance to express their views on the matter.

This example relates to an administrative procedure where the individual only has a relationship with the national authorities of the Member State, but whose guarantees must be upheld by the decision-making body, ie the Commission. It is completely illogical that, in such cases, it was not up to the Member State itself, as the valid interlocutor, to allow the beneficiaries to present their opinions on the possibility of reclassifying certain expenses as not qualifying for funding and, therefore, return the relevant sums. This judgment was appealed by the Commission, which was rejected by the ECJ, confirming its decision in Case C-32/95 *Commission v Lisrestal and others* [1996] ECR I-5373. Another more obvious example is the CFI's judgment of 10 May 2001 involving 12 joined cases (the first of which was T-186/97 *Kaufring and others v Commission* [2001] ECR II-1337). The case arose from the application of the Association Agreement of 1963 between the EEC and Turkey. An exemption from customs duties in a clause contained in the agreement was applied to the importation into the Community of colour televisions manufactured in Turkey. Subsequently, the Commission found that the certificates provided by the Turkish authorities for the purposes of benefiting from the exemption clause made false claims, as certain components of the televisions were made in other countries. As a consequence of this decision, the Commission asked Member States to reclaim the customs duties from companies importing the product in question, allowing them, however, to delay or even cancel payment altogether if they deemed it appropriate. Several months later, the Commission made a further request to Member States to reclaim the duties without delay given that the time-limit that governs the reclamation of such duties (three years) was due to expire. These decisions resulted in multiple claims in various Member States and were the basis of the 12 actions before the CFI. For present purposes, it must be said that the procedure for cancelling or reclaiming import duties has two phases. The first of these takes place at the national level: the national administration is in charge of hearing the application to annul the customs duty, and its decision is susceptible to appeal before national courts. However, if the national administration considers that any specific circumstance of the case do not allow it to take the decision, it can refer the case to the Commission. In the second phase, at the Community level, the Commission decides whether or not to demand the payment. In one of the cases in question, the Commission took its decision without allowing the parties affected to express their opinion. Moreover, in this type of procedure, the Commission's decision—as it has recognised—is based exclusively on the documents provided by national authorities, to which the affected parties did not have access because they were not included in the documentation sent to them by the national authority (the Belgian authorities in this case). In conclusion, this case also shows the advisability of applying the guarantees derived from the right to good administration to national authorities to ensure that the final decision adopted by the European administration complies with the right. On this question, see Maeso Seco (2004).

[73] As pointed out by Martín-Retortillo (2006) 92, who talks of 'expansive tension' to refer to the fact that, on the one hand, the Charter attempts to restrict its reach, while on the other hand it accepts that its expansion is unstoppable. In the same vein, Weber (2002) affirms that the Charter will produce 'harmonising effects'; see also Díez Picazo (2001).

[74] In this sense, Ponce Sole (2002) maintains that the limited reach of the Charter will not stop a process of filtering of the requirements relative to the right to good administration into national

Article 41 of the Charter does not mention national administrations in the field of application of the right to good administration; on the other are the national constitutional provisions relating to fundamental rights, which in the case of Spain are capable of granting validity to international treaties on human rights ratified by the State. In reality, there is nothing to prevent Member States, through their national courts, making use of the rights in the Charter—and, in particular, of the right to good administration—to decide cases brought before them. There are several ways: in some cases, it can be seen as the acknowledgement of rights more favourable to citizens than those contained in national orders; the openness of the clauses lends themselves to judicial interpretation; and, overall, it can provide solid support to national decisions resolving such conflicts.

This is exactly what is happening in Spain,[75] through the application of Article 10(2) of the Spanish Constitution, according to which 'Provisions relating to the fundamental rights and liberties recognized by the Constitution shall be construed in conformity with the Universal Declaration of Human Rights and international treaties and agreements thereon ratified by Spain'; the Charter is one of the international texts signed by Spain.[76] As has already been highlighted, numerous judgments make reference to the rights contained in the Charter—many even citing the Article in the Constitutional Treaty—and, specifically, the right to good administration in general or some of its particular manifestations.[77]

systems. For a very deep analysis on right to good administration in the Spanish legal system see his (2001). And, if so, important consequences and real legal changes in Member States have to be expected. In relation to the Spanish legal order, see Tomás Mallén (2004) 99 *et seq.*

[75] Considering the reports from other Member States, it seems that this is the view taken by judges and courts in the majority of Member States. The various national situations regarding the Charter of Fundamental Rights can been seen in the reports presented at the annual meeting of the European Public Law Group in 2001 in Spetses (Greece) and published in (2001) 14(1) *European Review of Public Law* (esp 275–746). For a general overview of right to good administration as a fundamental right of the EU in the Spanish legal order see Tomás Mallén (2004).

[76] See Nieto Garrido and Martín Delgado (2002). The interpretative value of the Charter in this way has been recognised in the jurisprudence of the Constitutional Court, the Supreme Court and the Superior Courts of Justice of the various judicial branches. To the judgments cited at the beginning of this chapter, we can add one from another judicial order: the Superior Court of Justice of Castilla-La Mancha, Social Chamber of 23 June 2004 (Case 325/2003) which invoked Art 46 of the Charter and found that 'the interpretative value [of the Charter] with respect to fundamental rights conforms with Article 10(2) of our constitutional text' (point 2).

[77] Among those that refer to Art 41(2)(c) or II-101(2)(c) in support of the solution found by courts to specific cases are the following: from the Supreme Court, judgment of 28 September 2004 (Case 4841/2001), judgment of 21 September 2004 (Case 2242/2001), and judgment of 2 June 2004 (Case 202/2002), among many others; of the judgments from the Superior Courts of Justice, judgment of the Superior Court of Castilla-La Mancha of 24 March 2004 (Case 790/2000), judgment of the Superior Court of Valencia of 14 May 2004 (Case 1196/2002), of 18 November 2005 (Case 407/2002), or 12 November 2004 (Case 1698/2003). The last of these judgements is significant: faced with an action for pecuniary damages against a health authority for negligence due to delay in diagnosing an illness which caused the death of a patient, the hospital involved seriously hindered the plaintiffs in their attempt to gain access to documents in order to bring the action. The Court found that 'the bad faith on behalf of the Requena Hospital administration in this case is patent, along with an ignorance of the basic principles of good administration recognized as citizens' rights . . . in our legislation. Moreover, the recent supranational instruments in the field of human rights serve to reinforce those rights, as Art 41 of the Charter of Fundamental Rights of the European Union makes clear [Art II-101 of the Treaty establishing a Constitution for Europe]'. The Court did not stop there; it went on to justify the use of this

The highest Court in Spain, the Supreme Court, has followed a similar path. It is not just willing to invoke Article 41 of the Charter in support of its decisions, as an additional argument to those based on national provisions, but it also frames the rights that those national provisions recognise within the right to good administration enshrined in the Charter. The judgment of 22 February 2005 (Case 3055/2001) illustrates this point, where the Court found that 'the duty on public

provision, stating: 'It's clear that the Treaty (and with it, the Charter) will only have legal force once the process of ratification of the twenty-five Member States is completed, but it's also clear, according to the Preamble to the Charter, that it "reaffirms" rights which have already been enshrined and developed in international human rights law and by the common constitutional traditions of the Member States of which Spain is a part, as expressed in Art 35 of Law 30/1992 which contains this right to good administration (which is in turn a manifestation of Art 105(b) of the Spanish Constitution of 1978)' (point 6). Indeed, the Court did not simply refer to the Charter, and specifically the right to good administration, to support its decision, it also justified such an invocation on the grounds that, given that the rights of the Charter reflect those contained in international human rights instruments and the common constitutional traditions of Member States, this fact in itself lends them a certain interpretative value.

This case law has been developed mainly by the Superior Court of Justice of the Autonomous Community of Valencia, the most active in invoking the Charter to support its findings and, more specifically, the right to good administration, independently of any link to Community law. This is illustrated by the judgment of 28 October 2002 (Case 30/1999), where in point 4 the Court affirmed that 'To summarize the arguments above, in the supranational instruments of human rights, the obligation on administrative organs to act within a reasonable time has been reformulated as a citizens' right within the broader right to good administration. This is reflected in Art 41 (the right to good administration) of the Charter of Fundamental Rights of the European Union . . ., whose paragraph 1 states that "Every person has the right to have his or her affairs handled impartially, fairly and within a reasonable time by the institutions, bodies, offices and agencies of the Union". On this point, two observations can be made: on the one hand, it is clear that the Charter was not created, in principle, as a binding legal document, but only as a solemn declaration at the highest European political level at the European Council of Nice in 2000; and, on the other, that the current case does not involve acts of the organs or institutions of the Union, nor administrative acts carried out by national organs in the implementation of Union law (Art 51 of the Charter). That said, it is also clear that the Charter reaffirms (as is expressed in its Preamble) "the rights as they result, in particular, from the constitutional traditions and international obligations common to the Member States, the European Convention for the Protection of Human Rights and Fundamental Freedoms, the Social Charters adopted by the Union and by the Council of Europe and the case law of the Court of Justice of the European Union and of the European Court of Human Rights". In fact, with respect to the principle of good administration (in its application as the right to be heard) the Court of Justice has repeatedly found (judgment of 4 July 1963, *José v Council* Case C-32/62), that this right is a general rule of administrative law applying in the Member States of the European Economic Community and "that this rule, which corresponds to the requirements of justice and good administration, must be observed by the Community organs". Finally, the parallels and connections between the declaration in the Nice Charter's preamble and Art 6(2) of the Treaty on European Union must be borne in mind, according to which "The Union shall respect fundamental rights, as guaranteed by the European Convention for the Protection of Human Rights and Fundamental Freedoms signed in Rome on 4 November 1950 and as they result from the constitutional traditions common to the Member States, as general principles of Community law". In sum, considering the challenge to the application of a controversial traffic offence within a reasonable time which the administrative authorities should have done, the court considers the challenged administrative resolutions null and void, thus rendering it otiose to consider the other grounds of action.'

A similar position was taken in the judgments of 4 of November 2002 (Case 2339/1998), 8 April 2003 (Case 19/2000), 15 March 2004 (Case 1513/2002), 14 May 2004 (Case 1356/2002) and 14 of September 2002 (Case 1079/2001). The judgments of this particular Superior Court of Justice have invoked the right to good administration in several of its manifestations specified in the Charter: the right to be heard (among others, judgment of 4 October 2002, Case 3348/1998); the duty to provide reasons (judgment of 14 May 2004, Case 1196/2002); and the right of access to the file (among others, judgment of 5 July 2002, Case 360/1997).

administrations to give reasons for their decisions should be incorporated into citizens' right to good administration, which is inherent in the constitutional traditions common to Member States of the EU, which has achieved the status of a legal provision as a fundamental right in Article 41 of the Charter of Fundamental Rights of the European Union' (point 4).[78] Moreover, the Supreme Court is conscious of the possible consequences for Member States of recognising the right to good administration as a fundamental right. In its judgment of 29 March 2004 (Case 8697/1999) it found that the duty to give reasons 'is a consequence of the principles of legal certainty and the prohibition of arbitrariness contained in paragraph 3, Article 9 of the Constitution and which, also, from another perspective, can be viewed as a constitutional requirement imposed by Article 103 (the principle of legality of administrative acts), which is reinforced in the Charter of Fundamental Rights of the European Union . . . which includes in its Article 41, on "the Right to good administration" the obligation incumbent upon the Administration to provide reasons for its decisions' (point 4). The inclusion of this right in the Charter 'reinforces' national legal provisions.

Even some internal laws have echoed this recognition of the right to good administration in the Charter. A paradigmatic example is Law 4/2006 of 30 June on the transparency and good practice of the public administration of Galicia (an autonomous law corresponding to the Autonomous Community of Galicia), whose preamble, after stating the importance of transparency in administrative action and the participation of citizens in the pursuit of the public interest, acknowledges that 'All in all, the measures included in this current law will contribute to making the right to good administration more effective, as a principle enshrined in our judicial *acquis* since the signing of the Charter of Fundamental Rights of the European Union'. It is unnecessary to elaborate any further to conclude that the right to good administration proclaimed in the Charter of Fundamental Rights affects national administrations.

In conclusion, it is clear that the important position of the right to good administration at the European level can and should have effects on national administrations when they apply EU law: the right to a hearing, which now applies not only in the field of state aid (Article 88 EC) but to the entire European administrative procedure; the right of access to one's own files; the duty to provide reasons for a decision; and all the other rights that are not explicitly mentioned in Article 41(2) but are integrated into the right to good administration—for example, those relating to the obligation to act with diligence and effectiveness[79]—

[78] The Supreme Court has given judgments in identical terms in the judgments of 23 May 2005 (Case 2414/2002) and 13 December 2005 (Case 120/2004), among others. All this is independent of the existence of a connection with Union law in the case in question.

[79] These requirements are more apt for a law of administrative procedure than a declaration of rights; probably for this reason there is no express mention of them in Art 41 of the Charter, which rightly limits itself to stating the right for everyone to have their affairs dealt with in an impartial, fair manner and within a reasonable time. However, they have been recognised by the ECJ and the CFI as conditions applying to Community administration by virtue of the principle of good administration. See eg Case C-49/88 *Al-Jubail Fertilizer Company and others v Council* [1991] ECR I-3187 and Case T-73/95

must be applied equally to national administrations when they act as part of the European administration pursuing the general interests of the EU, by virtue of the principle of loyal co-operation.[80]

For this reason, and keeping in mind that the rights explicitly mentioned in Article 41 of the Charter are directly applicable and can be relied upon without requiring further implementing measures, an eventual European law on administrative procedure which further develops the requirements should also be applicable in general terms to national administrations when they apply EU law.[81] Only in this way can it be ensured that the protection afforded to individuals does not change according to the national or European nature of the administrative organ.[82]

(b) The Right of Access to Documents

The right of access to documents is closely related to the principle of transparency and the right to good administration. In fact, when drafting the Charter of Fundamental Rights, it was proposed that such a right be included in the article on the right to good administration.[83]

Oliveira v Commission [1997] ECR II-381, both relative to the duty of due diligence; and Case C-374/87 *Orkem v Commission* [1989] ECR 3283, relating to the right to non-incrimination, which is connected to the right to a defence.

[80] The jurisprudence of the ECJ has used this principle on numerous occasions to demand specific action from and impose duties on the Member States, to the extent that it has become one of the basic principles of the Community system. It is sufficient to mention as well-known examples Case C-106/77 *Amministrazione delle finanze dello Stato v Simmenthal* [1978] ECR 629; Case 213/89 *The Queen v Secretary of State for Transport, ex parte Factortame* [1990] ECR I-2433; and Case 6/90 *Francovich and Bonifaci v Italy* [1991] ECR I-5357. In our opinion, the correct application of EU law, in those joint spheres of activity, requires the application of the requirements of the right to good administration. On the idea of the principle of loyal co-operation as the basis of every administrative action see Tomás Mallén (2004) 74.

[81] As was stated at the time, one of the consequences of the application of the Charter of Fundamental Rights to Member States is the existence of a legal basis whereby the Union can stipulate implementing measures based on a specific right which are binding, not only on the European institutions, organs and bodies but also on Member States. Although it is clear that, as Art 51(2) states, the Charter does not extend the field of application of Union law beyond the powers of the Union or establish any new power or task for the Union, or modify powers and tasks defined in the Treaties, it is also clear that national administrations act as part of the European administration when they apply EU law in the exercise of their executive or shared competences, and that such acts are closely connected with the acts of the European institutions. Thus, although the main addressee of an eventual law on administrative procedure would be the European administration and the administrative decisions taken by this administration in the sphere of the EU, it cannot be ruled out that it could also apply—within the limits of respect for the procedural autonomy of the Member States, which is being increasingly diluted—to administrative decisions taken by national administration or open administrative procedures for the adoption of implementing acts of the laws of the EU. For a more detailed analysis of an eventual European law on administrative procedure binding also on Member States, see ch 4.

[82] The terminology is taken from the ECJ's judgment in Joined Cases C-46/93 and 48/93 *Brasserie du Pêcheur v Bundesrepublik Deutschland and The Queen/Secretary of State for Transport, ex parte Factortame and others* [1996] ECR I-1029, confirming the principle of State liability for damage suffered by individuals due to a breach of European law: 'The protection of the rights which individuals derive from Community law cannot vary depending on whether a national authority or a Community authority is responsible for the damage' (para 42).

[83] CHARTE 4170/00 CONVENT 17, 20 March 2000.

In chapter two, the importance of this law for the achievement of the aims of transparency outlined by the Commission as part of the democratisation of the EU was explained. This will be further explored when considering the creation of law on administrative procedure and participation in the decision-making process. At this point it is worth examining the extent to which the principle of transparency, in one of its specific manifestations—the right of access to documents—is also applicable to Member States.

In principle, access to documents in the field of Community law arises—as contained in the Treaty and in secondary law—as a guarantee of the transparency of the acts of the European institutions.

Effectively, Article 255 of the EC Treaty, as well as Regulation No 1049/2001,[84] limits the obligation to furnish documents requested by citizens to the individual Community institutions.[85] However, this does not mean that the recognition of this right does not contain any obligation for Member States; on the contrary, according to Article 2 of Regulation 1049/2001, with respect to its sphere of application, 'This Regulation shall apply to all documents held by an institution, that is to say, documents drawn up or received by it and in its possession, in all areas of activity of the European Union', which includes documents given to the Community institutions by the Member States (Article 3(b)). Thus, any citizen can petition an EU institution for Member States' documents in its possession, unless the request falls under one of the exceptions to the right (contained in Article 4), which includes the situation where a Member State has specifically requested that the relevant document is not handed over pursuant to the request.[86] This has been interpreted by the CFI as constituting a right of veto for Member States who, moreover, are not obliged in any way to justify the exercise of their veto or to give reasons for their refusal to allow access to the documents.[87] In such cases, the rules on access to documents of the relevant Member State will apply.

Moreover, Member States are obliged to furnish documents of the European institutions in their possession on request. This much is clear from Article 5: 'Where a Member State receives a request for a document in its possession, originating from an institution, unless it is clear that the document shall or shall not be disclosed, the

[84] Regulation (EC) No 1049/2001 of the European Parliament and of the Council of 30 May 2001 regarding public access to European Parliament, Council and Commission documents [2001] OJ L145/43.

[85] Until the creation of this regulation, public access to documents was governed by different decisions from the Council, the Commission and the European Parliament: Decision 93/731/EC of the Council, of 20 of December 1993, on public access to Council documents [1993] OJ L340/43; Decision 94/90/ECSC, EC, Euratom, of the Commission, of 8 February 1994, on public access to Commission documents [1994] OJ L46/58; and Decision 97/632/EC, CECA, EURATOM, of the European Parliament, of 10 July 1997, on public access to the documents of the European Parliament [1997] OJ L263/27.

[86] As established by Art 4(5) of the regulation, which provides that 'A Member State may request the institution not to disclose a document originating from that Member State without its prior agreement'. Declaration No 35 to the Final Act of the ToA should also be taken into account.

[87] See Case T-76/02 *Messina v Commission* [2003] ECR II-3203; Case T-168/02 *IFAW Internationaler Tierschutz-Fonds v Commission* [2004] ECR II-4135; and Case T-187/03 *Scippacercola v Commission* [2005] ECR II-1029.

Member State shall consult with the institution concerned in order to take a decision that does not jeopardise the attainment of the objectives of this Regulation. The Member State may instead refer the request to the institution.'

Thus, in accordance with the relevant provisions of the Treaty, a double obligation exists—negative and positive—for Member States with respect to the right of access to documents,[88] an obligation which has been fortified by the transformation of the principle into a fundamental right by virtue of its inclusion in the Charter, as will be seen subsequently. In the same way, it must not be forgotten that there is a sector-specific framework with respect to the competences of the EU that is directly applicable to the Member States, requiring them to furnish any information requested by citizens. In this respect, Directive 2003/4/EC[89] requires Member States to create the provisions necessary to give effect to the right of any natural or legal person to gain access to information on the environment that is in the possession of the administration.

The Charter, in Article 42, and the Constitutional Treaty, in its Articles I-50 and III-399, preserves the status quo, identifying the Community institutions as entitled to the right of access to documents—although, as has been seen, it has been expanded to cover organs and bodies of the EU. In this way, Article I-50 provides that 'Any citizen of the Union, and any natural or legal person residing or having its registered office in a Member State shall have, under the conditions laid down in Part III, a right of access to documents of the Union institutions, bodies, offices and agencies, whatever their medium'.

However, the expression 'access to documents of the Union institutions, bodies, offices and agencies' should not be understood as only the documents originating from them; it also covers documents in their possession.

[88] Although the extension of the application of the right of access to documents was established by Regulation 1049/2001 (perhaps its most important innovation), it is envisaged that a future European law which, according to Art I-50(3) Constitutional Treaty, will lay down the general principles and limits applicable to the exercise of this right, will retain this double obligation on Member States given that it already constitutes an essential part of the right.

[89] Directive 2003/4/EC of the European Parliament and the Council, of 28 January 2003, on public access to environmental information [2003] OJ L41/26. This Directive was drafted with the aim of developing the obligations surrounding access to information on environmental issues signed up to in the Convention on Access to Information, Public Participation in Decision-Making and Access to Justice in Environmental Matters signed at Aarhus on 25 June 1998. The directive has been implemented in Spain by Law 27/2006 of 18 July, which regulates the rights of access to information, public participation and access to justice in environmental matters, and which also incorporates Directive 2003/35/EC of the European Parliament and the Council, of 26 May 2003, providing for public participation in respect of the drawing up of certain plans and programmes relating to the environment [2003] OJ L156/17, drafted as with the previous Directive in order to implement the Aarhus Convention, with respect to participation. The Spanish law enshrines the right to gain access to information regarding the environment which is in the possession of public authorities, without declaring a specific interest in the documents. The pioneer in this respect was, however, Directive 90/313/EEC of the Council, of 7 June 1990, which was implemented in Spain by Law 38/1995, of 12 of December, on the right of access to information in environmental matters.

This Convention is also binding on EU institutions: Regulation (EC) No 1367/2006 of the European Parliament and of the Council, of 6 September 2006, on the application of the provisions of the Aarhus Convention on Access to Information, Public Participation in Decision-making and Access to Justice in Environmental Matters to Community institutions and bodies [2006] OJ L264/13.

All in all, even though it is clear that the EU framework regulating the right of access to documents must respect national laws on the matter, the presence of an element of EU law in a national dispute means that EU law will supersede the application of national law. This is confirmed by the fact that all documents of the Community institutions (even if they are held by a Member State), as well as others which, even if not being their own are in their power, should be accessible to the public, albeit that certain conditions apply. This is confirmed by the fact that Article I-50 is an attempt to collate the existing regulatory framework in force on access to documents.[90]

This Article contains the most obvious manifestation of the rationale for broadening the sphere of application of fundamental rights to the activities of the administrations of the Member States connected to EU law, regardless of whether the provision regulating the right in question states that the right will apply to Member States: when a Member State acts as part of the European administration it should be subject to the same conditions as apply to this administration. When, in the exercise of shared competences in the framework of composite procedures or implementation competences—the application, strictly speaking, of policies within the exclusive competence of the EU—Member States must provide their own documents or, on the contrary, if they posses documents from a European institution (or body or office), they are bound by the right of access to documents, in such a way that both types of documents should be accessible by EU citizens, under the conditions and limits provided in the relevant regulatory framework. Measures taken by Member States in the sphere of application of EU law makes such a measure an act with European relevance, and EU law applies (in this case, the right of access to documents).

Moreover, it is with respect to this right that one of the most important innovations resulting from the conversion of this principle into a fundamental right contained in the Charter and the Constitution arises in terms of its implications for Member States. It has already been pointed out that, according to the current regulatory framework, simple refusal by a State is sufficient to halt the process of disclosing documents without having to justify the refusal with reference to the exceptions or provide reasons for such a refusal.[91] However, its inclusion in the Charter means that the case law of the ECJ will apply, according to which, when the Community rules allow an exception to a fundamental right it must be proportionate, making it inconceivable that the right of access will be unjustifiably deprived of any effect.[92]

[90] This can be seen in the Explanation provided by the Praesidium of the Convention, which cites both Art 255 of the EC Treaty and Regulation 1049/2001.

[91] For a critical analysis of this possibility with an exhaustive study of the jurisprudence of the CFI on the interpretation of Art 4(5) of Regulation 1049/2001 (which is flexible with respect to the validity of a refusal to hand over documents in such cases), see Cabral (2006). This author, after highlighting the incoherence of the jurisprudence with respect to the spirit of the Regulation and the right itself, concludes that 'only the protection of the specific interests mentioned in Art 4(1) to (3) of the Regulation can justify non-disclosure and ... all decisions totally or partially refusing access to documents held by the institutions (must be) properly reasoned, thus allowing an effective control of Member States' discretion by European citizens and the Community judicature' (p 388).

[92] The important judgment of the ECJ in Case C-5/88 *Wachauf v Bundesamt für Ernährung und*

Moreover, the need to provide reasons for every act (including implementing acts of European law, both national and European) as an expression of the right to good administration enshrined in Article II-101(2)(c), and in relation to Article I-38(2) of the Constitutional Treaty means that, in each individual case, any refusal to disclose documents must be accompanied by reasons for the refusal. Ultimately, the effect of the veto power of the Member States is mitigated, both due to the need to justify the refusal to provide access to a document and because each refusal must be proportionate. Moreover, if there is an obligation to provide reasons and avoid disproportionate refusals, there must also be the possibility of an appeal in order to protect the right of access.

Finally, a European law developing this right which does not recognise the exercise of the right with respect to Member States' documents in the possession of the European institutions would jeopardise the central core of the right of access to documents and, as a consequence, would be susceptible to challenge before the ECJ. This much can be gleaned from Article 52(1) of the Charter, which, moreover, requires that every limitation on the right is strictly necessary and corresponds to the general interest and that the need to protect other rights respects the principle of proportionality.

(c) The Right to Protection of Personal Data

The right to the protection of personal data recognised in Article 8 of the Charter is the only one of the three rights considered here whose field of application is demarcated in accordance with Article 51. Effectively, according to Article I-51 of the Constitutional Treaty[93]—to which reference must be made as provided by Article II-112(2)—not only does this right apply to national administrations, the EU is equipped with the legal basis to draft a European law or a European framework law on 'the rules relating to the protection of individuals with regard to the processing of personal data by Union institutions, bodies, offices and agencies, *and by the Member States when carrying out activities which fall within the scope of Union law,* and the rules relating to the free movement of such data' (emphasis added).

As was explained in chapter two, the main innovations in relation to this right—which was created by the Community legislator and not by the jurisprudence of the

Forstwirtschaft, explained in the first part of this chapter, found that the requirements deriving from the protection of fundamental rights in the Community legal order also bind the Member States when they apply Community laws which means that they are obliged as far as possible to apply the rules in a way that does not infringe upon those requirements (para 19), so long as restrictions on the rights correspond with objectives of general interest pursued by the Community and, taking into account the objective pursued, do not constitute a disproportionate and intolerable interference impairing the very substance of the rights (para 18).

[93] The text of this provision should be read with Declaration 10 attached to the Constitutional Treaty, relative to Art I-51, according to which 'The Conference declares that, whenever rules on protection of personal data to be adopted on the basis of Article I-51 could have direct implications for national security, due account will have to be taken of the specific characteristics of the matter. It recalls that the legislation presently applicable (see in particular Directive 95/46/EC) includes specific derogations in this regard'.

ECJ—are the creation of a single legal basis for the protection of the right within the ambit of the EU (which will be used to regulate the protection of this right by the EU institutions and the Member States), and its application to the third pillar of the EU. What is interesting for present purposes is that both the right and the law will be binding on Member States.[94] This will occur not 'when they are implementing Union law', but 'when carrying out activities which fall within the scope of Union law', an expression which corresponds to a broad interpretation of the sphere of application of the fundamental rights of the EU[95] and which confirms that the expression 'implementing Union law' should not be narrowly construed, but should have the same meaning as acting within the field of EU law. Consequently, when Member States act in the field of application of EU law,[96] they should respect the European regulatory framework regarding the protection of personal data.[97]

Thus, the definition of the term 'implement' provided in the first part of this chapter is clearly applicable with respect to Member States being bound by the right to the protection of personal data.[98]

III. FUNDAMENTAL RIGHTS OF THE EUROPEAN UNION AND MEMBER STATES: THE CASE OF STRUCTURAL FUNDS

To conclude this chapter on the effect of the binding nature of fundamental rights on the activities of Member States in the field of EU law, this final section will deal

[94] This has become regular practice since the entry into force of Directive 95/46/EC of the European Parliament and of the Council, of 24 October 1995, on the protection of individuals with regard to the processing of personal data and on the free movement of such data [1995] OJ L281/31. This was based on Art 95 EC Treaty (approximation of laws for the establishment and functioning of the internal market).

[95] The final draft of this text was obviously influenced by the existing Community Regulation: Art 3 of the 1995 Directive provides that with respect to its sphere of application, it will not apply to the handling of personal data in activities which do not fall within the sphere of application of Community law.

[96] It should not be ruled out, however, that, along with the right to good administration and, in general, with the rights contained in the Charter, the right to protection of personal data can be relied on before national courts even in situations unconnected with EU law. For an example see the judgment of the Spanish Supreme Court, Criminal Division, of 14 October 2005 (Case 739/2005).

[97] This constitutes more than a simple shift from national regulation of the protection of personal data to a European regulation thereof; it implies the integration of the European system into national law.

[98] An example prior to the signing of the Constitutional Treaty—in fact prior to the solemn declaration on the Charter—is the ECJ's judgment in Joined Cases C-465/00, C-138/01 and C-139/01 *Österreichischer Rundfunk and others* [2003] ECR I-4989, analysed in depth in the ch 2. It is interesting to note that, in response to one of the three questions posed in the preliminary reference by the various Austrian courts regarding the possible violation of Community law by a national law obliging a national body to gather and hand over information on salaries and pensions in order to publish the names and earnings of the employees of specific public bodies, the Court stipulated that 'It should also be noted that the provisions of Directive 95/46, in so far as they govern the processing of personal data liable to infringe fundamental freedoms, in particular the right to privacy, must necessarily be interpreted in the light of fundamental rights, which, according to settled case law, form an integral part of the general principles of law whose observance the Court ensures' (para 68).

with the application of the theoretical argument developed in the previous pages to a specific sector of European law: the EU's structural funds.

The choice of this sector in particular can be justified by the need to provide an example of joint administration—an example of direct administration by a European institution and indirect administration by the Member States—which involves mixed organs in which both administrations are represented and, moreover, the adoption of decisions affecting individuals.[99]

One of the principal objectives pursued by the EU, as indicated by Article 2 EC, is the development of economic, social and territorial cohesion among the Member States. For this reason Article 158 EC deals with the development of this objective and lays down the bases for shared competences in establishing that 'In order to promote its overall harmonious development, the Community shall develop and pursue its action leading to the strengthening of its economic, and social cohesion'. Article 159 sets out Member States' obligation to co-ordinate economic policies to this end and mentions specifically the instrument to be used to achieve such ends: structural funds.

Currently, Regulation (EC) No 1083/2006 of the Council, of 11 July 2006, laying down general provisions on structural funds, regulates this sector.[100]

In general terms (and bearing in mind the purpose of this analysis—namely to give an example of joint administration necessitating the application of the fundamental rights of the EU to the acts of Member States, independently of the wording of the relevant provision), the case of structural funds shows that the difference between direct and indirect implementation[101] is of decreasing practical value, exactly because of the inexorable expansion of areas of shared competence. As a consequence of this, the principle of the autonomy of Member States when establishing organs, rules and procedures for the application of EU law should be qualified in the light of the need to regulate mixed organs and complex procedures laid down by the EU law regulating the specific subject matter.[102] This can be clearly seen in Regulation 1083/2006, which on the one hand provides that the application of the principles of proportionality and subsidiarity mean that it is for the Member

[99] Shared management must be understood as the 'management of those Community programmes where the Commission and the Member States have distinct administrative tasks which are interdependent and set down in legislation and where both the Commission and the national administrations need to discharge their respective tasks for the Community policy to be implemented successfully'. See the Committee of Independent Experts Second Report on Reform of the Commission (10 September 1999), Vol. I, at 3.2.2, cited by Craig (2006) 78.

[100] [2006] OJ L210/25. These provisions focus on each of the individual funds through the following measures: Regulation (EC) No 1080/2006 of the European Parliament and of the Council, of 5 July 2006, on the European Regional Development Fund [2006] OJ L210/1; Regulation (EC) No 1081/2006 of the European Parliament and of the Council, of 5 July 2006, on the European Social Fund [2006] OJ L210/12; Council Regulation (EC) No 1084/2006, of 11 July 2006, establishing a Cohesion Fund [2006] OJ L210/79 (those general provisions apply also to the Cohesion Fund).

[101] On the difference between direct and indirect execution see Isaac (2000).

[102] Alongside this, the principle of the autonomy of Community law itself is also influenced by national legal systems. In the words of Alonso García (2005), 'such autonomy can only be understood in the context of interaction with the laws of Member States, characterized by a dynamic and permanent conceptual symbiosis, at the European and national levels' (p 47–48).

States to administer and control structural funds and, on the other, that it is necessary to establish the general principles applicable to the control and management systems of the operational programmes with a view to guaranteeing their proper functioning.[103] This explains the fact that the ultimate decision is taken by the Commission, that this institution controls the management of the activities carried out by national authorities, and that the national organs of control (monitoring committee, as established by Article 63) should include a Commission representative.

The effect of the two situations mentioned above—confusion regarding direct and indirect administration and the qualification of the principle of autonomy—is a growing interdependence between European and national acts, which mutually influence each other. The conclusion reached on observing this reality, with respect to the specific question being analysed in this chapter, is the need to guarantee respect for the fundamental rights recognised by the European legal order independently of the authority—national or European—that is acting in the specific phase of the complex procedure. And the explication for this conclusion lies in the fact that both the acts and the interests pursued are shared.

An analysis of the functioning of structural funds[104] highlights the following elements: application of the regulatory provisions of such funds is carried out by a joint administration (Regulation 1083/2006 mentions associations between the Commission and Member States in Article 11 and joint management in Article 14) in which, broadly speaking, the Commission is charged with planning and the national administration acts as the implementing arm of the Commission; the administrative function developed in this procedure is one; and, finally, it pursues a common interest. Formally speaking, the performance is ultimately imputed to the Commission, although in fact it is the result of a series of acts carried out at the national and the European level; any challenges to the acts will be heard at either the national or European level depending on the specific act being contested. Ultimately, what is involved is a procedure (in reality made up of various procedures) that pursues the adoption of a decision in the application of an EU policy for the achievement of a shared objective, such as economic, social and territorial cohesion.

Three levels of activity—European, national and individual—are interrelated in the three main phases of action—planning, execution, and evaluation and monitoring. The European Commission (Article 32) is charged with adopting the decision to provide a specific sum from the structural funds in order to finance a specific project put forward by a Member State and elaborated on the basis of the needs of the sector and in collaboration with the interest groups affected; moreover, it is also up to the Commission to monitor and evaluate the process, a function it

[103] This is set out in a general way in Recitals 65 and 62 of the Regulation.

[104] For a more complete study in relation to the phenomenon of co-administration in field of structural funds (albeit focused on the general provisions contained in Regulation (EC) No 1260/1999, now superseded by Regulation 1083/2006) see the Articles published in 2002 in *Rivista Giuridica del Mezzogiorno*: Casini and Midena (2002); Saltari and Savino (2002); Caroli Casavola and Greco (2002).

shares with national authorities (Article 47), given that it is ultimately the body responsible for the decision to grant funds and, where applicable, the decision to reduce or withdraw funds (Article 99). National authorities are the necessary (and the only) interlocutors with the European Commission. They present the various requests to the Commission, select the specific projects to benefit from the programme, supervise the development of activities, certify that those activities have been developed and, in general, guarantee the correctness of the application of the programme as well as having charge of the management of the projects (Articles 60–68 and 70–71). The ultimate recipients of funds present their projects within the framework of the funding procedure, elaborate their specific financial activities and receive the corresponding financial amount. They deal exclusively with the national authority that constitutes the bridge between them and the Commission.

With regard to the relationship between the administration and the individual, the most interesting phases for the purposes of the current analysis are those relating to execution and monitoring, due to the fact that they are a clear example of co-administration: the European administration and the national administration on occasions join to form one body (the monitoring committee during the monitoring phase), and at the same time, carry out complementary actions. In this way the Commission receives first-hand information and the Member States influence the final Commission decision, thereby participating in the management of a European policy. Although the final decision rests with the Commission, it is heavily influenced by national administrations, to which it grants an important decision-making autonomy, in such a way that it can be asserted that both act together and between them create a relationship of mutual dependency.

Essentially, the management and control functions are granted to the Member States by Regulation 1083/2006. Deepening their relationship through this connection and mutual influence, the Commission's final decision is influenced by the acts of the national authorities, to the point where it can be said that a deficient act on the part of the latter can negatively affect the final decision of the former.[105] For example, the national administration is in charge of signing off the accounts presented by the beneficiary of structural funds for the project approved by the fund (Article 61), while the Commission takes the final decision and, in doing so, it will take into account the certificates and files prepared by the managing, certifying and auditing authorities.[106]

[105] This is highlighted by Case C-32/95 *Commission v Lisrestal and others* (n 52), where the appeal of a decision of the CFI to the ECJ was rejected (the details of which are provided above). The Commission argued that, under the system for aid provided under the European Social Fund, whereby the Commission entrusted the Member State with the role of administering the funds for the approved project, imposing a duty to give individuals a hearing would cause a change in the system. However, the ECJ rejected this contention, stating that 'an argument based on practical grounds is not sufficient to justify infringement of a fundamental principle such as the observance of the rights of the defence' (para 37). Ultimately, the essential procedural guarantees that have now been integrated into the right to good administration must be respected independently of whether the act in question is taken by the European or the national administration.

[106] In Case C-413/98 *Frota Azul-Transportes e Turismo* [2001] ECR I-673, the ECJ confirmed that

Thus, the authorities of the Member States have a certain decisional autonomy with respect to the aid granted within the framework of structural funds, although the final decision always rests with the European Commission, which releases the funds and takes the final decisions approving the relevant programme. For this, it is necessary to guarantee that the activities of the national administrations comply with Community requirements[107]. In other words, maladministration at the national level could result in maladministration at the European level, jeopardising the overall procedure.[108] This is the main argument for the application of the right to good administration—but also the other rights applicable to the relationship between the administration and citizens—to the acts of the national administrations. Moreover, given that in terms of challenging these acts there is a division depending on which the acting authority is (national or European),[109] the criteria

Member States should not limit themselves to a simple technical verification of the expenditure, but must satisfy themselves that such expenditure was incurred pursuant to the development project at the market price for the relevant goods and services involved. The risk of inequality in the application of the criteria, as indicated by the Court, should be mitigated by the fact that the Commission is the ultimate decision-maker (paras 27–31).

[107] Craig (2006) insists on the importance of reconciling the tension between collective interest and individual interests of Member States and the tension between decentralisation and effective supervision of regional policy (p 96).

[108] An example of this situation can be seen in the case brought before the CFI in Case T-346/94 *France-Aviation v Commission* [1995] ECR II-2841, regarding an action for annulment of a Commission decision based on a request from the French Republic with respect to the devolution of particular rights of importation whose extension was not justified. The beneficiary of the importation rights acted with the utmost diligence but the responsible French authorities did not ensure that all the relevant requirements applicable to the case were complied with. During the procedure—which developed in two phases, national and Community—the individual affected did not have the opportunity to present his version of the facts. The influence that the national measured exercised over the Community decision caused the CFI to opine that 'the applicant's right to be heard in a procedure such as that to which these proceedings relate must actually be secured in the first place in the relations between the person concerned and the national administration. Regulation No 2454/93 provides only for contacts between the person concerned and the administration, on the one hand, and between the administration and the Commission, on the other. Although that legislation does not provide for direct contacts between the Commission's departments and the person concerned, it does not necessarily mean that the Commission may deem itself satisfied in every case where an application for repayment has been brought before it with the information transmitted to it by the national administration. Suffice it to say, in this connection, that Art 905(2) of Regulation No 2454/93 provides that the Commission may ask the Member State concerned to supply additional information. Consequently, the Court should consider whether in the instant case the Commission should have made such a request in order to ensure that the applicant's right to be heard was respected through the provision of additional explanations first provided by the applicant to the French administration and subsequently transmitted to the Commission' (para 30). In other words, the European administration was supposed to use the legal means available to 'oblige' the national administration to hear the views of the individual affected. Most interestingly, the Court recognised that 'It appears therefore that the Commission took the contested decision on the basis of an incomplete case' (para 35); for this reason, taking into account that the French authorities had recognised that they could not impute any negligence to the individual, the Commission, which attempted to distance itself from the national authorities (who were in favour of not seeking the devolution of importation rights), 'had a duty to arrange for the applicant to be heard by the French authorities' (para 36).

[109] Regulation 1083/2006, just like its predecessor, emphatically insists on the division of responsibilities. Recital 28 speaks of the necessity to specify the necessary conditions so that the Commission can exercise the responsibilities incumbent on it in relation to the execution of the general budget of the EU and clarify the responsibilities of co-operation with the Member States, because this allows the

for the control and legality of such acts cannot be left completely to the national legal systems, in such a way that national judges must take into account the parameters of control stemming from the recognition of fundamental rights at the European level, especially the right to good administration. This does not entail a change of jurisdiction given that the decisions adopted by the national authority will still be controlled by the internal jurisdictions, while those taken by the Commission will be controlled by the European jurisdiction; it simply presupposes the application of the requirements applicable to the Community institution to national institutions due to the influence that their acts can have on the activities of the latter.[110] The direct/indirect administration dichotomy and the consequent principle of the autonomy of Member States cannot persist as though composite procedures do not exist, in the same way that it cannot be maintained that fundamental rights such as the right to good administration are not binding on national authorities because of purely formal considerations. Composite or joint procedure highlights this point, and one arrives at the same conclusion if one takes into account the fact that the Constitutional Treaty contains a new legal base for the acts of the EU which undoubtedly will have an influence on this question: administrative co-operation, enshrined in Article III-285.[111]

To conclude, it can be said that co-administration takes place, in the words of Cassese, 'when a Community function is divided between Community organs which develop the activity of the direction and share the management and national organs which develop the implementation, paying attention to both national and Community interests'.[112] There is a common administration which pursues common interests, so that the requirements and guarantees of their acts must also be shared, as well as those relative to fundamental rights and, in particular, the right to good administration.

Commission to determine whether the Member States are using the funds in a legal and proper way according to the principle of good financial management. As García de Enterría (1993, 319), referring to mixed and shared procedures, points out, 'the peculiar thing here . . . is the fragmentation of procedure in two parts affects of its ability to be challenged. The procedure in itself is mixed, in the way that it is influenced by the acts of national administrations and Community acts but is united in its objective, conception, process and conclusion. This unity is fragmented when different parts of the acts are challenged separately before different courts'.

110 Perhaps the most obvious example of this is the well-known judgment in Case C-97/91 *Oleificio Borelli v Commission* [1992] ECR I-6313. Having received a negative report from a regional authority with respect to securing financing under the European fund of Agricultural Orientation and Guarantee, the applicant received a rejection from the Commission. Having brought an appeal for the annulment of this decision, the Court found that it lacked jurisdiction to decide upon the compliance of a act emanating from a national authority to a fundamental right; however, noting that the internal judicial order in question (Italian in this case) did not provide any way of challenging the decision of a regional authority, in being a simple procedural measure, it found that once 'the requirement of judicial control of any decision of a national authority reflects a general principle of Community law stemming from the constitutional traditions common to the Member States and has been enshrined in Arts 6 and 13 of the European Convention for the Protection of Human Rights and Fundamental Freedoms . . . that Member State is obliged to comply with the aforesaid requirement of judicial control' (paras 14–15).

111 Although this provision does not cover the possibility of creating measures harmonising the administration provisions of the Member States, it will contribute to increasing the areas of join and co-administration.

112 (2003c) 201.

IV. CONCLUSION

Independently of the current situation regarding the application of EU fundamental rights to national authorities—they are binding in any case as general principles of law[113]—and the innovations introduced by the Constitutional Treaty by including the Charter of Fundamental Rights in its Part II, the analysis undertaken in this chapter leads us to the conclusion that there is a tendency to apply the same requirements as apply to the European administration to national administrations with respect to the rights enforceable against administrative acts when they act in the sphere of application of EU law.[114] The Charter is part of the *acquis communautaire.* [115]

The repeated interconnection of legal orders and institutional acts, the mutual influences between national and European systems,[116] the expansion of the fields of joint action and the inexorable advance towards enhanced integration are all elements that clearly illustrate the existence of a single European administration, with the Commission at its apex in conjunction with national administrations,[117]

[113] The Charter cannot mean in any case a negative change in the existing European legal order, in such a way that those guarantees granted to individuals by means of general principles of law continue to be applicable. In the same vein, see Carrillo (2003).

[114] One fact supporting this conclusion is the Regulation (EC) No 168/2007 of the Council, empowering the EU Agency for Fundamental Rights to pursue its activities in areas referred to in Title VI of the TEU. Its objective, as specified in Art 2, is *'to provide the relevant institutions, bodies, offices and agencies of the Community and its Member States when implementing Community law* with assistance and expertise relating to fundamental rights in order to support them when they take measures or formulate courses of action within their respective spheres of competence to fully respect fundamental rights' (emphasis added). This proposes not only to give a bigger role to fundamental rights in the sphere of the EU, but will also provide a useful—and, more importantly, common—instrument of assistance advice to the institutions of the EU and the Member States in their decisions on fundamental rights. On the idea about general principles of good governance in the EU valid for the European Community and for its Member States, see Chiti (1995a) esp 245.

[115] Craig (2006) 539. As affirmed by the Court of Justice in several occasions, fundamental rights are general principles of Community law stemming from the constitutional traditions common to the Member States, which has been reaffirmed by the Charter of fundamental rights of the European Union. Among others, Case C-432/05 *Unibet,* para 37, and Case C-303/2005 *Advocaten voor de Wereld,* para 45 (not yet published).

[116] See Schmidt-Aßmann (2001).

[117] As Ortega Álvarez (2004) maintains, the Community administration operates like a federal administration when actuating executive function, while it acts like a centralised administration regarding inter-institutional relations with national administrations.

All of these issues have been expertly analysed by Cassese in several of this works compiled in a single volume entitled *Lo spazio giuridico globale,* recently translated into Spanish by Ortega Álvarez, Martín Delgado and Gallego Córcoles with the title *La Globalización Jurídica* (Marcial Pons, Madrid, 2006). At pp 116 *et seq* he highlights how the Union and its legal order has changed in its 50 years, to the point that it can now be considered a 'a Community domain of Administrative law'. In the words of the author, 'European administrative law goes beyond simply direct and indirect administration (state administration carrying out Community functions). The links between the two systems are increasingly numerous and complex. Functions are not attributed to the state or the Union, but are rather shared, in such a way that creates a functional nexus. The order is therefore mixed but where the Community element is preeminent. This not only influences the activity of the national administration but also establishes an organizational and functional equilibrium. They constitute common administrative organs within the Community' (p 120). As has already been pointed out, one of those forms of influence occurs through

and also allows for a common European administrative law in the field of fundamental rights and Public Administration. The upshot of all this is a trend towards the europeanisation of administrative procedure.[118]

the shaping of a national administrative law: through a law dictated by the EU national administrative apparatuses are created, procedural rules which nation authorities are bound to follow are promulgated, and certain activities are determined according to the interests of the Community. In this way the autonomy of States is limited. Some of the contributions contained in this work include studies of the Community regulatory framework that support this conclusion and should be consulted for a more in-depth study of this issue. See in particular Chiti and Franchini (2003).

118 This is highlighted by Nehl (1999) 87: 'The continuing growth of regulation relating to EC administrative process, the strengthening of executive complexity and the increasing entwinement of joint EC and national administrative activity suggest that further federalising tendencies on the basis of fundamental procedural rights protection are to be expected. It is assumed that a development is triggered, at the final stage of which the Member States would have to comply with harmonised standards of procedural protection in the event of acting, so to say, as "Community agents", in the sphere of substantive EC competence'. Ultimately, the issues considered in this chapter, as the author himself points out, 'would only be the very first step in a development towards harmonising the basic procedural conditions under which EC and national administration, whether acting jointly or severally, will be called upon to implement substantive Community law' (p 91).

4

Towards a Law on Administrative Procedure

I. AN OLD ISSUE REVISITED: WHY NOW A EUROPEAN LAW ON A COMMON ADMINISTRATIVE PROCEDURE?

1. General Considerations

The European Union is a Community of administrative law.[1] It contains binding norms which are directly effective not only on Member States but also on individuals.[2] Administrative procedure is a fundamental theme in European administrative law[3] which has been expanded with the development of the Community legal order and is still developing, as was illustrated in chapter two of this book. Since the original Coal and Steel Community and up to the current European Union with its distinct objectives of political integration, many developments have taken place in the last 50 years in administrative procedure. The prophetic words spoken by Robert Schuman on 9 May 1950 in the *Salon de l'Horloge* in Paris have become reality—especially with respect to European administrative law—'Europe will not be made all at once, or according to a single plan. It will be built through concrete achievements which first create a *de facto* solidarity.'

Despite the breadth of the topic and the importance of the reform of the EU's administrative model,[4] this chapter will focus on the developments contained in the Treaty establishing a Constitution for Europe (Constitutional Treaty) which, despite their diversity, all basically raise questions surrounding the development of a law that regulates the fundamental aspects of administrative procedure within the EU. This involves highlighting and analysing the constitutional foundations of European administrative procedure in order to establish the dimensions—form and content—of a future law on administrative procedure.

This is not, of course, a new question. Despite the emphasis on simplicity when the organs and procedures of the European Communities were created, the

[1] Schwarze (1992).

[2] Chiti (2002) 100.

[3] According to Chiti (2002) this law is 'the combined result of the autonomous development of the Community and the influence of the administrative law of national legal systems' (p 115). For a general overview of the bases of European administrative law see de la Sierra (2005) 29 *et seq.*

[4] For debate on this aspect of the topic see Della Cananea (2003b) 1922.

progressive expansion of the Community's competences has increased in complexity to the extent that nowadays one speaks of a Community public administration, with its own agents, its own resources and its own rules of procedure.[5] Despite this phenomenon, the Community 'legislator' has remained passive in the face of questions regarding a law of administrative procedure integrating the substantial aspects of the activities of the organs that make up European administration. However, as with developments in other areas of Community law, the ECJ has taken the opportunity to formulate a series of general principles which Community executive organs must respect in carrying out their functions. This has led various authors to question the advantages and disadvantages of an eventual uniform codification of administrative procedure.[6]

Thus the issue is not new, but it is important, because 'the establishment of an administrative procedure in Community law is regarded as essential, having regard to the general principles of the rule of law and in particular of legal protection'.[7] Moreover, it directly influences the attainment of the goals of the Union[8], including economic goals (in the sense that excessive bureaucracy impedes the activities of market actors).

The passing of the Constitutional Treaty has raised new questions relating to this issue. They will be outlined first, and will receive more detailed treatment later. There are two important arguments in favour of such a law, which touch on the issues surrounding the development of a law of European administrative procedure: on the one hand, the literal interpretation of Article III-398, along with the other articles of the Constitutional Treaty, could serve as the legal basis for the development of a law of administrative procedure; on the other hand, the inclusion

[5] As Chiti (2002) points out, 'the role of the Administration is, in fact, directly proportional to the expansion of competences at the Community level, as well as the "state-like structure" of the Community', in such a way that, as the Community becomes less like an international organisation and more like a federal state through the integration process, European administration in general, as well as administrative procedure, acquires increasing relevance (p 238). Franchini (2003) provides an in-depth analysis into this idea and examines one of its consequences: the diffusion of mixed administrative procedures.

[6] This was not just questioned in academic circles. The European Parliament has, on several occasions in questions put to the Commission, also highlighted the necessity of producing a general regulation on administrative procedure: Question 3093/92 (93/C145/38); Question 1275/93 (93/C350/93); Question 78/98 (H-0947/98/rev. 1). Of course, on each of these occasions, the Commission avoided speaking out in favour of a particular law, deeming the explanatory manuals, the internal rules of procedure and the initiatives to simplify procedure sufficient.

[7] Schwarze (1992) 1197.

[8] In fact, as affirmed by the European Economic and Social Committee, well-defined and effective national political and administrative procedures in Member States are, together with better lawmaking, implementation and enforcement, an integral part of EU good governance. They will also enhance transparency and clarify the impact of EU law and policies towards society at large, Opinion on EU and national administration practices and linkages, [2006] OJ C325/3. Smichdt-Aßmann (2001) insists on the importance of administrative procedure within the administrative legal system and connects procedure to protection of individual rights, respect of law and prosecution of public interests. Also Craig (2006), taking into account that legal systems of the Member States possess various precepts of administrative law concerning procedural and substantive review and that the idea that administration should be procedurally and substantively accountable before the courts has been central to the rule of law, shows that administrative procedure and judicial review have special force in the Community legal order (pp 270 and 271).

of the Charter of Fundamental Rights in the Constitutional Treaty (which recognises the right to good administration), gives it binding force. According to the Presidency Conclusions of the Brussels European Council (21/22 June 2007) it seems that both contents shall be maintained in the reform in process.

Arguments highlighting the necessity of creating a law on administrative procedure invariably discuss its possible content, paying attention to the various provisions of the Treaties. For this reason, an attempt will be made to provide an approximation of the principles that would regulate a law on administrative procedure.

The Constitutional Treaty 'wants to create a fundamental order';[9] that involves analysing the constitutional foundations of administrative procedure.

2. A Public Administration without a Law of Administrative Procedure

It is clear that a European public administration exists, and that it is becoming increasingly prominent.[10] However, the activities carried on by this administration lack general formal regulation. The situation is well described by Lenaerts and Vanhamme:

> The European Community has no comprehensive legislation on the procedural rights of private parties to be respected throughout the administrative process that precedes the adoption of decisions which might adversely affect the interests of such parties. Rather it has a variety of ad hoc legislative enactments applicable to specific fields of substantive law supplemented with unwritten general principles of law whose observance conditions the legality of administrative proceedings and thus the legality of the decision adopted as a result of these proceedings.[11]

(a) Separated Procedural Norms in Primary and Secondary Law

According to standard legal literature, administrative procedure is both the blueprint for administrative activity and an instrument for the adequate protection—after appropriate consideration—of the interests affected by a decision involving the exercise of public power inherent in the administration.[12] More specifically, it is defined by a series of concrete acts aimed at gathering and processing information,[13] resulting in the production of a measure capable of producing legal effects,

[9] Schwarze (2006). The complete citation is as follows: 'The Treaty consists of two elements: treaty and constitution. On the one hand the term constitution indicates that, regarding its content, it wants to create a fundamental order. On the other hand the expression treaty makes it quite clear, that the realisation of this constitution is dependent on the agreement of the Member States.'

[10] Although European administration was originally formed on an *ad hoc* basis and thus was a minimalist governing apparatus, as the integration process has progressed, it has assumed new responsibilities, new tasks and ultimately assumed proper administrative functions, in this way becoming an administration of control. In this sense see Della Cananea (2003b) 1800–13.

[11] Lenaerts and Vanhamme (1997).

[12] In the words of Ortega Álvarez (1993).

[13] Schmidt-Aßmann (1993) 318. The notion of administrative procedure as the accumulation of functions which have as their objective the provision of information, communication or interaction with others comes from German law: see Barnés (2003) 6 and 7.

by public or private agents who act in the pursuit of public functions.[14] Although it is a way of adopting an act, it has its own (independent) legal effects, and thus fulfils a triple function: it is a mechanism for guaranteeing the rights of citizens, a method of pursuing the general interest, and a vehicle by which individuals can participate in administrative decision-making.

Even if the EU is not equipped in the same way as its constituent Member States with respect to the division of powers, the functioning of the administration or the procedural rules, it still constitutes a Community based on the rule of law[15] in which public powers are subject to Law's Empire; moreover, it recognises a series of fundamental rights of its citizens which can be relied upon in the application of European law. As a consequence of the above, the institutions and various offices and bodies that exercise executive functions in the European order—that is, apply specific polices within the Union's competences—either at the Community level or at the national level, act in the pursuit of the aims stated in the Treaties by virtue of the competences contained in it through the production of rules designed to carry out those aims according to a specific procedure. Within this framework, community administrative acts are the most important and can take the form of expressions of will, judgment, desire or knowledge coming from a Community executive institution in the exercise of a particular administrative power separate from the regulatory power[16] aimed at the Member States or individuals. Such acts must follow a particular procedure for their adoption. In this sense, the Community administrative process constitutes the formal procedure through which the European administration applies Community law by adopting acts applicable to Member States or natural or legal persons.

The administrative implementation of European law is governed by three principles established in the Treaty: the duty of co-operation or institutional loyalty, institutional and procedural autonomy, and subsidiarity. The second of these principles explains, in part, why there is currently no general corpus of common procedural norms that govern the entire sphere of administrative implementation—understood as a collection of rules and acts aimed at applying Community rules to society—:[17] each particular sphere of activity of the EU has its own norms and procedures without common rules applying to the entire procedure and without a law of general application regulating a common European administrative procedure[18].

[14] Morbidelli (2001) 1229.

[15] As much was established by the ECJ in Case C-294/83 *Les Verts v Parliament* [1986] ECR 1339. This has been explicitly acknowledged in Art I-2 Constitutional Treaty. As the Commission stipulated in its White Paper on Governance, COM (2001) 428 of 25 July [2001] OJ C287/1, 'The Union is built on the rule of law; it can draw on the Charter of Fundamental Rights, and it has a double democratic mandate through a Parliament representing EU citizens and a Council representing the elected governments of the Member States' (p 7).

[16] This definition is provided by de la Quadra (2000), who translated Zanobini's well-known definition to the Community level.

[17] See Moreno Molina (2000). For a more in-depth analysis see Moreno Molina (1998).

[18] Principle of procedural autonomy, however, is being toned down in different ways. A good example is Directive 2006/123/CE of the Parliament and the Council, of 12 December 2006, on services in the

Thus, until now, in each of the different pillars of the Union, there has been a specific procedure (regulated by primary Community law in certain situations—for example, the excessive budget deficit procedure in Article 104 EC—and secondary law for most of the rest[19]) channelling the actions of the competent administration.[20] The one exception to this is the Community Regulation, which governs the language used in the procedure.[21] Moreover, each institution has its own internal rules of procedure. In particular, the Rules of Procedure of the Commission[22] contain the distinct decision-making procedures relative to this Community institution and deal more with rules of internal functioning than with rules of procedure. All in all,

> currently, the regulation of administrative procedure in the Community system is full of lacunae and is unsuitable as a frame of reference for procedures which are increasingly important, executed directly by Community organs or the Administrations of the Member states or concurrently in the sense of being exercised at both Community and Member State levels.[23]

Thus, there are many different procedures: internal procedures, procedures of indirect co-operation, procedures of horizontal co-operation, procedures of direct application,[24] instrumental and final procedures and, with respect to the latter, there are prescriptive, contractual procedures, adjudicative procedures, etc.[25]

The administrative or executive function at the European level is carried out principally by the Commission (Article 211 EC); however, national administrations play a predominant role by virtue of the principle of the indirect execution of Community law[26] as required by the principle of subsidiarity. The concept of a European administrative procedure, in a strict sense, is only used for the direct execution of Community law by the Community administration,[27] including the

internal market [2006] OJ L376/36, which obliges Member States to cooperate with other Member States (mutual assistance), to simplify administrative procedures, to create points of single contact and to lay down provisions concerning internal aspects of procedure (right to information, use of electronic means, period to process the applications, etc.).

19 In these cases, as MP Chiti points out (1995a), those procedural rules are of value only for the sector under consideration.

20 The regulation of Community administrative procedure is, in this sense, incomplete. See Weber (1993) 60–62; (1992) 395–6.

21 Regulation 1/1958, determining the languages to be used by the European Economic Community [1958] OJ 17/401.

22 [2000] OJ L308/26. An Annex to the rules of procedure includes a Code of Good Administrative Behaviour for Staff of the European Commission in their Relations with the Public, and contains a series of directives for staff of the European Commission which must be observed in their relationship with citizens. This will be analysed later.

23 Chiti (2002) 257.

24 The distinction is drawn by Parejo (2000a) 235.

25 For an analysis of this classification see Della Cananea (2003b) 1893–906.

26 Parejo (2000a), in this vein, notes the model in internal systems known as federal execution (p 45).

27 Picozza (1994); Weber (1992) 393; Arzoz Santisteban (1998) 453. The rules on Community administrative procedure regulate the direct execution of Community law, but also have an influence on indirect execution. In a strict sense, as Weber (1993) highlights, 'only the former case can be properly called community execution, given that Community organs, applying the forms of action contained in the Treaty, orient juridical acts towards European citizens or at the Member States in conformity with the

European institutions exercising executive power (principally the Commission but also the Council in specific circumstances), EU bodies (the Central Bank and the European Investment Bank) and organisations (Committees[28] and Community Agencies, referred to in chapter two). However, we should not forget the fact that the progressive expansion of the activities in which European public power is exercised tones down the principle of indirect execution: through the increasing diffusion of complex or mixed procedures, the intervention of national administrations is added to the European administration.[29] Moreover, in particular sectors such as the internal market, the elaboration of regulations or directives which establish measures for the approximation of legal, regulatory and administrative provisions of the Member States—the purpose of Article 95 EC[30]—undoubtedly exercise an influence on procedure.

The Constitutional Treaty, as with the EC Treaty, establishes certain rules relating to administrative procedure: the duty to state reasons (Article I-38(2)), the duty of consultation (Articles III-392 and III-388), and the right of access to documents (Articles I-50 and II-102). Along with this, the Constitutional Treaty establishes rights and principles that affect procedure: the principle of legality (which is subject to the control of the ECJ as established in Articles III-365 and III-376), the principle of equality (Articles I-4 and I-45 for citizens[31] and I-5 for Member States; II-80 and II-81 in general), the principle of subsidiarity (Article I-11(1)), the principle of institutional loyalty (Article I-5(2)),[32] the principle of transparency (Article I-

juridical principles contained in primary law or secondary law, while the beneficiaries of indirect application are Union citizens in their respective Member States, in accordance with the requirements of national administrative law—whether substantive or procedural—of its rules of execution, and national administrative justice' (p 58).

[28] See the framework decision on Comitology, Council Decision 1999/468/EC, of 28 June 1999, laying down the procedures for the exercise of implementing powers conferred on the Commission [1999] OJ L184/23, which supersedes the previous Decision 87/373 of 13 July 1987.

[29] Chiti (2002) 240. It is for this reason that Della Cananea (2003b) maintains that, in reality, it is not possible to draw a clear line between direct and indirect execution of Community law or Community policy, precisely because of the increasing incidences of co-administration. See pp 1871–3. For an analysis of mixed administrative procedures from the point of view of the implementation of Community law, arguing in favour of codification see Maeso Seco (2005) (the proposal for codification can be found at pp 108–110). For an analysis of the complex procedures in the sphere of European law, see Della Cananea (2003a), and S Cassese (2003b). This author highlights how the (numerous) complex procedures at the EU level on occasion appear to be regulated by the Member States—subject to general limits which are focused on facilitating the exercise of the rights recognised by the supranational order—and at other times seem to be regulated by Community law through the establishment of general binding principles; the diffusion and lack of homogeneity explain, in his opinion, the arguments for codification from authors over the past 20 years (see in particular 18–24 and 26).

[30] Arts III-172 III-173–III-176 Constitutional Treaty contain similar provisions in this respect.

[31] This Article deserves special mention for establishing the principle of equality from a democratic perspective, in requiring that all Union citizens receive equal attention from its institutions, organs and bodies.

[32] The principle of institutional loyalty is complemented by the competence of the Union to carry out supporting, co-ordinating or complementary action in the area of administrative co-operation (Art I-17(g)), in order to ensure the effective implementation of EU law by Member States (Art III-285). Indeed, administrative co-operation is one of the few new legal bases introduced by the Constitutional Treaty to increase the scope of action of the EU. The Convention justifies the introduction of this clause by underlining the assumed common interest in the effective application of EU legislation by Member States and allows the EU to support this legislation with supplementary measures.

47(3)), the right to access relevant files (Article II-101(2)(b)),[33] the right to be heard (Article II-101(1)(a)), the right to compensation for damages (Article II-101(3)), the right to an expeditious resolution (Article II-101(1)), and the duty to publish and notify normative acts (Article I-39(2) and (3)). All of these principles are found in the Code of Good Administrative Behaviour adopted by the Commission on 13 September 2000[34] (thus before the solemn declaration on the Charter of Fundamental Rights of the European Union). As an internal form of self-regulation, this Code undoubtedly goes some way to making up for the lack of a general law on administrative procedure and attempts to serve as a guide for the administrative staff of the Commission. It contains a series of principles governing all activity in the field of European administration that directly influences procedure: its ultimate aim is to submit the Commission to the principle of legality in its day-to-day activities. Although its content is not that of a law of administrative procedure, it contains a series of requirements relative to procedure and demands conformity with them.

Essentially, it helps to encourage good administration in the Commission and this is achieved by submitting the activities of the Commission to the following principles: general principles such as legality, the prohibition of discrimination, equality of treatment, proportionality and coherence; directives for good administrative conduct: impartiality, objectivity, and information on administrative procedures; information on the rights of interested parties: right to a hearing for interested parties, obligation that the administrative decision contain the possible means of appeal against it. Any complaint made by a citizen regarding the activities of the Commission relating to the fulfilment of the relevant requirements may be heard by the European Ombudsman.[35]

(b) Shaping of the General Principles of Administrative Procedure by the Court of Justice

The legal status of the general principles of law is one of the most important characteristics of Community law: the ECJ has, through these principles, given form to the law of the EU while at the same time expanding the protection of the rights of citizens.[36] The absence of a general law on administrative procedure and the resulting plethora of measures has made the ECJ the protagonist in developing general rules on procedure through these principles.

An analysis of the collection of European norms and jurisprudence on Community administrative procedure highlights one fact in particular: while the

[33] See Nehl (1999) 28–30 and 43–69.

[34] Commission Decision 2000/633/EC, ECSC, Euratom, of 17 October 2000, amending its Rules of Procedure [2000] OJ L267/63 (the Code is included as an Annex). For a general analysis on the Code see ch 2.

[35] The Ombudsman has competence to take action only against the institutions, organs and agencies of the Union and not against Member States, according to Art 2 Decision of the European Parliament 94/262/ECSC, EC, Euratom, of 9 March 1994, on the regulations and general conditions governing the performance of the Ombudsman's duties [1994] OJ L113/15.

[36] Chiti (1995b).

essential elements of procedure have been developed by the EU legislator systematically and according to each sector with respect to the specific issues that they regulate, the jurisprudence of the ECJ defines common principles systematising a general procedure at the European level. [37] Thus, it was the ECJ and, subsequently the CFI, that carried out the progressive shaping of the essential principles of European administrative procedure through the application of the law. [38] This development has been extensive: 'the case law of the Court is characterised by a tendency to give an extensive interpretation of provisions on legal protection within its own court procedure as well as to develop general procedural guarantees for the parties concerned in administrative procedure.'[39] The following principles of EU law were developed in this way: the principle of legal certainty, the principle of legitimate expectations, the right to a hearing, the right to a defence,[40] and the right to good administration.[41] The reader is referred to chapter two of this book, where the jurisprudence of the ECJ on some of the principles of the Community legal system is analysed.

In sum, as Della Cananea points out, the intervention of the ECJ has given prescriptive value to the notion of administrative procedure, in a such way that 'the judge finds that all procedure of this type, if not all procedure, should respect a series of general rules in at least some categories or classes. This confirms the fact that procedure is "a general method of developing of public activity", not limited to the public power of states, but also for other types of public power',[42] such as European administration.

[37] See Cassese (2003b) 7.

[38] A thorough study of the principles 'created' by the ECJ regarding administrative procedure can be found in Weber (1992) 397–411, who concludes by stating that 'procedural administrative law constitutes, along with administrative judicial protection, an essential part of the *ius administrativum europeum*, whose development is principally due to judicial construction rather than the harmonization of rules' (412).

[39] Schwarze (1992) 1188. At pp 1189–97 he offers many examples of this proposition. Nehl (1999) notes the danger inherent in an extensive interpretation of the principle of good administration in the sense that on occasions the Court has been the victim of its own tendency to create new principles without adequate argumentation and the desirable transparency (p 35).

[40] In relation to the right of defence Case C-259/85 *France v Commission* [1987] ECR 4393 should be emphasised: 'observance of the right to be heard is, in all proceedings initiated against a person which are liable to culminate in a measure adversely affecting that person, a fundamental principle of community law which must be guaranteed even in the absence of any rules governing the procedure in question' (para 12). For a complete analysis of the jurisprudence of the Court regarding the rights of defence—broadly understood—in administrative procedure see Barbier de la Serre (2006). This article highlights two facts: on the one hand the extent to which the construction of a European administrative procedure from the perspective of the rights of individuals is an essentially judicial construction; and, on the other, that the ECJ has developed principles applicable to procedure in respect of the power exercised by the decision-making organ in a specific case, ensuring the role of procedure as an instrument to control of the exercise of administrative discretion.

[41] For a general overview see Chiti (2002) 246–50.

[42] Della Cananea (2003b) 1871.

3. New Arguments for the Creation of a Law on Administrative Procedure

It was mentioned at the beginning of this chapter that the question of the codification of Community administrative procedure is not new. At different stages of the integration process, this issue has been approached from different perspectives with various arguments. The Constitutional Treaty has preserved the status quo with respect to this question (the normative dispersion still continues; Article I-19 provides that 'Each institution shall act within the limits of the powers conferred on it in the Constitution, and in conformity with the procedures and conditions set out in it'), but there are other innovations in relation to other areas.

Generally speaking, it is true, as Barnés points out, that 'in reality, all that happened was that a large part of the pillars and bases of the administrative procedure which form part of the *acquis communautaire* were formalized in text', in such a way that 'it doesn't constitute, in effect, a qualitative change or reform of the concept, its sense or its aims nor a change in the principles and the structures which have characterized community administrative procedure';[43] however, it is also certain that the Constitutional Treaty introduces minor, but nonetheless important, qualitative changes.

Thus, along with the general argument that a strong Europe needs a strong modern administration, discharging its functions under the Treaty efficiently, transparently, responsibly and with independence,[44] there are also certain requirements that must be respected in all administrative procedure, mainly those relating to the fundamental rights in Part II of the Treaty; universal values which have an influence on procedure when shaped by secondary law (equality, transparency); and the expressly established limits that act as the conditions with which procedure must comply in the final instance (subsidiarity, proportionality, respect for the basic conditions of fundamental rights).[45] We will return to this topic later on.

II. CODIFYING EUROPEAN ADMINISTRATIVE PROCEDURE

Thus, administrative procedure, understood as the channel of the administrative action of the European Union, needs a law on European administrative procedure, a corpus of rules, norms and principles that regulate procedure in view of the aims to be achieved and the functions that must be carried out.

The European Union has been gradually shaped over the years as a political system, one which increasingly resembles a State. Whereas it is still far from becoming a true political union of a federal nature, the presence of Community acts

[43] Barnés (2003) 8. The author also showed that it must be acknowledged, however, that the Constitutional Treaty has created an environment conducive to administrative procedure playing a stronger role in Community affairs.

[44] See Reforming the Commission: A White Paper, Part I, COM (2000) 200, 5 April, p 3.

[45] Continuing with the triple distinction relating to levels of intensity—specific provisions, values and limitations—that can be found in national constitutions regarding the rules on administrative procedure proposed by Schmidt-Aßmann (1993) 325–6.

and national acts coming from Union Law in the ordinary lives of European citizens—which have become the majority of its purely internal acts—means that it is increasingly necessary to avoid the proliferation of measures and strive for uniformity. In a way, parallels can be drawn between the EU and the experience of certain European countries such as Spain, Austria, Germany and Italy, which, at the end of the 19th century and during the 20th, passed laws on a common administrative procedure and, in doing this, placed administrative procedure among the fundamental institutions of administrative law. Increasingly at the European level, a European public power with a major executive reach is emerging, which in consequence has an increasing influence on individual citizens. For this reason, it can be asserted that the next logical step that should follow at this stage is the regulation of procedure through a common system, or at least a series of rules governing the entire administration—European or national—in the application of European law.[46] In other words, as with national legal systems, procedure has gone from being simply a method of administrative action to an instrument securing the public aims required from the system, the adequate consideration of the interests involved, the correct exercise of administrative discretion and the resolution of conflicts,[47] thus acquiring its own proper autonomous function. At the level of the EU, the progressive expansion of administration and the effect of European administrative activity on individuals increase the need for a disciplined system governing procedure. Along with this, another thing is clear: the more decisions regulating various aspects of life that are taken in Brussels rather than in national capitals,[48] the greater the interest in transparency and participation.[49]

Many arguments have been used by various authors to defend and justify the necessity of proceeding with the codification of administrative procedure in the sphere of the EU:[50] the principle of legal certainty (clearly the regulation of

[46] See Shapiro (1996). In this article, the author explains the experience of the US around the time of the passing of the Administrative Procedure Act—a similar experience to what the EU is currently undergoing—arriving at the conclusion that the US experience should be considered in the debate at the EU level.

[47] It has to be taken into account that in the Community legal system, in contrast with what happens in national legal systems, not every administrative act can be appealed—be it administrative or judicial—by individuals. Thus, for this reason, procedure is particularly important so that citizens can be guaranteed protection—in the sense of sufficient consideration of the issues involved in the matter—in relation to the interests involved in the act, something whose effect must be guaranteed when developing the principles that guide European administrative procedure. In this sense, Schwarze (1992) affirms that 'improvements in administrative procedure serve the aim of improving legal protection generally', such that 'if the interests of those involved are already protected through an appropriate administrative procedure, the need for subsequent judicial protection may be less urgent' (pp 1178–9).

[48] In the words of Chiti (2002), 'the expansion of community administration seems to be connected to the progressive development of the community order as a complex order, with functions which increasing deal with natural and legal persons of the Member States' (p 181).

[49] 'If you are "in", you do not concern yourself with participation and transparency, that is to the interest of the "outs" . . . But if you are beginning to feel "out", participation and transparency suddenly seem more attractive': Shapiro (1996) 43.

[50] Among the most important works are the following: Harlow (1996); Della Cananea (1995); MP Chiti (1995a); Shapiro (1996). Nehl (1999) is in favour of codifying a series of minimal procedural rules on good administration as a method of creating a better framework for decision-making in the EU and for the development of administrative law (see p 170). For a general perspective see Chiti (1995b).

procedure through judicial maxims is incomplete and causes uncertainty, while regulation using rules is—in theory—clearer, less ambiguous and more coherent); the principle of transparency (a complete regulation of administrative procedure is more recognisable for citizens); the principle of legitimacy (through the intervention of the Parliament); the control of administrative discretion (the existence of a structured procedure helps to avoid arbitrariness); and even the principle of better protection of the individual (by providing a legal framework for administrative procedure, taking into account that this is defined as the legal course of administrative performance and the appropriate forum for consideration of the interests involved, procedure contributes to providing better protection of these interests). All in all, it is clear that it is extremely beneficial to administrative staff, citizens and the system in general that a uniform procedural law is promulgated with basic guarantees governing the exercise of administrative power in every decision-making procedure.

To all this we can add two more reasons: the increasing impossibility of drawing a clear distinction between the direct and indirect execution of Community law, along with the spread of functions shared between the European administration and national administrations in the application of EU law, makes it very difficult to separate one from the other. A law on administrative procedure applicable to both the national and European levels through the implementation of standard-setting principles would help to overcome this difficulty. The principle of equality and the prohibition of discrimination would also favour such a law: administrative decisions, in the light of these principles, must be applied equally to every citizen and every Member State, independently of the territory in which it is being applied, the type of administrative entity acting and the nature of the administrative power being exercised.

On the other hand, there are also objections to codification: if codification is characterised by the presence of a State and a long legal tradition, the EU lacks both; there is no pressing need to codify the administrative procedures of Community law and, in any case, any specific requirements can be satisfied under the current regime of rules and European jurisprudence; codification can freeze administrative procedure and leave limited room for evolution.[51]

In any case, a legal base permitting the drafting of such a law would be required. And, although there is apparently no general will to proceed with a general codification of administrative procedure,[52] what is certain is that the Constitutional Treaty has introduced new arguments in favour of codification.

[51] Such arguments are considered by Della Cananea (1995) 975, who is not convinced by them. Arguments against general codification (mainly, the lack of a well defined European administrative organisation) are also provided by Chiti (1995a). In the same way Chiti states that the codification of the principles does not add much in terms of binding legal force. However, he does not deny the advantages that such codification could bring (p 669).

[52] Chiti (2002) 258 highlights the resistance of certain Member States to such a proposal and the sheer complexity of the Community legal system as reasons why such a codification project is not realistic at the moment, and predicts more sectoral regulation for the foreseeable future.

1. Legal Foundation

The European Union can only act within the competences attributed to it by the Treaties according to the principle of conferral of competences. The promulgation of a law on administrative procedure by the European legislator that applies equally to European and national administrations insofar as they are applying EU law, would require a proper foundation. In this sense, it is necessary to consider the extent to which the Union has the competence to draft a law binding national administrative procedure when applying European law. A distinction must be drawn between the distribution of competences and the distribution of powers:[53] whereas the first refers to the catalogue of competences that Community institutions can exercise according to the Treaty, the second type refers to the ceding of part of Member States' sovereignty to the EU.

Procedural competence is inextricably linked to material or substantive attributions: once procedure constitutes the form of administrative action and all administrative action follows a procedure carried out by the institutions by virtue of the competences attributed to them, the Union could be said to possess the relevant competence for a general law on procedure.[54] However, this interpretation only legitimates the promulgation of binding norms for the European administration. A question then arises as to national administrations. In our opinion, such norms would be equally binding on national administrations due to the recognition of the right to good administration: the insertion of the Charter into the Constitutional Treaty means that the status of the right to good administration is elevated (with all that that entails in terms of supremacy, direct effect and the jurisdiction of the Court). More importantly, it implies that the right will be enforceable against national administrations when they apply EU law even if the internal order does not recognise such a right (as seen in chapter three). Both arguments will now be analysed.

(a) Formal Basis: Article III-398 of the Treaty establishing a Constitution for Europe

One of the most cogent arguments against the creation of a generally applicable law on common administrative procedure in the EU is the absence of a legal basis to permit its creation.[55] However, an article has been introduced into the

[53] On this distinction see Díez-Picazo (2002) 181.

[54] Barnés (2003) sees the EU possessing the capacity 'to determine the administrative procedures which are seen as advisable, either for direct relations with citizens or other administrations or respecting the indirect application of Community law' (p 10). In the Spanish legal system, competence in administrative procedure is attributed to the central State or to the Autonomous Communities according to who has the material competence.

[55] Even so, some authors have invoked Art 308 EC—Art I-18 Constitutional Treaty—as a legal basis for codification; see Della Cananea (1995) 979. Cobreros Mendazona (2002) maintains that the flexibility clause could provide a basis for the creation of a regulation with the same content as the Europe Code of Good Administrative Behaviour, which will be analysed subsequently. The Working Group on Complementary Competencies (W6 375/1/02) came to the conclusion that Art 308 of the EC Treaty

Constitutional Treaty which might be used as a legal basis for this purpose. It is Article III-398, and it states:

> 1. In carrying out their missions, the institutions, bodies, offices and agencies of the Union shall have the support of an open, efficient and independent European administration.
> 2. In compliance with the Staff Regulations and the Conditions of employment adopted on the basis of Article III-427, European laws shall establish provisions to that end.

This article speaks of institutions, bodies, offices and agencies, thereby covering the large variety of forms of administrative organisation that exist within the EU.[56] It is a horizontal provision, applicable to all the public powers of the Union,[57] through which the progressive expansion and the form and function of the European administration are constitutionalised; it also provides a broad base by which procedure may be regulated. A literal reading of the second paragraph clearly shows a broad basis to act, which would cover all measures aimed at creating an open, efficient and independent administration. A law on administrative procedure would simply constitute one of those measures.[58] In this way, the EU can be said to have a legal basis for the elaboration of common legislation on administrative procedure.

The validity of the aforementioned article as a legal basis for the creation of a European law on procedure is confirmed by the Introduction to the Code of Good

should be preserved, but within definite limits: it should not be used as a basis for harmonising measures in areas where they are explicitly excluded in the Treaty. In this way, taking into account that administrative co-operation—a new legal basis provided for in the Constitutional Treaty for the performance of the institutions of the EU—expressly excludes any harmonising measures, it is not possible to create a law harmonising administrative procedure binding upon national administrations through Art I-18 Constitutional Treaty. Moreover, given that there is a legal basis for the creation of a law on administrative procedure applicable to Member States based on fundamental rights, it is not necessary to rely on the flexibility clause.

[56] The legal literature talks of administration with a polycentric or star-shaped structure: Della Cananea (using the terms of Cassese) (2003b) 1833. This author delimits four models of organisation: the Commission and the machinery through which it acts, the administrative organs that serve the other European institutions, the agencies, and the national bodies dependent on the Union (pp 1839–42).

[57] The English version speaks of 'offices and agencies', as well as 'institutions and bodies', while the Spanish version uses the term 'organismos', along with 'instituciones' and 'órganos'. Interestingly, the initial version of the Article (then III-300) used the term 'agencias', not instead of 'organismos', but alongside it: 'En el cumplimiento de sus cometidos, las instituciones, agencias y organismos de la Unión estarán respaldados por una administración europea abierta, eficaz e independiente'. Note also the change in emphasis between 'estar respaldado' and 'apoyarse'; whereas the first invokes complementarity, the second implies fundamentality. Moreover, the element of compulsion also changes with respect to the adoption of a European law establishing provisions to this effect: the initial version said 'podrá adoptarse' (CONV 727/3, p 94). In conclusion, the version finally accepted reinforces the initial version from the point of view of the legality of the acts of the administration.

[58] Barnes is of this opinion: (2003) 11, as is Ladenburger (2005a) 170. In his opinion, that article, 'though not drafted with perfect clarity, in fact establishes a legal basis for the definition of a body of European general administrative law, and in particular of principles of administrative procedure. The provision thus ends a long-standing academic controversy on whether the Union ... had competence to enact provisions of general administrative law'. Also Craig (2006) maintains that Art III-398 would serve as legal foundation for a general code of administrative procedure (p 280). By contrast, Della Cananea (2005) claims that the EU does not have the power or provisions to create rules on a general administrative law, including procedure (p 79).

Administrative Behaviour published by the European Ombudsman, which states that Article III-398 establishes the legal base for the creation of a regulation that includes the obligations contained in the Code.[59]

(b) Substantive Basis: The Right to Good Administration as a Binding Fundamental Right and the Principles of Democracy and Legality

As Schmidt-Aßmann notes,

> From the point of view of its 'facticity', that is, of its practical application as a real fact, procedure is very important in Administrative law in the sense that the correct application of procedural rules are questioned, such as those relating to participation, competences or the publication and notification of administrative acts. Such is the area of the so-called 'formal legality of administrative action' and the related doctrine of infringement of an essential procedural requirement. In other words, procedure adds what can be called an ordering element to Administrative law. That is, administrative procedure as an organized process which provides transparency and rationality, coordination and contact; aims which, in themselves, entail and develop important judicial principles.[60]

In other words, procedure aims at substantive legality. For this reason, along with the formal base, a natural base must be found for the promulgation of a law on administrative procedure.

Since the TEU introduced the concept of European citizenship into the Community legal order, the status of Union citizenship—contained in Article I-10 of the Constitutional Treaty—has complemented this concept with the express acknowledgement of a series of rights for European citizens.[61] The greatest expression of this development can be seen in the binding legal status of the provisions of the Charter of Fundamental Rights.[62] In effect, the Constitutional Treaty, as well as recognising the rights and freedoms of citizens at the level of the Union (Article

[59] *European Code of Administrative Behaviour* (Luxembourg, Office for Official Publications of the European Community, 2005) 9.

[60] Schmidt-Aßmann (1993) 321.

[61] Among those related to the status of citizen as individual, the right to petition the European Parliament, the right to apply to the Ombudsman, and the right to address the institutions and advisory bodies of the EU in one of the official languages and receive a reply in the same language, as required by Art I-10(2)(d) and developed in Arts III-128, III-333 and III-334 Constitutional Treaty. Art III-129 stipulates that these rights must be supplemented by laws or framework laws adopted unanimously in the Council, with the prior consent of the Parliament and after their ratification by Member States in accordance with their national constitutional requirements. It is necessary to underline that, although all these rights are granted to the citizens of the Union, some apply to all persons, even if they are not nationals of Member States. This is the case with the right of access to documents and the right to good administration. For a very critical revision of the current status of European citizenship and proposals to transform it into a real attribute of European citizens, see Fraile Ortiz (2003) esp 351–409.

[62] In fact, the right to good administration 'is also an attempt to add a new (supranational) dimension to the notion of Community citizenship ... Empowering citizens with European administrative rights contributes to an expansion of citizenship beyond the national framework (citizens vis-à-vis national authorities), which is a consequence of a gradual transfer of powers from the Member States to the Community': Kanska (2004).

I-9(1)) and providing for the accession of the Union to the ECHR (Article I-9(2)),[63] integrates the Charter of Fundamental Rights into Part II of the Treaty, thereby giving it legally binding effect;[64] thus, the Constitutional Treaty provides not only for a Community based on the rule of law but also a Community of rights.[65] What must now be considered is whether this new addition can serve as a basis for the creation of a general law of European administrative procedure. At first blush, the answer would seem to be negative: Article II-111(2) of the Constitutional Treaty (Article 51.2 of the Charter) is clear when it states:

> This Charter does not extend the field of application of Union law beyond the powers of the Union or establish any new power or task for the Union, or modify powers and tasks defined in the other Parts of the Constitution.

Thus, a fundamental right cannot be used as a way of conferring a competence that the Treaty does not attribute to the Union. However, it is clear that rights do exist whose exercise can only be rendered effective through an administrative procedure;[66] and indeed, from the point of view of procedure, the Charter contains a right of general application: the right to good administration.

If it is considered that Article III-398 grants the Union the competence to promulgate a law of administrative procedure, the answer to the question posed above changes completely: the right to good administration which, in essence, presupposes that the administration, when dealing with individuals, will correctly apply the laws (and thus comply with the specific interests recognised in them of individuals) and will aim to be in the general interest, allows for the creation of a law on administrative procedure which contains the guarantees implicit in the right to good administration,[67] given that procedure in itself guarantees the legality of administrative action.[68] Moreover, administrative procedure is a guarantee of good

[63] It should not be forgotten that the rights contained in the Constitutional Treaty and those that come from the common constitutional traditions of the Member States form part of the law of the EU as general principles, as is established by the third para of Art I-9; nor that the rights in the Charter that correspond with the rights in the Convention will have the same meaning and application as those of the Convention, as Art II-112 provides. An interesting issue, which cannot be considered here, is the relative influence on administrative procedure of the right to a fair trial which is enshrined in Art 6 of the Convention, in relation to European administrative procedure in cases where judicial control of administrative activity is not always possible. See Cassese (2003d) 168–72; Zampini (1999); and Rodríguez Pontón (2004).

[64] Adopting the most 'constitutionalising' proposal of the three proposed by the Working Group on Incorporation of the Charter/Accession to the European Convention on Human Rights (Group II of the European Convention). See the Final Report (CONV 345/02). The two remaining proposals involved were the inclusion in the Constitutional Treaty of a reference to the Charter of Fundamental Rights or its incorporation into the Treaty as an Annex, and the introduction of an indirect reference to the Charter in order to give it binding force but not constitutional status.

[65] Della Cananea (2003b) 1818.

[66] This is the case with the right to asylum, for example: Directive 2005/85 EC of the Council, of 1 December, on minimum standards on procedures in Member States for granting and withdrawing refugee status [2005] OJ L326/13.

[67] Effectively, a law of this type would make citizens aware of the courses of action available to protect their interests with respect to the issue at hand and would make staff aware of how they are to act.

[68] According to Díez-Picazo (2002), the contention that the Charter does not change the distribution of competences, even if it implies that the Union cannot adopt legal measures aimed at promoting the

administration, in the sense that it ensures that the administration respects certain rules, thereby contributing to the legality of the acts of the administration. This notion is highlighted by the definition of maladministration given by the European Ombudsman: 'Maladministration occurs when a public body fails to act in accordance with a rule or principle which is binding upon it.'[69]

In accordance with this definition, on the other side of the coin from the right to good administration is the duty of good administration, which requires that every office, institution and body of the Union acts according to the rules established by the Treaty, the provisions of secondary law and the ECJ or emanating from a general principle of Community law. In this way, procedure, as a way of guaranteeing the proper exercise of power and respect for the principle of legality, becomes an instrument of good administration and, at the same time, a parameter of it. In other words, the right to good administration 'is procedural in character'.[70] The content of the right to good administration will not be considered in this chapter (it was analysed in chapter two); it is nonetheless interesting to make some reference to this right from the perspective of administrative procedure.

Article II-101 of the Constitutional Treaty provides that:

> 1. Every person has the right to have his or her affairs handled impartially, fairly and within a reasonable time by the institutions, bodies, offices and agencies of the Union.
> 2. This right includes:
>
> (a) the right of every person to be heard, before any individual measure which would affect him or her adversely is taken;
> (b) the right of every person to have access to his or her file, while respecting the legitimate interests of confidentiality and of professional and business secrecy;
> (c) the obligation of the administration to give reasons for its decisions.
>
> 3. Every person has the right to have the Union make good any damage caused by its institutions or by its servants in the performance of their duties, in accordance with the general principles common to the laws of the Member States.
> 4. Every person may write to the institutions of the Union in one of the languages of the Constitution and must have an answer in the same language.[71]

As can be seen, the right to good administration, which has its essential basis in the rule of law, is made up of a series of general principles governing the process of

rights contained in the Charter, 'cannot mean that the European institutions cannot take those rights into account when making Regulations or Directives in areas of community competence, and, in this indirect way, there is clearly scope for a community policy on fundamental rights' (p 36).

[69] *European Code of Administrative Behaviour* (2005) 8. This definition, as explained by Söderman (2001), was contained in the European Ombudsman's Annual Report of 1997 and also includes the violation of human rights (or, in the terminology of the EU, fundamental rights). The Ombudsman receives complaints from citizens relating to cases of maladministration in the activity of the institutions, offices and bodies of the EU as established by Arts I-49 and II-103 Constitutional Treaty and developed in Art III-335.

[70] Kanska (2004) 301.

[71] Generally speaking, this provision captures the recent jurisprudence of the ECJ and the CFI, even if certain aspects thereof have already been assimilated into the Treaties, such as the right to make good any damage caused by European institutions, the requirement to give reasons for decisions and the right to use any language of the Community.

administrative decision-making: objectivity and impartiality, participation, transparency, information and effectiveness. Accompanying these principles are rights and duties, such as the right to a hearing, the duty to give reasons for decisions, the right to have one's case heard within a reasonable time, the right to use one's own language, and the duty to compensate for damage caused by an administrative act.

The right to good administration is directly related to the duty of the good governance of European public power, which, under the concept of European governance, entails the principles of openness, participation, responsibility, effectiveness and coherence contained in the principles of proportionality and subsidiarity.[72] Once this right acquires binding nature due to its incorporation into the Constitutional Treaty, a European law is necessary in order to make explicit the rules and principles contained in the right and give it uniformity, transparency and legal certainty. In this way, administrative procedure is essential. Moreover, the Constitutional Treaty—in line with the general trend towards the constitutionalisation of procedural requirements—contains a series of concrete provisions that must be respected in all administrative procedure and which also contribute to good administration from the external or democratic point of view, such as the principles of openness and transparency of the workings of the institutions of the EU, access to documents (Articles I-50 and II-102), the publication of decisions, and the protection of personal data (Article I-51, specifically in relation to the acts of public authorities, and Article II-68 in general).

These principles have been included in the European Code on Good Administrative Behaviour passed by the Resolution of the European Parliament of 6 September 2001[73] (this is distinct from the Code of Good Administrative Conduct of the Commission cited earlier), whose objective is 'to explain in more detail what the Charter's right to good administration should mean in practice'.[74] In the words of the Ombudsman, 'the Code tells citizens what this right means in practice and what, concretely, they can expect from the European administration. With the Charter making up Part II of the Treaty establishing a Constitution for Europe, we can be sure that this right will become increasingly meaningful in the coming years'.[75] Given that this text is not legally binding in the way that a provision of the Treaty or secondary legislation would be, the European Parliament requested that a regulation be passed setting out the contents of the Code. This request has been ignored.[76] Thus, the Code is a temporary solution to the need to develop and

[72] White Paper on Governance in Europe, COM (2001) 428 (n 14), p 10. See particularly pp 12 *et seq.* For a critical commentary on the White Paper, see *Response to the Commission White Paper on European Governance by the LSE Study Group on European Administrative Law*, March 2002.

[73] [2001] OJ C72. See ch 2 in relation to its origins and content.

[74] At p 7. In the Spanish version of the text it is easier to understand the aim of the Code: 'to ensure in practice the right to good administration established in the Charter', in other words, to develop this right in the day-to-day activities of the European institutions.

[75] *European Code of Administrative Behaviour* (2005) 5.

[76] However, the importance of its existence should not be ignored: a proof of that is the fact that the right of access to documents, which is now constitutionalised in the Constitutional Treaty and already existed in the Treaty of Rome, began life as a Code of Conduct concerning public access to Council and Commission documents: Decision 93/731/EC, of 20 December, on public access to Council documents

substantiate the right to good administration, binding on all the European institutions, its staff and agents,[77] whose application is subject to the control of the European Ombudsman. However, its provisions could provide a useful reference point for determining the content of an eventual European law on a common administrative procedure.

Given the impossibility of identifying all the situations of fact that can arise in administrative activity, administrative procedure is presented as a method of linking administration to the principle of legality.[78] Moreover, this is the original function of administrative procedure, which arose precisely with the aim of reforming the administration from within, in order to gradually subject it to legality. In this way, administrative procedure is a vital aspect of the rule of law[79] and is directly related to good governance. In fact, as the Commission highlighted in its White Paper on European Governance, 'governance' means rules, processes and behaviour that affect the way in which powers are exercised at the European level, particularly with respect to openness, participation, accountability, effectiveness and coherence.[80]

The right to good administration, once constitutionalised and legally binding, entails two consequences. On the one hand, it changes the logic of the system: if previous cases of good administration (or, rather, maladministration) involved the Ombudsman, a legally binding right to good administration will involve the ECJ; the bridge between one and the other is procedure. On the other hand, it is also binding on Member States when they apply Union law as provided for in Article II-111(1) of the Constitutional Treaty (Article 51(1) of the Charter), as shown in chapter three. This increases the need for a law on administrative procedure containing the general principles of procedure, which, at the same time, are a consequence of the right to good administration.

To sum up, the fact that the right to good administration is not sufficient to enhance the efficiency of the European administration and national administrations acting as European agents, or to meet the interests of individuals, is a factor contributing to the elaboration of a European law on a common administrative procedure.

As indicated in the title of this section procedure also enhances the effectiveness of the administrative action[81] and, at the same time, effectiveness requires the improvement and simplification[82] of the internal and decision-making procedures of the European administration and national administrations when they apply Union law. In other words, 'efficient and transparent procedures would not only

[1993] OJ L340/43 and Decision 94/90/ECSC, EC, Euratom, of 8 February, on public access to Commission documents [1994] OJ L46/58.

[77] It is clear that Art 2, in using the term 'institution', must be understood as including both the Community institutions and the Community bodies.

[78] This idea belongs to Barnés (2003) 6.

[79] Weber (1993) 75 and (1992) 400.

[80] COM (2001) 428 (n 14), p 8.

[81] Craig (2006) 278 and 279 and Della Cananea (2003b) 1893.

[82] Reforming the Commission: A White Paper, Part I, COM (2000) 200, 1 March, p 8. The Commission understands simplification as 'designing and re-designing procedures to offer the quickest, simplest and more transparent way to achieve an objective' (Part II, p 22).

foster the rule of law, but they would also add to better communication between the EU and business circles, social partners and civil society, creating better understanding, and eventually, participation and commitment'. [83]Finally, from a democratic perspective, procedural unity has the effect of bringing European administration closer to the citizen.[84] Furthermore, the existence of a law on European administrative procedure in the form of a European law promulgated through the ordinary legislative procedure contained in Article III-396 of the Constitutional Treaty—thus with the intervention of the European Parliament—would enhance the democratic character of the Union.[85] Moreover, it should not be forgotten that when European citizenship was granted constitutionally recognised status, it became necessary to guarantee that citizens receive equal treatment from the European administration and from the various national administrations independently of the nationality of the citizen and the territory of the Union in which he or she was located, a principle strongly expressed in Article I-45 of the Constitutional Treaty. It can be maintained then that the democratic principle exercises an influence over administrative procedure.[86] It is not a bottom-up influence, in the sense of there being greater participation by citizens in administrative procedure that grants this enhanced democratic character; it is top-down, in the sense that an explicit recognition of the principle of participatory democracy forces the procedure to open up to participation,[87] thereby democratising administrative action.[88]

Thus, the principle of good administration, the principle of democracy and the principle of legality are factors favouring the creation of a European law of common administrative procedure, which, for its part, would contribute reciprocally to good governance, to the democratisation of the executive function and to the legality of administrative action.

[83] European Economic and Social Committee, Opinion on EU and national administration practices and linkages, p 8.

[84] S Cassese (2003b) 24.

[85] In this sense, Della Cananea (1995) stipulates that the intervention of the Parliament in the regulation of administrative procedure has been viewed by many of the Member States as a better democratic control of administrative action (p 977).

[86] The former Ombudsman maintains in this sense that 'dedication and service for citizens are the only means in the hands of the European civil servants in order to gain the confidence and support in a Europe which faces the most difficult challenges of its 50 year history' (Söderman 2001, 14).

[87] Participation, of course, not of those individually affected—they participate through the principle of the right to a hearing which is derived from the rule of law and is explicitly required by the Constitutional Treaty—but of interested citizens and their representatives. In this sense, see E Schmidt-Aßmann (1993) 335–6. The opening up of the decision-making procedure to participation from pressure groups and society in general is one of the central objectives of the European Commission in its action plans and proposals for the future. In this sense see the document Reforming the Commission: A White Paper, Part II, COM (2000) 200, 1 March, pp 6–7; and the Commission initiative on transparency in Europe, http://ec.europa.eu/commission_barroso/kallas/transparency_es.htm. See also the Communication from the Commission on Follow-up to the Green Paper 'European Transparency Initiative, COM (2007) 127 final of 21 Mar 2007.

[88] As Della Cananea (1995) points out, 'the regulation of administrative procedures is a useful tool . . . to ensure that policy decisions are responsive to the interests or preferences expressed by citizens' (p 978).

2. Content: Putting the Individual at the Centre of Procedure

Although it may seem somewhat odd, the expression employed by the Preamble to the Charter of Fundamental Rights[89] is apt as a heading for what we are attempting to convey in this section: the novelties of the Constitutional Treaty that directly or indirectly influence procedure, even if they are scarce, are sufficiently relevant to require a leading role for individuals in the decision-making processes of administrative acts that affect their interests.[90]

(a) Prior Considerations: A Law of General Principles or a Law of Particulars? A Law on European Administrative Procedure or a Law of European Administrative Procedures?

Community law tends to seek unity, although not thoroughness or uniformity. However, as was underlined in the opening lines of this chapter, currently normative dispersion prevails within administrative procedure. Questions arise as to whether work on the harmonisation of procedure should be done through a law of particular situations, which takes procedure in all its stages (offering a common model for all procedures) or, on the contrary, whether it is easier to create a law of general principles, including all the general principles that should govern procedure, the rights of individuals that must be respected during procedure and the general requirements with which the administrative decision and the performance of executive function must comply.[91]

[89] Specifically, in the second paragraph of the preamble, it states, 'Conscious of its spiritual and moral heritage, the Union is founded on the indivisible, universal values of human dignity, freedom, equality and solidarity; it is based on the principles of democracy and the rule of law. *It places the individual at the heart of its activities*, by establishing the citizenship of the Union and by creating an area of freedom, security and justice' (emphasis added).

[90] Many of the European Commission's documents dealing with this material highlight the importance of the European citizen and their involvement in the work of the EU as vital and necessary elements in continuing the integration process. This is captured in the document of Strategic objectives 2005–2009 *Europe 2010: A Partnership for European Renewal Prosperity, Solidarity and Security* COM (2005) 12, 26 January, p 2: 'Europe is therefore at a crossroad. The Union has to convey to Europeans a new sense that we understand the challenges of the future and that we have credible strategies in place to address them.'

[91] The Commission has, in its documents, shown two ways of organising administrative procedure: detailed codification, and a code with various procedural models which would serve as precedents when creating new procedures and reforming pre-existing ones. Harlow (1996) is against detailed regulation because the nature of the application of Community law, being for the most part an indirect application, creates a dual problem of normative transposition of Community norms and compliance issues (p 14). In her work on the codification of European administrative procedure, she distinguishes between 'code', which refers to a general system of principles, and 'codification' which designates the collation of all norms dealing with the same subject; in her opinion, 'codes can be seen primarily as a convenient way to index and articulate connected and interlocking rules' (p 9).

For his part, J Barnés (2003) understands the codification in question as 'a collection of principles and procedural guarantees both general and common, or even particular or ordered according to subject matter, which governs administrative procedure in every situation . . . Codification, in sum, which is not synonymous with simplification or unification but relates to a common denominator—or common denominators due to various procedural types—capable of influencing, governing and inspiring

The answer to this question must begin by acknowledging a recent phenomenon that is exercising a strong influence in law: globalisation. The globalisation of law, which is intimately linked to economic globalisation, has resulted in the blurring of the borders of legal systems and markets, especially in the EU, where a reciprocal influence between the Community system and national systems has been established.[92] This reality makes it reasonably easy to extract a series of general principles[93] that apply both to European administration and to national administrations when they apply European law.[94] Moreover, new technologies are an important feature[95] of this development and play an increasingly important role in the shaping of a common European administrative procedure. It could be argued that

multiple specific procedures, whether they are formal or informal' (p 14). In the same way, Nehl, in his book on the principles of administrative procedure in Europe (1999), defends his preference 'to identify certain *basic process rules* which, it is assumed, are coming to be recognised as a common standard of reference in various fields of policy implementation', rules which revolve around the right to good administration (pp 4–5) (emphasis in original).

[92] This is highlighted in Schwarze (1992). Also interesting in this sense is Cassese (2006). This influence has been further evidenced in the area of procedure, as Chiti (2005) highlights by maintaining that the characteristics of European procedural administrative law are the result of mutual influence between the ways of acting in national administrations and their equivalent at the European level, as well as the horizontal influence between the administrative law of the various Member States, which leads to the harmonisation of procedural standards (p 9).

[93] All the principles developed by the ECJ are binding on Member States as general principles of EC law. In consequence, even if they are not contained in any Article of the Treaty, Regulation or Directive, they still produce effects for national administrations. Such principles, moreover, can have the effect of contributing to the Europeanisation of administrative law. This is clearly exposed by Ladeur (2002): 'Member states act autonomously when creating and developing the general administrative infrastructure on which specific European laws rest in each jurisdiction, so it seems entirely consistent that the procedural law is expected to be more-than-usually "rational" in relation to the effectiveness of specific European administrative laws. This helps to guarantee its implementation in a practical sense. It also has broader effects for the process of integrating European law as a whole: this is a process that requires greater transparency so that both Europe and its member nations can work towards achieving a co-operative transnational administrative law through a pattern of mutual learning. Enhancing procedural law would seem to be a goal that is thoroughly compatible with those of the various national administrative legal systems. It meanwhile has the side effect of enabling "autonomy" for administrative procedures to be used for purposes of Europeanisation' (p 9). In the same vein, Franchini (2003) notes that 'this results in a virtuous circle, given that, on the one hand, national legal systems influence the legal system of the European Union, in the sense that national administrative law is promoted at the supranational level; on the other hand, the Community legal system conditions internal legal systems by using the Institutions and applying the principles of the legal order, adjusting the latter accordingly to the relevant national circumstances, refining and harmonizing them, and thereby promoting their acceptance from the point of view of European integration . . . [M]oreover, the general principles of European law also gain acceptance in the legal systems of the member states, due to their status as a source of law, and because national administrations and judges are competent and indeed, under an obligation, to apply the rules of Community law' (p 1054).

[94] Ladenburger (2005a) regrets that the principles of general administrative law to be adopted under Art III-398 Constitutional Treaty probably cover only European administration and not national administrations implementing EU law (p 170).

[95] There are numerous Community documents relating to e-government and e-administration, including COM (1999) 687 final, of 8 December 1999; COM (2000) 200 final of 1 March, Reforming the Commission: A White Paper, Part II, pp 8–10. Within the framework of the simplification programmes of Community law new technology features extensively. Finally, the e-Government Action Plan elaborated by the Commission—COM (2006) 173 final of 25 April—includes as one of the most important aims of this action plan strengthening participation and democratic decision-making in Europe (p 10).

the creation of a European administrative procedure can only be developed in conjunction with telematic procedures. This involves not so much the application of new technology to administrative procedures as the development of procedures, taking new technologies into account. In other words, the creation of a law on administrative procedure must take into consideration the possibilities offered by new technologies when shaping the content of a European administrative procedure in aspects such as the right to a hearing, participation, access to documents, etc. Thus, a European law on administrative procedure should not simply collate and codify principles; it should also take the opportunity to innovate.

As far as we can discern, the key to understanding the content of an eventual law on administrative procedure in the EU must be based on the ideas of simplification and standardisation: it must be a general unifying law, containing principles that simplify and unify, without being too detailed. Simplification can be achieved through general procedures according to the more important sectors;[96] stan-

[96] The Constitutional Treaty makes both normative and administrative advances on simplification. This is evidenced in the new classification of legal instruments in Art I-33 and, at the administrative level, the provisions of Art 163(b), for example (see ch 1). Both the normative and the administrative simplification influences the matter of administrative procedure: indirectly in the first case—it is necessary to clarify the regulatory rules of the multiple European administrative procedures that are currently in force in the Union; and directly in the second case through the simplification of administrative practice. Commission initiatives in the areas of legislative and administrative simplification are numerous and go back a long way, although only recently have they been put into practice at a general level. Since the foundation of the European Communities, the Community judicial corpus has not been subject to structural revision. Simplification has acquired a fundamental relevance in recent years. This is reflected in the way in which the European Convention that produced the text of the Constitutional Treaty formed a Working Group on Simplification (Group IX), whose final report can been consulted in CONV 424/02.

Since a group of Independent Experts was appointed to write a report (the summary and proposals of this report can be found in COM (95) 288, 21 June), simplification has been viewed as an effective method of achieving Community objectives in the various areas of EU competence and efforts have been made to create a culture of simplification. Comments of the European Commission on this report, which listed and endorsed most of the initiatives proposed, can be found in SEC (95) 2121, 29 November. Subsequent initiatives have been varied, particularly with respect to rules that have attempted to refine, clarify and simplify the laws of the EU. The first initiative occurred in 1997; in 2001 the Commission launched a programme to codify all Community secondary law with its Communication to the European Parliament and the Council, regarding the *acquis communautaire* COM (2001) 645, 21 November; the second programme commenced with the communication of the Commission to the Council, the Parliament, o the Economic and Social Committee and the Committee of Regions, on the updating and simplification about the *acquis communautaire*, COM (2003) 71, 11 February (indeed, this document puts the date at which the *acquis* reached 97,000 pages in the Official Journal as December 2002 and states that, after the application of the initiatives proposed, the volume would be reduced to 20,000 pages); the White Paper on Governance in Europe, COM (2001) 428 also contains simplification measures (pp 26 and 27); there is also a Commission Communication to the European Parliament and the Council, the Economic and Social Committee and the Committee of the Regions on the application of the Community program to the Lisbon Agenda: A strategy for the simplification of the regulatory framework, COM (2005) 535, 25 October. Finally, the Communication from the Commission to the European Parliament, the Council, the European Economic and Social Committee and the Committee of the Regions, Annual Policy Strategy for 2007—Boosting Trust through Action, COM (2006) 122, 14 March, also highlights simplification as a way of building trust between the EU and its citizens, together with a modern, efficient and accountable administration that delivers on its policies.

Moreover, simplification and codification go hand in hand in the Commission's documents. In this sense, again the abovementioned Commission Communication regarding the codification of the *acquis communautaire*. Finally, it must be mentioned that the regulation on procedure could help to achieve

dardisation must apply to all administrative procedure with the aim of creating common minimum standards—based on the general principles of procedure, which includes a regulation on procedure itself[97]—guaranteeing the equal application of European law to European and national administrations and have the same effect on individuals.[98] Simplification and standardisation—distinct but complementary measures—are the basis of codification.[99]

Another argument in favour of a law of general principles instead of a detailed one is the fact that the national identity of Member States must be respected (as established in Article 6(3) TEU). Member States have procedural autonomy—as the manifestation of the more general principle of autonomy in complying with community provisions (Article I-37(1) Constitutional Treaty)[100]—in such a way that European law, in those areas where it lacks exclusive competence, cannot replace the identity of national legal orders.[101]

some of the objectives of good governance in Europe. Particularly when speaking of the objective of 'focusing the institutions', the White Paper on Governance proposes legislation that would define the conditions and limits within which the Commission discharges its executive role and a simple juridical mechanism which would allow the Council and the Parliament to monitor and control the acts of the Commission in relation to the principles and policy orientation adopted in legislation (COM (2001) 428, p 36).

Administrative procedure is the solution to these initiatives. Moreover, it would help to achieve other objectives such as the more effective participation of national agents in the creation, application and control of Community laws and Community programmes (p 39). It would also help to clarify the form in which the Union acts and uses its competences, another of the grand objectives proposed by the Commission to correct deficiencies in clarity, responsibility, proximity and effectiveness in the acts of the community institutions (Commission Communication: A Project for the European Union, COM (2002) 247, 22 May 2002, p 19). Internally, the Commission has implemented an initiative regarding the simplification of its administrative procedures, which, under DG ADMIN, aims at simplifying internal procedures of staff and agents of the Community administration, with the ultimate aim of eliminating bureaucracy. In the words of this initiative, the aim is to 'transform the administration to a personnel service and to aid personnel'. In sum, even when there is no specific initiative for the simplification of administrative procedures '*ad extra*', the aforementioned initiatives undoubtedly have an influence. Recently, in the frame of the Strategic Review for Better Regulation in the EU, the Commission has elaborated a working document to the end of measuring administrative costs and reducing administrative burdens in the European Union: COM (2006) 691 final.

For a general overview of the simplification of the legal orders of the member States of the Union see Sandulli (2000).

[97] In this sense see Della Cananea (1997) 248.

[98] It is evident that the principles of equality and non-discrimination cannot justify complete uniformity in the application of the law in the EU; however, they can be used as complementary arguments to support the usefulness of establishing a series of common principles which must be respected in all Member States in the application of EU law related to procedure.

[99] Codification is defined by the European Commission in the following terms: 'Codification seeks to clarify the law by bringing together, in a new legal act, all the provisions of an act together with any subsequent amendments. This process renders the law simpler by establishing a single authoritative text, notably by deleting obsolete and overlapping provisions; by harmonising terms and definitions; and by correcting errors without substantive change. Codification brings major benefits by providing legally secure texts that are more readily understood by users' (COM (2003) 71, 11 February, p 12). Note that this is not the type of codification proposed in the present chapter. The arguments put forward here lead to the positivisation of the principles of European administrative procedure. In this work, 'codification' is used in the sense of creating a methodical and systematic normative text of general application.

[100] In this sense Art I-33(1) Constitutional Treaty leaves it to national authorities to choose the form and methods to achieve the aims established in the European Regulation (when this is the measure adopted).

[101] However, there are limits to this principle. For example, Art III-134(b), within the framework of

In this sense, although the principle of subsidiarity and respect for national identity would exclude a general codification of administrative procedure applicable to national administrations when they act as the executive administrations of European law,[102] at the same time neither subsidiarity nor respect for the identities of the Member States can justify the complete dispersion of administration, given that this would have a negative effect on the application of European law for the citizens of the Union. Thus, the tension between aspirations for unity and the reality characterised by dispersion finds its point of equilibrium in the principles that inform administrative procedures, in the principles that make up the right to good administration, which would be applicable to the procedures followed by national administrations in the implementation of EU law.

Supporting the notion of a regulation setting out general principles—ruling out a specific regulation with a model uniform procedure—is the notion of the multi-functionality of procedure: procedure does not have one single goal; it can respond to various goals depending on the case,[103] in such a way that a detailed regulation would be unable to because the necessary flexibility would be lost.

A final issue must be considered: 'if the codification of Community administrative procedures is to be more than a symbol, we need to tailor it carefully to the needs of administration'.[104]

In conclusion, the arguments laid out above argue for a law on administrative procedure—and not a law of administrative procedures—based on general principles.[105]

However, this does not conclude the issue definitively. The kind of law that could be used to give expression to the principles and requirements of an administrative procedure contained within a written text of general application remains to be determined. Article III-398 speaks of 'provisions', leaving the choice of a suitable normative instrument to the legislator to achieve an open, effective and transparent administration. In our opinion, this should be a binding legal norm, in the form of a regulation and/or directive,[106] created through the ordinary legislative

the free movement of workers, provides that a European law or framework law which develops this freedom will have the aim of 'abolish[ing] those administrative procedures and practices and those qualifying periods in respect of eligibility for available employment, whether resulting from national legislation or from agreements previously concluded between Member States, the maintenance of which would form an obstacle to liberalisation of the movement of workers'. Art III-138 contains similar provisions regarding the freedom of establishment.

With regard to asylum procedures, Art III-266 provides for the establishment of common procedures to extend or withdraw the status of asylum or subsidiarity protection. Similar provisions are contained in Articles 40(b) and 44 EC.

[102] Harlow (1996) is of this opinion (p 21).

[103] E Schmidt-Aßmann (1993) 322.

[104] Harlow (1996) 18.

[105] The greatest advocate of this idea is Harlow (1996), for whom 'a Community Code or Charter of Good Administration would reinforce Basic administrative Standard within national administrations and, at the same time, clarify and fortify the twin images of legality and good administration in the public perception' (p 22).

[106] Della Cananea (1997) maintains that the establishment of a series of general rules applicable to administrative procedure could be achieved with a Regulation in the case of procedures carried out directly by the Commission and with a Directive for those that are developed at the national level (p 249).

procedure—with the intervention the European Parliament—and applicable to the European administration as well as to national administrations.

Having decided upon the necessary type of law, its content must now be analysed.

(b) General Considerations regarding the Content of the Law on European Administrative Procedure

The declaration on the Future of the European Union of 15 December 2001 provides a few clues as to the aims to which the EU should aspire (which, although they are not specifically referred to in administrative procedure, affect it). Beginning with citizens—they demand clear, transparent, effective and democratic action by the Community institutions—which in turn require simplification, democracy, transparency and effectiveness as ways of improving the functioning of the Union, increasing its legitimacy and thus coming closer to its citizens.[107]

In relation to this point of the Constitutional Treaty, as is the case with the majority of Member States' constitutions, it is clearly fundamental to stipulate the criteria, conditions and requirements that all European administrative procedure must respect, leaving secondary law to spell out the particulars. Similar to the current situation, each sector can have its own procedural norms and each institution, body and agency can make use of its own rules of procedure.[108] What it offers is a basis for the shaping of common elements to all procedure. In this way, an eventual law on administrative procedure should consider the elements that have been shaped by both primary and secondary Community law, and also the jurisprudence of the ECJ and the CFI. This process is reasonably simple: Community law is already codified in some sectors (such as the rules on state aid); entire procedures can be taken as procedural models (the procedure in the area of competition, for example[109]); and there are principles newly created but sufficiently studied in legal literature (the best example is right to good administration, the key when elaborating a law on administrative procedure), which can act as guidelines.

Administrative procedure is related to democracy, the rights of the individual, transparency, legality and the limitation of discretion, which are all elements that must be included in a law on European administrative procedure. Such a law must ensure the effective application of the various rules regulating administrative action and, at the same time, ensure respect for the rights and interests of natural and legal persons as well as Member States, which in their respective spheres are affected by decisions emanating from the administration. Specifically, the Act should cover the

[107] The Heads of State or Government of the Member States of the European Union, in their declaration on the ratification of the Draft Constitutional Treaty done at the European Council of June 2005 (SN 117/05), declared that the Constitutional Treaty was 'the fruit of a collective process, designed to provide the appropriate response to ensure that an enlarged European Union functions more democratically, more transparently and more effectively'.

[108] This is how Barnés (2003) understands it (p 13).

[109] Regulated by Council Regulation (EC) No 1/2003, of 16 December 2002, on the implementation of the rules on competition laid down in Arts 81 and 82 of the Treaty [2004] OJ L1/1, replacing the previous Regulation 17/62.

following principles:[110] general principles, such as the principle of legality, the principle of legal certainty, the principle of proportionality, the principle of equality, the principle of objectivity, impartiality and independence and the principle of good administration; principles of procedure, such as respecting competences, the official nature of the process, rights of defence, the right to a hearing,[111] the right to receive legal advice, the right of access to one's own file and the right to a resolution within a reasonable time; and requirements regarding administrative acts themselves, such as the requirement to give reasons, the right to judicial review of the act, the requirements of publication and notification of acts, presumption of validity and validity after notification,[112] and the right to contest breaches of procedural requirements, whether the acts in question are provisional or final.[113]

Without doubt, the provisions of the European Code on Good Administrative Behaviour, discussed above, could serve as a model to determine the principles of administrative procedure to be included in a European law on common administrative procedure. Until now, even though it has had some successes, Community law constitutes a 'system of imperfect procedural justice: whilst EC law contains substantive rules defining the fairness of an outcome from a legal perspective, it does not provide for procedural principles capable of always guaranteeing such outcomes'.[114]

In the next sections, the three most important issues that will have to be taken into account in an eventual law on administrative procedure will be briefly developed.

(c) The Development and Guarantee of the Rights of the Parties in Procedure

In Council Regulation (EC) No 1/2003, point 37 of the recital states:

> This Regulation respects the fundamental rights and observes the principles recognised in particular by the Charter of Fundamental Rights of the European Union. Accordingly, this Regulation should be interpreted and applied with respect to those rights and principles.

[110] A very interesting and useful catalogue of principles governing administrative procedure in the Council of Europe area is provided in *The Administration and You. A handbook* (Strasbourg, Council of Europe Publishing, 1996). The aim of this book is 'to set out . . . those principles of substantive law and administrative procedure which are considered to be of primary importance for the protection of private persons in their relations with the administrative authorities' (p 5). See Franchini (2003) 1037–59, which contains very useful references to the ECJ's case law.

[111] In its dual characteristic both as an instrument that contributes to a revision of the facts of the case and as a way of protecting the interests of the parties.

[112] Even if not expressly stipulated in the Constitutional Treaty or in the Treaty of Rome, the literature has interpreted that Art 254(3) EC Treaty gives Community acts a presumption of validity. In this sense see de la Quadra (2000) 215–16.

[113] With respect to decisions that are not final and which can be contested see Case T-64/89 *Automec v Commission* [1990] ECR II-367, in which the CFI found that the relevant criterion to be used was the possible effect of the decision on the rights of the interested party. The grounds for appeal are broadened when fundamental rights are binding: citizens can use such rights to defend the fundamental rights contained in Part II of the Constitutional Treaty.

[114] Barbier de la Serre (2006) 227.

This general clause is illustrative of what the creation of a European law on administrative procedure should represent, from the point of view of the rights and interests of individuals that can be affected by administrative action, and in our opinion, it should be included in any such subsequent law; a framework by which individuals can make their interests known relative to administrative acts that affect them must be created and should be guaranteed as a right.[115] As Craig notes, 'process rights are extremely important, because they constitute one method whereby the individual can gain access to the particular legal system in question. In any system of administrative law, you have access points or gateways . . . and any administrative law regime will normally have two crucial access points: there will be procedural rules determining who is entitled to be heard, or intervene before the initial decision is made, or who is entitled to be consulted before a legislative act . . . and there will be rules of standing to determine who should be able to complain to the Court that the decision maker has overstepped its powers'.[116] In this way, the fundamental rights of the parties involved in the administrative decision have to be protected, paying attention to their essential content (as required by Article 52 of the Charter). This will increase the legitimacy of challenging an administrative decision,[117] which will have the desired effects relative to the system of judicial review within the EU.

(d) The Rise of Transparency, Impartiality, Equality and Legal Certainty

It is insufficient to simplify administrative procedures and protect the rights of individuals that can be affected by the exercise of administrative power. It is also important to ensure that administrative acts are transparent, as a necessary element in guaranteeing good administration or, in negative terms, in order to avoid maladministration. The procedure itself and the introduction of processes enabling information and debate effectively contribute to the transparency of administrative decisions. Transparency implies that the decision-making procedure is comprehensible, that reasons are given for the decision, that the information upon which the decision is based is available to the public, that the meetings of the decision-making institutions and organs are held in public, and that a political debate emerges prior to the taking of the decision.[118]

[115] This implies the guarantee of the right to a defence in procedure, through the recognition of other rights entailing this right: the right to information, the right to a hearing, the right of access to relevant files, the right to examine the evidence, the right to legal assistance, etc: Barbier de la Serre (2006) 232.

[116] Craig (2005) 25.

[117] This is Nehl's idea, who states that 'The development can be described as *circular* or recursive: the participation of individual parties (not necessarily on the basis of procedural rights) in proceedings on the administrative level leads to *locus standi* and, accordingly, allows opportunities for challenging the result of the decision-making process in the courts. The courts, in turn, in their decisions on the substance, generally tend to reinforce the applicant's procedural status . . . and thus lay the foundation of increased participation and procedural protection in administrative decision-making' (1999) 22–23 and 62–64 (the citation can be found on pp 63 and 64).

[118] Söderman (2001) 12.

Article I-46 of the Constitutional Treaty, which contains the principle of representative democracy, establishes in the third paragraph that 'Every citizen shall have the right to participate in the democratic life of the Union. Decisions shall be taken as openly and as closely as possible to the citizen'. This must be compared with the first paragraph of Article III-398, which also requires transparency and openness in the acts of the institutions, bodies, offices and agencies of the Union. The European Commission has already adopted certain initiatives in this area,[119] because of the relationship between transparency and the enhanced legitimacy of the decision-making process and, furthermore, the integration process.[120] The right of access to documents contributes to transparency,[121] whose field of application—similar to that of the right to good administration—has been expanded by Articles I-50 and II-102, from the institutions and bodies of the Union to the offices and agencies, regardless of their form.[122] However, Article I-50 embodies the obligation of transparency, providing that: '1. In order to promote good governance and ensure the participation of civil society, the Union institutions, bodies, offices and agencies shall conduct their work as openly as possible. 2. The European Parliament shall meet in public, as shall the Council when considering and voting on a draft legislative act'. This obligation is extended to become an obligation on all Community institutions in Article III-399 of the Constitutional Treaty.

Moreover, the existence of established procedures contributes to impartiality, which is another requirement of the right to good administration,[123] and it consists of examining the legal and factual issues of the particular case.[124] It also presupposes the equal treatment of all those potentially affected by an administrative decision (in this sense it is important to highlight the principle of democratic equality, enshrined in Article I-45 Constitutional Treaty,[125] which is a new feature in the Treaty—in the sense that it is explicitly enshrined—and must be translated into administrative procedure). Finally, it ensures legal certainty as much for individuals as for the staff of the administration.

[119] Some of which have been around for some time now: Communication from the Commission to the Council, the Parliament and the Economic and Social Committee: *Openness in the Community*, COM (1993) 258 final, 2 June 1993 [1993] C166/4; Resolution on democracy, transparency and subsidiarity and the Interinstitutional Agreement on procedures for implementing the principle of subsidiarity; the regulations and general conditions governing the performance of the Ombudsman's duties; the arrangements for the proceedings of the Conciliation Committee under Art 189(b) EC, 25 October 1993 [1993] OJ C329/132. See also the Declaration n 17 TEU.

[120] In the opinion of Commission President Durao Barroso, 'we need increased transparency and a more strict obligation to be accountable to the public if we want to maintain the legitimacy of the European decision-making process' (Press Release IP/06/562).

[121] Regulation (EC) No 1049/2001 of the European Parliament and of the Council of 30 May 2001 regarding public access to European Parliament, Council and Commission documents [2001] OJ L145/43. See ch 2.

[122] For this reason, on the basis of this modification and the requirements formulated over the years in terms of the application of Regulation 1049/2001, Kranenborg (2006) argues for the need to amend the regulation with regard to the right of access of documents.

[123] Among the most recent see Case T-54/99 *Max.mobil v Commission* [2002] ECR II-313, para 48.

[124] For an exposition of the requirement of impartiality from the point of view of the principle of care see Nehl (1999) 106 *et seq.*

[125] 'In all its activities, the Union shall observe the principle of the equality of its citizens, who shall receive equal attention from its institutions, bodies, offices and agencies.'

In any case, recognition of the principle of transparency and its inclusion into a law on administrative procedure must be introduced in such a way that it does not have a detrimental effect on decision-making procedures.[126]

(e) The Strengthening of Participation Rights: Towards a More Democratic and Open European Administration

Clearly, any natural or legal person or Member State affected by the exercise of administrative functions must be able to voice their opinions in the procedure through which the function is exercised. Thus it is essential that the decision-making body gives due consideration to the circumstances of the case and therefore complies with the requirements of the legality of administrative action. In this sense, there is an interest in participating in the procedure through which administrative action is channelled, due to the legal effect of the decision on the individual (or Member State).

Along with the interest created through legal effect, there is another situation that is similar but distinct: the impact of interests. Whereas the first relates to the right to good administration, the latter relates to other rights such as the right of access to documents and the principle of transparency.[127] This occurs in cases where, because of the special nature or the reach of the procedure—in this sense procedures relating to environmental regulation come to mind—third parties as well as interested individuals should be given the opportunity to submit their observations. The rationale for this is simple: 'Democracy depends on people being able to take part in public debate.'[128]

Public administration is increasingly shedding its authoritarian and hierarchical character and becoming more co-operative, with increased participation. In fact, at the Community level, the administration was created more as a co-operative administration than an authoritarian one.[129] The Commission has adopted numerous initiatives in recent years—mainly since the White Paper on Governance—in the sense of opening up avenues to increase the participation of citizens, associations, interest groups and generally anyone involved in EU decision-making processes.[130] In particular the 'Commission Communication Towards a Reinforced

[126] As Nehl (1999) states, it will always be necessary to have a 'reasonable balance between the functional needs of the administration on the one hand and the protection of individual rights and interest on the other' (p 25).

[127] Nevertheless, it is obvious that participation, even if not necessarily included under the right to good administration, encourages good administration as a duty for public authorities: participation contributes to better realisation of the public interest. See Kanska (2004) 299.

[128] White Paper on Governance, COM (2001) 428, p 12.

[129] Barnés (2003) states, 'the peculiar structure of Administration at the European level requires cooperative application and execution, whether it is direct or indirect (combined procedures; mixed organs)' (p 4).

[130] Among others, the following can be mentioned: Commission Communication Towards a reinforced culture of consultation and dialogue—General principles and minimum standards for consultation of interested parties by the Commission, COM (2002) 704, 11 December; Communication from the Commission to the Council, the European Parliament, the European Economic and Social

Culture of Consultation and Dialogue' contains the general principles and minimum standards for consultations by the Commission to citizens, agencies, associations and groups, as well as the procedure to be followed in such consultations. All of these initiatives are based on the principles of participation, responsibility, openness, effectiveness and coherence.

The Preamble to the Constitutional Treaty captures this idea by providing that Europe 'wishes to deepen the democratic and transparent nature of its public life'. This declaration is further developed in Article I-47, according to which, '1. The institutions shall, by appropriate means, give citizens and representative associations the opportunity to make known and publicly exchange their views in all areas of Union action. 2. The institutions shall maintain an open, transparent and regular dialogue with representative associations and civil society.'

The notion of citizen participation in public affairs enshrined in these provisions must have the desired effect with respect to procedure in which executive decisions that affect the individual as much as the public interest are taken.[131] Moreover, procedure provides a bridge between the administration and the citizen, through which the Commission makes contact with citizens, directly or through national administrations.[132]

From the Member States' point of view, furthermore, indirect administration necessarily implies participation in procedure; in this way procedure aids the joint exercise of shared competences (Articles I-12–I-17 Constitutional Treaty). Moreover, the Constitutional Treaty itself, in Part III, enshrines the principle of collaboration and co-operation between national administrations and the Community administration with a view to achieving the more effective application of EU law in each of the different areas of Community policy. From the perspective of the individual, another important argument applies: citizens who have had the possibility of participating in the adoption of a particular administrative act will be more willing to accept the end result, especially if it contains their suggestions or revisions.[133]

Committee and the Committee of the Regions: The Commission's contribution to the period of reflection and beyond: Plan-D for Democracy, Dialogue and Debate, COM (2005) 494, 13 October 2005. In fact, participation is one of the most useful and important instruments by which the aims of the Union can be achieved by 2010: Strategic objectives 2005–2009 Europe 2010: A Partnership for European Renewal Prosperity, Solidarity and Security, COM (2005) 12, 26 January, esp pp 5–6. Moreover, there are many programmes that try to promote citizens' participation. As an example, see Decision No 1904/2006 of the European Parliament and the Council, of 12 December 2006, about the programme 'Europe for Citizens' [2006] OJ L378/32; and Decision No 252/2007 of the Council, of 19 April 2007, about the programme 'Fundamental Rights and Citizens' [2007] OJ L110/33.

[131] It must be borne in mind that the third para of Art I-47 contains an obligation on the Commission to engage in 'broad consultations' with interested parties regarding EU acts.

[132] In this sense, Cassese maintains that 'the creation of homogenous procedural standards . . . results in reducing the distance between the Commission and citizens, bringing them close together' (2003b) 24.

[133] Schwarze (1992) 1178. In order to strengthen the participation of citizens in decision-making procedures it is important to use new technology. This is the aim of the EU's website, where citizens can express their views on any aspect of the Union: www.europa.eu.int/yourvoice.

However, Article 47 of the Constitutional Treaty, which has no equivalent in any of the previous Treaties, is not exactly a revolutionary measure.[134] For this reason, the application of the constitutional provision will be limited. Nonetheless, what does emerge is the notion of the individual gradually becoming a co-administrator, through their participation in the administrative procedure.

III. CONCLUSION

The correct direction for the reform of community public administration is that of opening up to citizens, working for them and providing a transparent, dedicated and honest service.[135]

European administration must channel its activities through a procedure that simultaneously guarantees the legality and effectiveness of administrative acts. It is necessary to substantiate all the good intentions of the European Commission, in general, by the institutions of the EU, into rules that result in real benefits for individuals, without abandoning the aim of administrative action—the satisfaction of the general interest—which demands efficiency and effectiveness. With respect to these ends, procedure is an essential instrument.

This common procedure should consist of standard stages, independent of the acting body, the subject-matter and the nature and type of act adopted within it. In this respect, the protection of interests—whether they belong to legal or natural persons or Member States—should occupy a fundamental part of procedure, as well as the participation of individuals, agents, associations and groups when the type of procedure calls for it.

The new provisions introduced by the Constitutional Treaty are sufficient to assume the consitutionalisation of the legal basis of European administrative procedure. Without doubt, they will affect the European administration and national administrations in the exercise of executive functions, the ECJ in exercising judicial functions and the Council and the Parliament in their legislative functions.

In this chapter we have argued in favour of a European law on common administrative procedure which establishes a series of general principles applicable to all European administrative procedure, regardless of the rules governing specific

[134] Doubting the practical effect of this constitutional innovation, Craig (2005) argues that the principle of democratic participation will not make any difference to the decisions of the ECJ (p 28). This is correct if we take into account that the right to participate in the democratic life of the Union, which in the draft of the Constitutional Treaty presented by the Praesidium contained an article relative to the principle of participative democracy, has finally become part of the principle of democratic representation. In addition, other amendments proposed by the members of the Convention in the sense of extending the right not only to the democratic life of the Union but also to the decision-making procedures of the European institutions were rejected. For this reason, a member suggested that in continuing with the draft as it was, the principle of democratic involvement rather than the principle of democratic participation should be included. Moreover, Art I-47 mentions only institutions without referring to the organs, bodies and agencies of the Union. In the end, it is not a fundamental right—which would be contained in Part II of the Treaty—but a programmatic principle.

[135] Söderman (2001) 14.

procedures in certain sectors in each case. Such a law would help to eradicate the current diffusion of rules and guarantee the application of basic principles by the institutions, offices and bodies of the Union and national administrations when applying EU law in their relations with citizens. Moreover, it would result in the strengthening of the position of citizens, in the sense that they will be more prominent in the taking of administrative decisions and have a greater ability to challenge such acts.

5

Judicial Protection

I. INTRODUCTION

This chapter deals with the modifications that the Union needs in the field of judicial protection. Its aim is not to debate the federalist tendency of the Community Courts or the relationship between the Community Courts and national courts.[1] On the contrary, this chapter analyses the extension of the Courts' competences by the Constitutional Treaty in order to review the legality of Union and Member States' acts when implementing EU law. In other words, the chapter explains how the drafters within the Convention wanted to fill gaps in the EU's judicial system and in the Constitutional Treaty. This chapter highlights the main problems in the current Union legal system regarding the right to effective judicial protection within the scope of EU law. Some of those problems have been the subject of much doctrinal discussion in the light of recent case law (eg the need to modify the rule of standing of Article 230(4) EC and the competence of the ECJ in relation to police and judicial co-operation in criminal matters under Article 35 TEU);[2] others may be the subject of partial modification promoted by the Commission due to the paralysis in the Constitutional Treaty ratification process (eg the scope of jurisdiction of the ECJ in the fields covered by Title IV of the EC).[3]

The chapter is divided into four sections below, which deal with the main issues concerning the jurisdiction of the Community courts. Firstly, it deals with the modification of the rule of standing of individuals in the annulment action; secondly, the extension of the Community Courts' jurisdiction to review the legality of agencies and bodies' acts, such as those of Europol and Eurojust, is discussed; the third section deals with the possible implications of the obligation on Member States to provide remedies sufficient to ensure effective legal protection in the fields covered by EU law; and finally, the extension of the Community Courts' competence to the present third pillar is considered.

[1] Sarmiento (2004); Arnull (2005).

[2] Case C-50/00 *Unión de Pequeños Agricultores v Council* [2002] ECR I-6677 and Case C- 263/02 *Commission v Jégo-Quéré & Cie SA* [2004] ECR I-3425 (see section II of this chapter); Case C-105/03 *Maria Pupino* [2005] ECR I-5285 (see section V of this chapter).

[3] Communication from the Commission to the European Parliament, the Council, the European Economic and Social Committee, the Committee of the Regions and the Court of Justice of the European Communities on 'Adaptation of the provisions of Title IV of the Treaty establishing the European Community relating to the jurisdiction of the Court of Justice with a view to ensure more effective judicial protection', COM (2006) 346 final, 28 June 2006.

Changes in this field are necessary due to the need to guarantee the effectiveness of fundamental rights and their judicial protection in a Union defined as a Community of law made up of citizens and Member States. Guaranteeing the right to effective judicial protection is essential in a Community of law such as the EU,[4] with a Constitutional Treaty drafted 'on behalf of the citizens' and 'reflecting the will of the citizens'.[5] Whereas the preamble to the current Treaties refers to peoples, the Constitutional Treaty consciously underlines the double basis of the Union's legitimacy as a Union of the citizens and the States of Europe.[6]

It is submitted that the improvements to judicial protection within the EU legal system dealt with in this chapter tend towards the traditional model of administrative law, which aims to control any excess of institutional power and subject it to legal and, especially, judicial control. This reflects the model described by the red light theory of Harlow and Rawlings.[7] However, the features of a growing European administrative law, to which the Constitutional Treaty makes important contributions, do not belong exclusively to that traditional model but also belong to a model focused on the implementation of principles of transparency, participation, effectiveness and accountability in the daily operation of public administration. This modern model of administrative law, contained in the green light theory,[8] is also part of the growing body of European administrative law, as the preceding chapters of this book have shown.

II. THE RULE OF STANDING AND THE RIGHT TO EFFECTIVE JUDICIAL PROTECTION

This section focuses on the changes introduced by the Constitutional Treaty to the rule of standing in Article 230(4) of the EC. Recent case law, in which the right to effective judicial protection was at stake, highlights the need for such amendments (the *UPA* and *Jégo-Quéré* cases).[9] This second part of the chapter is divided into four sections: the first explains the current rule of standing. The second analyses the *UPA* and *Jégo-Quéré* cases in which the right to the effective judicial protection of the applicants was *de facto* violated. The third deals with the modification of the rule of standing in Article 230(4) of the EC by the Constitutional Treaty and, finally, the fourth sets out a conclusion.

[4] Case 294/83 *Parti écologiste «Les Verts» v European Parliament* [1986] ECR 1339, para 23.

[5] Constitutional Treaty, preamble and Art I-1.

[6] This was a step forward consciously made by the Convention after a majority of its members requested the modification of a previous draft of Art 1 that referred to peoples rather than citizens. Ladenburger (2005a) 159.

[7] Harlow and Rawlings (1997) 37.

[8] *Ibid*, 67–90.

[9] At n 2.

1. Brief Description of the Current Rule of Standing found in Article 230(4) of the EC

Any natural or legal person may challenge the validity of a Community measure before the CFI when he or she fulfils the requirements of standing found in Article 230(4) of the EC according to the interpretation given by the ECJ. There is plenty of literature on these requirements, which will not be entered into here.[10] On the contrary, the aim of this section is merely to highlight the key case law in relation to these requirements, which will prove useful for understanding the debate in the sections that follow.

Currently, review proceedings under Article 230(4) of the EC can only be brought in three situations: firstly, when there is a decision addressed to the applicant—in this case, the addressee can challenge the decision before the CFI; secondly, when there is a decision addressed to another person, but the applicant claims that he or she is directly and individually concerned by it; and thirdly, when there is a decision in the form of a regulation and the applicant claims that he or she is directly and individually concerned by it. The problems with the rules of standing arise (a) when the applicant has to prove that he or she is directly and individually concerned by a decision and (b) when he or she tries to show that the regulation is a decision addressed to him or her. According to the Court, a person is directly concerned by a Community measure when the measure:

> directly affects the legal situation of the individual and leaves no discretion to the addressees of that measure who are entrusted with the task of implementing it, such implementation being purely automatic and resulting from Community rules without the application of other intermediate rules.[11]

The following paragraphs explain the meaning of 'individual concern' according to ECJ case law and the conditions that an individual must fulfil in order to challenge the validity of the measure in (a) and (b).

(a) The applicant has to prove that he is directly and individually concerned by a decision which is not addressed to him. The ECJ set out the meaning of 'individual concern' in the *Plaumann* case:[12] the applicant's commercial activity was affected by the Decision of the Commission of 22 May 1962, which did not authorise the Federal Republic of Germany to suspend in part the customs duties applicable to mandarin oranges and clementines freshly imported from third countries. The applicant applied for the annulment of that Decision under Article 173(2) (current Article 230(4) EC), which establishes that:

[10] Albors-Llorens (1996); Arnull (1995) and (1999); Craig (1994); Hartley (1998); Cassia (2002b); Ward (2000).

[11] Case T-177/01 *Jégo-Quéré et Cie SA v Commission* [2002] ECR II-2365, para 26. The first time the ECJ interpreted the condition was in Case 106–107/1963 *Toepfer v Commission* [1965] ECR 405 and Case 41-44/1970 *International Fruit Company v Commission* [1971] ECR 411, paras 23–27.

[12] Case 25/62 *Plaumann & Co v Commission of the European Economic Community* [1963] ECR 95.

> Any natural or legal person may . . . institute proceedings against a decision . . . which, although in the form of . . . a decision addressed to another person, is of direct and individual concern to the former.

In that case the ECJ interpreted the meaning of 'individual concern' in the following way:

> A person other than those to whom a decision is addressed may only claim to be individually concerned if that decision affects them by reason of circumstances which are peculiar to them or by reason of circumstances in which they are differentiated from all other persons and by virtue of these factors distinguishes them individually just as in the case of the person addressed.[13]

As the applicant was affected by the Decision as an importer of clementines—someone performing a commercial activity that may be practised by any person—the action for annulment was declared inadmissible.

However, in the *Extramet* case[14] the ECJ recognised the standing of the applicant, who was the largest importer of the product forming 'the subject-matter of the anti-dumping measure and the end-user of the product'.[15] In the *Codorníu* case, the applicant brought an action for annulment against a Decision that reserved the right to use the term 'crémant' for French and Luxembourg vine producers.[16] The provision prevented Codorníu from using that term, which was one of its visible trade marks. Hence, the ECJ considered that Codorníu had established the existence of a situation which from the point of view of the contested provision differentiated it from all other traders. Therefore, the objection of inadmissibility put forward by the Council was dismissed and the contested provision annulled.

To sum up, since the *Plaumann* case, the doctrine of the ECJ on the concept of individual concern within the rules of standing of Article 230(4) of the EC is based on whether the applicant was a member of a class that was closed at the time the measure was adopted.[17] Craig has defined a closed category as one in which the membership is fixed at the time of the adoption of the measure and an open category as one in which the membership is not fixed at the time the measure was adopted.[18] The ECJ grants standing to those who belong to a closed category. Therefore, in the *Plaumann* case the applicant did not have standing because he was a trader who imported fruit (an open category) and the Community measure was only applicable to anyone who commenced operations after the decision came into effect.[19]

(b) Under the rules of standing as set out in Article 230(4) of the EC, an individual or legal person may have difficulties getting *locus standi* when he or she wants to challenge the validity of a regulation. The applicant faces two obstacles:

[13] Case 25/62, para 1 *in fine*.
[14] Case C-358/89 *Extramet Industrie SA v Council* [1992] ECR I-3813.
[15] *Ibid*, para 17.
[16] Case C-309/89 *Codorníu SA v Council* [1994] ECR I-1853.
[17] Arnull (1995) 42.
[18] Craig (1994) 510.
[19] Hartley (1998) 344–5.

firstly, he or she must prove that formally speaking the measure is a regulation but substantively it is in fact not a regulation. And, secondly, he or she must prove that he or she is directly and individually concerned by the decision in the form of a regulation. Here the leading case is *Calpak*,[20] in which the ECJ explained the reason for giving *locus standi* to those who want to challenge the validity of a Community regulation:

> To prevent the Community institutions from being in a position, merely by choosing the form of a regulation, to exclude an application by an individual against a decision which concerns him directly and individually; it therefore stipulates that the choice of form cannot change the nature of the measure.[21]

The criterion used by the Court to distinguish between a regulation and a decision is whether or not the measure at issue is of general application[22] (Article 249 EC).

In the *Calpak* case, the applicants were producers of William pears. They complained that the calculation of production aid granted to them was void. Under the terms of a previous regulation, production aid was calculated on the basis of average production for the previous three years, in order to avoid the risk of over-production.

The new method of aid calculation was based on a marketing year in which the production was particularly low. The applicants also claimed that they were directly and individually concerned by the regulation because they were 'not merely a closed and definable group but equally a group, the members of which were either known to or at least identifiable by the Commission at the time when it adopted the disputed provisions'.[23]

Using the criterion established by the current Article 249 of the EC, the ECJ held that:

> A provision which limits the granting of production aid for all producers in respect of a particular product to a uniform percentage of the quantity produced by them during a uniform preceding period is by its nature a measure of general application within the meaning of Article 189 of the Treaty [Article 249]. In fact the measure applies *to objectively determined situations and produces legal effects with regard to categories of persons described in a generalised and abstract manner.* The nature of the measure as a regulation is not called into question by the mere fact that it is possible to determine the number or even the identity of the producers to be granted the aid which is limited thereby.[24]

Therefore, the applications were dismissed in the *Calpak* case because the applicants had not established the existence of circumstances that justified the changes in the regulations as a decision adopted specifically in relation to them. The regulations were not just formal but substantive regulations because they

20 Cases 789 and 790/79 *Calpak SpA et Società Emiliana Lavorazione Frutta SpA v Commission* [1980] ECR 1949.
21 *Ibid*, para 7.
22 *Ibid*, para 8.
23 *Ibid*, para 5.
24 *Ibid*, para 9 (emphasis added).

applied 'to objectively determined situations and produced legal effects with regard to categories of persons described in a generalised and abstract manner'. The use of the language describing categories of persons in a generalised and abstract manner as a criterion to determine whether there is a substantive regulation has been criticised because the Community institutions could always use abstract language in order to immunise a provision from annulment actions by individuals[25] and because the Rome Treaty does not mention that only individual decisions could be the object of annulment action by private parties.[26]

Before ending this section, it should be noted that the Court has adopted a more liberal approach in three cases—concerning dumping, competition and state aid matters. Anti-dumping duties can only be imposed by regulation and, as in the other cases (competition and state aid matters, the Court has recognised the *locus standi* of an applicant who enjoyed the right to be heard during an administrative procedure culminating in the adoption of the challenged decision/regulation.[27] There are two similar elements in the cases where the ECJ has adopted the liberal approach as to the standing of applicants: the first is the participation of the applicant in the administrative procedure before the challenged measure is adopted. The second pays regard to the 'substantive nature of the subject matter in these cases',[28] which has made the Court receptive to an argument that shows how a Community measure could negatively affect the interests of the Community.[29]

Having described the requirements of the rules of standing according to the case law of the ECJ, the following section deals with the *UPA* and *Jégo-Quéré* cases in which AG Jacobs and the CFI highlighted the deficiencies of the Union's judicial system in guaranteeing the right to effective judicial protection. It is submitted that these cases provoked the modification of the rule of standing introduced by the Constitutional Treaty.

2. *UPA* and *Jégo-Quéré* Cases and the Gaps in Judicial Protection in the Union

In the *UPA* case an association of farmers (UPA) sought the annulment of Regulation 1638/98, which substantially amended the common organisation of the

[25] Craig (1994) 515.

[26] Cassia (2002b) wrote: 'Manifestement, la Cour réécrit ici le traité de Rome, où il n'est nulle part fait mention du fait que seules les décisions individuelles pourraient faire l'objet d'un recours en annulation de la part des particuliers . . . Il faut insister sur le fait que l'assimilation des décisions à portée générale aux règlements ne découle pas de la lettre du traité: au contraire, on peut même estimer que celui-ci envisage les règlements comme une catégorie juridique spécifique, qui ne comprend pas les décisions à portée générale' (p 339).

[27] Arnull (1995) 33.

[28] Craig (1994) 527.

[29] One of the examples used by Craig (1994) involves state aid: 'The provision of such aid is contrary to the Community's interest, since it places the recipient firms at a competitive advantage as compared to firms in other countries. The Court is, therefore, likely to be receptive to an argument, such as that put in the *COFAZ* case, that the Commission has been mistaken in thinking that the transgressing state has corrected its past illegal behaviour' (p 527).

olive oil market.[30] UPA appealed to the ECJ against a CFI judgment. The CFI had dismissed UPA's application for annulment because the members of UPA were not individually concerned by the contested Regulation. According to the CFI, UPA did not fulfil the conditions of Article 230(4) of the EC. The CFI held that the Regulation concerned UPA members only on the basis of their objective capacity as operators trading in the olive oil market, in the same way as all other operators who traded in this market[31] (ie they belonged to an open category). What was important and different about the *UPA* case was that the applicant focused its action on its right to effective judicial protection. The ECJ had recognised that 'the requirement of judicial control of any decision of a national authority reflects a general principle of Community law stemming from the constitutional traditions common to the Member States and has been enshrined in Articles 6 and 13 of the European Convention for the Protection of Fundamental Rights and Fundamental Freedoms'.[32] The right was *de facto* denied by the CFI on dismissing its application: as far as the provisions of the Regulation did not require any national implementing measure, the applicant could not seek the annulment of a national measure. In other words, UPA could not attack the Regulation via a preliminary ruling (Article 234 EC).

Although the ECJ mentioned that the EU was a community based on the rule of law where the institutions' acts should respect fundamental rights, it rejected the applicant's arguments and the Opinion of AG Jacobs. Basically, the Court held that the Treaties established a complete system of legal remedies and procedures designed to ensure judicial review of the legality of institutions' acts and, according to that system, natural or legal persons could not directly challenge Community measures of general application if they did not fulfil the standing requirements of Article 230(4) of the EC.[33] With respect to the role of national courts, the Court held that they should interpret national procedural rules in a way that facilitates an indirect challenge of the Union's regulation via a preliminary ruling.[34] Here again we can see how the ECJ restricted the autonomy of national judges who must

[30] Case C-50/00 *Unión de Pequeños Agricultores v Council* (n 2).

[31] Case T-173/98 *Unión de Pequeños Agricultores v Council* [1999] ECR II-3357, para 10.

[32] Case 222/84 *Johnston v Chief Constable of the Royal Ulster Constabulary* [1986] ECR 1651, para 18; Case 222/86 *UNECTEF v Heylens* [1987] ECR 4097, para 14; Case C-97/91 *Oleificio Borelli SpA v Commission* [1992] ECR I-6313, para 14.

[33] On the Community legal order the ECJ held in its Opinion 1/91 [1991] ECR I-06079 that 'the EEC Treaty , albeit concluded in the form of an international agreement, none the less constitutes the constitutional charter of a Community based on the rule of law. The Community treaties established a new legal order for the benefit of which the States have limited their sovereign rights and the subjects of which comprise not only Member States but also their nationals. The essential characteristics of the Community legal order which has thus been established are in particular its primacy over the law of the Member States and the direct effect of a whole series of provisions' (para 1).

[34] Case C-50/00, n 2, paras 38–42. According to the ECJ's interpretation of the role of national courts when satisfying the right to effective judicial protection, the British courts have accepted the control of the validity of a Directive before its transposition into the national legal order (Case C-491/01 *British American Tobacco* [2002] ECR I-11453). The Spanish Constitutional Court has held that the right to effective judicial protection includes the preliminary ruling procedure before the ECJ when the appeal is before a last instance court and the *acte claire* doctrine is not applicable (judgment of the Constitutional Court 58/2004, 19 April, point 14).

guarantee the effectiveness of individual rights within their legal systems, such as the right to effective judicial protection.[35] The ECJ's narrow interpretation of the rule of standing in Article 230(4) of the EC resulted in the individual's claim being made through the preliminary ruling procedure.[36]

With respect to the finding that the Treaty establishes a complete system of legal remedies and procedures, the Opinion of AG Jacobs in the *UPA* case highlighted, as never before, the gaps in the EU's judicial system guaranteeing an effective right to judicial protection to private parties who do not fulfil the standing requirement, even though they have suffered negative effects of a Community measure. AG Jacobs, in his Opinion, analysed the legal remedies and procedures established by the Treaties to ensure the judicial review of the legality of acts of the institutions. Specifically, AG Jacobs began by analysing whether the assumption that the preliminary ruling procedure provided full and effective judicial protection against a general Community measure was correct, which was answered in the negative. According to him, proceedings before national courts are not capable of guaranteeing that individuals seeking to challenge the validity of Community measures are granted fully effective judicial protection, firstly, because national courts are not competent to declare measures of Community law invalid, and secondly, because the principle of effective judicial protection requires that applicants have access to a court which is competent to grant remedies capable of protecting them against the effects of unlawful measures, and thirdly, because access to the ECJ via Article 234 of the EC (the preliminary ruling procedure) is not a remedy available to individual applicants as a matter of right.[37]

These arguments led AG Jacobs to conclude that proceedings before the CFI under Article 230 of the EC are generally more appropriate for determining issues of validity than preliminary rulings.[38] The arguments used in that Opinion in favour of the action of annulment were as follows. First, the institution that adopted the impugned measure is a party to the proceedings from beginning to end because a direct action involves a full exchange of pleadings. Secondly, for reasons of legal

[35] On this topic see Cassia (2002a) 2828–9; see also Ward (2000) 323.

[36] Regarding the role of the preliminary ruling procedure as a tool used by the Court to introduce a federalist integration see Sarmiento (2004).

[37] The arguments used by AG Jacobs were the following: (a) National courts may refuse to refer questions and appeals within the national judicial systems could produce delays incompatible with the principle of effective judicial protection. (b) When national courts refer a question of validity to the ECJ, the former may reformulate the questions referred by limiting them, eg the range of Community measures that an applicant sought to challenge. (c) In some cases it may be impossible, as in the *UPA* case, to challenge a Community measure that does not require any act of implementation by national authorities. In these cases, there will no measures for providing a basis for an action before national courts. In other cases, although there was a national measure implementing EU law, individuals could not be required to breach the national law in order to gain access to justice. (d) Compared to a direct action before the CFI, proceedings before the national courts via the Art 234 EC procedure presents serious disadvantages for individual applicants, such as substantial extra delays and costs. Opinion of AG Jacobs of 21 March 2002, Case C-50/00 (n 2), paras 38–44. In addition, we should not forget that interim measures awarded by a national court would be confined to the Member State in question, so an applicant might have to bring proceedings in more than one Member State. *Ibid*, para 44.

[38] *Ibid*, paras 45–48.

certainty, it requires that the validity of Community acts be brought as soon as possible after their adoption: Article 230(5) of the EC set up a time-limit of two months, whereas Article 234 does not establish a time-limit, so the validity of Union measures could be raised before a national court at any time, depending on national procedural rules.

Regardless of whether an action for annulment under Article 230(4) of the EC is the most appropriate proceeding for issues regarding the validity of the Union's measures, the ECJ should adopt a formula other than 'individual concern'. According to AG Jacobs, the argument as to how many operators could be affected by the measure is unacceptable, because the right to an effective judicial review of individuals and the legal certainty of the EU legal system cannot depend on the number of individuals that are affected by a measure. He proposed the following concept of 'individually concerned':

> A person should be regarded as individually concerned by a Community measure where, by reason of his particular circumstances, the measure has, or is liable to have, a substantial adverse effect on his interests.[39]

Following the arguments of AG Jacobs in the *UPA* case in March 2002, the CFI, on 3 May 2002, declared admissible the appeal of *Jégo-Quéré et Cie SA*[40] (a fishing company established in France which operates on a regular basis in the waters south of Ireland). Jégo-Quéré et Cie SA appealed for the annulment of some provisions of Commission Regulation No 1162/2001, which established measures for the recovery of the stock of hake and associated conditions for the control of activities of fishing vessels. The CFI's main concern was to guarantee the right to effective judicial protection taking account of AG Jacobs' Opinion in the *UPA* case. The CFI was aware of the disadvantages of using the preliminary ruling procedure to challenge the validity of Community legislation by an individual who was not the addressee of the measure. Following AG Jacobs' Opinion, the CFI held that:

> [There was] no compelling reason to read into the notion of individual concern, within the meaning of the fourth paragraph of Article 230 EC, a requirement that an individual applicant seeking to challenge a general measure must be differentiated from all others affected by it in the same way as an addressee . . . In the light of the foregoing, and in order to ensure effective judicial protection for individuals, a natural or legal person is to be regarded as individually concerned by a Community measure of general application that concerns him directly if the measure in question affects his legal position, in a manner which is both definite and immediate, by restricting his rights or by imposing obligations on him. The number and position of other persons who are likewise affected by the measure, or who may be so, are of no relevance in that regard.[41]

Therefore, the CFI dismissed the objection of inadmissibility raised by the Commission and ordered that the action proceed. The Commission appealed

[39] *Ibid*, para 60.

[40] Case T-177/01 *Jégo-Quéré et Cie SA v Commission* [2002] ECR II-2365.

[41] *Ibid*, paras 49 and 51.

against this judgment and, in the interim, the *UPA* judgment[42] was decided by the ECJ without a change in the rules of standing under Article 234(4) of the EC. Following the arguments used in the *UPA* judgment,[43] the ECJ insisted on the responsibility of national courts to provide a system of legal remedies and procedures that ensures respect for the right to effective judicial protection:

> In that context, in accordance with the principle of sincere cooperation laid down in Article 10 EC, national courts are required, so far as possible, to interpret and apply national procedural rules governing the exercise of rights of action in a way that enables natural and legal persons to challenge before the courts the legality of a Community act of general application, by pleading the invalidity of such an act.[44]

According to the judgment, the ECJ cannot extend its jurisdiction to examining and interpreting national procedural law in order to see whether those rules allow an individual to bring proceedings to contest the validity of the Community measure at issue.[45] The ECJ was not able to modify its interpretation of the condition of being individually concerned even though such an interpretation damaged a fundamental right of the applicant (the right to effective judicial protection). However, the Court imposed on national judges the duty to interpret their procedural law in such a way that the applicant's right to effective judicial protection will be protected.[46]

These ECJ decisions can be criticised not just because they increase the tension in the relationship between the Court and national judges but, particularly, because the Court does not appear to be aware of the increasing role of fundamental rights within a Union of citizens. The Court made its decisions based on a doctrine developed before the proclamation of the European Charter of Fundamental Rights. Although the Charter did not have binding effect when the judgments were handed down, this does not mean that the Courts could ignore them.

It is submitted that both judgments represent a missed opportunity to update the ECJ's doctrine according to a legal system that has, for the first time, its own Charter of Fundamental Rights.

3. Modifications to the Rule of Standing of Private Parties Introduced by the Constitutional Treaty

The Convention's plenary discussions on 5 and 6 December and 20 and 21 January 2003 revealed that some members of the Convention felt that there was a need to

[42] The CFI's judgment on the admissibility of the *Jégo-Quéré* application was delivered in May 2002 and the Judgment in the *UPA* case was given in July of the same year.

[43] See the beginning of this section.

[44] Case C-263/02 *Commission v Jégo-Quéré & Cie SA* (n 2) para 32.

[45] *Ibid*, para 33. The Court recognised that the conditions established in Art 230(4) EC must be interpreted in the light of the principle of effective judicial protection; but, almost at the end, the Court stated that such an interpretation cannot have the effect of setting aside the condition in question expressly laid down in the Treaty (para 36).

[46] Case C-312/93 *Peterbroeck, Van Campenhout & Cie SCS v Belgian State* [1995] ECR I-45599, para 12.

look at the implications that certain proposals might have for the operation of the ECJ. In recognition of these concerns, the Praesidium set up a discussion circle on the operation of the Courts, in which members of both Courts (the ECJ and CFI) had the opportunity to express their views on matters concerning them.

The discussion circle was chaired by Mr Antonio Vitorino and its purpose was to look at those matters on which the Convention had not yet adopted fixed positions, such as the procedure for appointing judges and Advocates General to the ECJ and the CFI, and renaming the ECJ and the CFI. The circle also discussed judicial review of the acts of agencies or bodies, the effectiveness of the system of penalties for non-compliance with a judgment of the Court, the possible modification of the rule of standing in Article 230(4) of the EC, and other questions aimed at facilitating the application of Articles 225A, 229A and 245 of the EC.[47] In addition, the circle was open to any other concern that its own members or members of the ECJ or the CFI considered worth examining. In order to address these issues, the discussion circle met four times, with an additional meeting on the possible jurisdiction of the ECJ on CFSP matters.[48]

The question of liberalising the conditions for direct action before the ECJ and the proposal to introduce a constitutional appeal that would enable any individual to challenge directly any Community act, even those of a legislative nature, for violating his or her fundamental rights were discussed by Working Group II.[49] With regard to the modification of the rule of standing in Article 230(4) there was no consensus. However, on the proposal of introducing a constitutional appeal for violation of fundamental rights, most members of the Group observed that 'a new form of legal action based on the violation of fundamental rights would be difficult to distinguish from other legal actions since these rights may be adduced in nearly every dispute'.[50] The proposal was rejected due to the problems it might cause in the distribution of competences between the ECJ and the constitutional courts of Member States.[51]

When the discussion circle discussed the rules of standing, the members split into two groups. For some, the current wording of the provision (Article 230(4) EC) satisfied the essential requirements to provide effective judicial protection of the rights of litigants. This group had in mind the present decentralised system based on the subsidiarity principle, which leaves to national courts the defence of the rights of individuals and which might (or should, at the last instance) refer questions to the Court for a preliminary ruling on the validity of a Union act. Therefore, this first group thought it unnecessary to make any substantive change to the fourth

[47] See *Final report of the discussion circle on the Court of Justice* CONV 636/03 CERCLE I 13, 25 March 2003, Annex, p 12.

[48] The four meetings of the discussion circle took place on 17 and 24 February and on 3 and 17 March 2003. An additional meeting was held on 4 April 2003. During these meetings the circle heard Mr Rodríguez Iglesias, President of the Court of Justice, Mr Vesterdorf, President of the CFI, and a delegation from the Council of the Bar and Law Societies of the European Union. CONV 636/03 (*ibid*), p 1.

[49] *Incorporation of the Charter/Accession to the ECHR* CONV 116/02, 18 June 2002, pp 15–17.

[50] *Ibid*, p 16.

[51] Arguments in favour of the introduction of a fundamental rights complaint at Community level are explained by Schwarze (2004).

paragraph of Article 230. However, they were in favour of mentioning explicitly in the Constitutional Treaty that:

> In accordance with the principle of loyal cooperation as interpreted by the Court of Justice, national courts are required, so far as possible, to interpret and apply national procedural rules governing the exercise of rights of action in a way that enables natural and legal persons to challenge before the courts the legality of any decision or other national measure relative to the application to them of a Community act of general application, by pleading the invalidity of such an act. It is in fact for the Member States to establish a system of legal remedies and procedures which ensures respect for the right of individuals to effective judicial protection as regards rights resulting from Union Law.[52]

Therefore, this group picked up the case law of the Court by considering the need for stronger integration in the matter of judicial protection. This position seems to be the origin of Article I-29(1)(2) of the Constitution.[53]

Others within the discussion circle considered the conditions of admissibility established in Article 230(4) too restrictive for proceedings by individuals against measures of general application. Some of the solutions proposed were to substitute the formula 'of direct and individual concern' for one of following options:[54]

(a) Separate the two conditions (direct or individual concern);
(b) Replace 'and individual' with 'and affects his legal situation';
(c) Maintain the current wording and add 'or against a measure of general application which is of direct concern to him without entailing any implementing measure';
(d) Leave the current wording for legislative acts and allow referral to the ECJ for regulatory acts when the applicant is directly *or* individually concerned; or
(e) Leave the current wording but give individuals the right to appeal against legislative acts of the Union which do not entail any implementing measure, when the applicant is directly *or* individually concerned.

Eventually the wording of Article 230(4) was changed as follows:

> Any natural or legal person may, under the same conditions, institute proceedings against an act addressed to that person or which is of direct and individual concern to him or her, and against a regulatory act which is of direct concern to him or her and does not entail implementing measures.[55]

Our first remark regarding the amendments introduced by the Constitutional Treaty in Article 230(4) of the EC relates to the replacement of the word 'decision' by 'act'. This was in accordance with the case law of the ECJ, which held that measures were acts, within the meaning of Article 230(4), depending on their substance and not their form. Any measure with binding legal effects and capable of affecting the

[52] CONV 636/03 (n 47), para 18, p 6.
[53] See below.
[54] See CONV 636/03 (n 47), para 19, p 7.
[55] Art III-365(4) Constitutional Treaty.

interest of the applicant is an act or decision, which may be subject to an action under Article 230. Therefore, the general rule under the Constitution is, as it was previously, that an individual who challenges an act not addressed to him or her must show that he or she is directly and individually concerned by it. The same conditions are applicable when the challenged act is a European law or framework law.

The second remark relates to the most important amendment introduced to Article 230(4) by the Constitutional Treaty:

> Any natural or legal person may . . . institute proceedings against . . . a regulatory act which is of direct concern to him or her and does not entail implementing measures.

The aim of this provision is to give standing to individuals negatively affected by the Union's self-executing regulations; this means regulations that impose prohibitions upon individuals without giving rise to national implementation measures challengeable before national courts (recently, the *UPA* and *Jégo-Quéré* cases). This provision puts an end to those problematic cases in which the individual is directly concerned by a regulation but does not fulfil the condition of individual concern according to the ECJ's case law. These are cases in which the individual concerned must infringe the general measure in order to gain access to a national judge, because he or she does not have standing before the ECJ in an annulment action. Whether or not the Constitutional Treaty enters into force, the applicant would obtain standing by proving that he or she is directly concerned simply by a regulatory act, which does not entail national implementing measures.[56]

A final remark on Article III-365(4) relates to the wording of 'a regulatory act', which was chosen instead of 'an act of general application'. Both options were analysed by the discussion circle. The first was preferred because it made a clear distinction between legislative and regulatory acts. By doing so, the constitutional provision reflects a restrictive approach to proceedings by private individuals against legislative acts, where the condition 'of direct and individual concern' still applies, and a more open approach concerning proceedings against regulatory acts.

One problem with the terminology used in that provision could be the conceptual delimitation of a regulatory act. Article I-33(1)(4) of the Constitutional Treaty establishes a negative definition of a regulatory act as a non-legislative act of general application for the implementation of legislative acts and of certain specific provisions of the Constitution. It is clear from the report of the discussion circle that the concept of regulatory acts within the meaning of Article III-365(4) is to be understood as covering not just regulations but also decisions of general application. Furthermore, a regulatory act within the meaning of Article III-365(4) may be a delegated regulation or an implementing act. To complicate matters further, the

[56] On the meaning of 'direct concern' the Court said: 'For a person to be directly concerned by a Community measure, the latter must directly affect the legal situation of the individual and leave no discretion to the addressees of that measure who are entrusted with the task of implementing it, such implementation being purely automatic and resulting from Community rules without the application of other intermediate rules' (n 11).

delimitation of a regulatory act within the meaning of Article III-365(4), the provision contained in Article I-35(3) adds that:

> The Council of Ministers and the Commission, in particular in the cases referred to in Articles I-36 and I-37, and the European Central Bank in the specific cases provided for in the Constitution, shall adopt European regulations and decisions.

It is submitted that this provision contains an open clause on the meaning of delegated regulations which extends the meaning of the term 'a regulatory act' within Article III-365(4) of the Constitutional Treaty.[57]

What is the rationale behind these changes in the wording of Article 230(4)? What is behind the wording of Article III-365(4) of the Constitution? Two causes of tension can be seen in this provision: on the one hand, the need to draft the provision in accordance with the second part of the Constitutional Treaty, which contains the Charter of Fundamental Rights, specifically the right to effective judicial protection, and, on the other, the need to shield primary legislation from challenges by individuals.

Currently, regulations and directives constitute the primary legislation of the Union, and the ECJ has interpreted the rule of standing in Article 230(4) being aware that Member States do not provide a general and unconditional judicial remedy against legislative acts.[58] The Constitutional Treaty establishes a hierarchy of norms that will help to clarify which norm of primary legislation should be preserved from challenges by individuals. According to the Constitutional Treaty, individuals could have standing to challenge a 'regulation' that does not need a national implementing measure if they are directly concerned by the regulation. However, they could not challenge a European law or European framework law even if they are directly concerned by that law. Individuals would need to be directly and individually concerned by a European law in order to attain the standing required for its challenge.

4. Modifications to the Rule of Standing of Private Parties and the Action for Failure to Act

Article III-367 of the Constitutional Treaty contains the procedure for failure to act with two modifications: one direct modification in the wording of this provision (the extension of this action to bodies and agencies acts), and another indirect modification regarding the requirements for individuals and legal persons to appeal against a failure to act.

[57] See ch 1.

[58] For instance, in Germany and Spain, direct judicial protection is only granted against administrative acts of general application. As against acts of the legislature only an extraordinary legal remedy is admissible at the German Constitutional Court (Verfassungsbeschwerde) and at the Spanish Constitutional Court (Recurso de amparo). Both remedies require that the plaintiff be 'directly, individually and presently concerned by the contested law'. See Schwarze (2004) 288.

This action has been considered the other side of the coin of the action for annulment,[59] with private parties being in the same position to assert their rights before the CFI. Therefore, the Court has interpreted Article 232 of the EC with reference to Article 230 of that Treaty, because both provisions describe one and the same method of recourse:[60]

> Just as the fourth paragraph of Article 173 [Article 230 EC] allows individuals to bring an action for annulment against a measure of an institution not addressed to them provided that the measure is of direct and individual concern to them, the third paragraph of Article 175 [Article 232 EC] must be interpreted as also entitling them to bring an action for failure to act against an institution which they claim has failed to adopt a measure which would have concerned them in the same way. The possibility for individuals to assert their rights should not depend upon whether the institution concerned has acted or failed to act.[61]

The conditions in Article III-367 of the Constitutional Treaty are: first, the institution or body concerned must be under an obligation to act; secondly, the institution or body must have been called to act; thirdly, if within two months of being so called the institution or body has not acted, the action can be brought before the Court within a further period of two months.

This section analyses the impact of reform of the rule on the standing of private parties by the Constitutional Treaty upon the action for failure to act that individuals and legal persons could take; that is, the indirect modification mentioned above. The extension of the action for failure to act to Union bodies and agencies will be dealt with in the next section.

As we saw in previous sections, the rule of standing of individuals and legal persons under the Constitutional Treaty remains the same as it was under the EC in terms of challenging an act not addressed to them. They must prove they are directly and individually concerned by the act. However, the requirement has varied when individuals or legal persons have wished to challenge a self-executing regulation, that is 'a regulation which directly imposes prohibitions upon individuals without giving rise to national implementation measures challengeable before national courts'.[62] Under the Constitutional Treaty, individuals and legal persons would be able to challenge a 'regulatory act' by proving that they are directly concerned by its provisions.[63] Nevertheless, it is difficult to imagine an individual or legal person requesting a declaration from an institution or body from the CFI on infringement of the legal order because it did not enact a regulatory act that would impose restrictions upon the freedom of the applicant. Therefore, the modification of the rule of standing of private parties in Article III-365(4), in theory applicable to Article III-367(3) of the Constitutional Treaty, would not have any effect in practical terms upon the standing required to bring an action for failure to act before the CFI.

59 Albors-Llorens (1996) 209.
60 Case 15/70 *Chevalley v Commission* [1970] ECR 975, para 6.
61 Case C-68/95 *T Port* [1996] ECR I-6065, para 59.
62 Ladenburger (2005a) 176.
63 Constitutional Treaty, Art III-365(4).

5. Conclusions

The case law of the Community courts shows the minimal options that, currently, an individual or legal person has to obtain *locus standi* for challenging the validity of Union legislation, whether or not he or she is directly and individually concerned by the measure. The modifications introduced by the Constitutional Treaty represent a small variation to the current scenario. However, the elimination of the condition of being 'individually concerned' in order to challenge a European regulation that does not imply implementing measures for the Member States might help to end those cases in which the right to effective judicial protection of the applicant was *de facto* violated (*UPA* and *Jegó-Queré* cases).

The solution adopted by the Constitutional Treaty helps to solve a legal lacuna that was difficult to justify: the right of an individual to challenge a regulation which impinges on his or her legal status and does not entail implementing measures by a Member State.

The idea behind the Constitutional Treaty is that it falls to national judges to interpret their procedural law in order to satisfy the right to effective judicial protection of individuals.[64] In spite of the Charter of Fundamental Rights and the efforts towards the democratisation of the Union via civil society's and citizens' participation in decision-making processes, in the field of judicial protection, citizens and legal persons are still non-privileged applicants.

III. THE EXTENSION OF ARTICLES III-365 AND III-367 TO UNION BODIES AND AGENCIES INCLUDING EUROPOL AND EUROJUST

So far, the standing of natural and legal persons who appeal against the validity of the acts of an institution has been the object of discussion. Nonetheless, the Constitutional Treaty has introduced new provisions that extend the jurisdiction of the Court to review the legality of the EU's agencies and acts of other bodies. The Court will also have jurisdiction to review their failure to act.[65] This section analyses the implications of those provisions. To this end, we have classified the EU's agencies into three groups depending on their tasks: data-collecting agencies, regulatory agencies and executive agencies. The implications of the constitutional modifications are different for these three groups and for Europol and Eurojust, which do not fit into any of these groups. Therefore, I will analyse the impact of the constitutional amendment on Europol and Eurojust separately, at the end of the section.

[64] See n 34.

[65] Constitutional Treaty, Arts III-365(1)(5) and III-367.

1. Agencies and Bodies of the Union: General Framework

Before giving a definition of the groups of agencies mentioned above, the general framework of the agencies and bodies of the EU will be introduced. More than 17 agencies and bodies are created under the EC,[66] one under the Euratom Treaty,[67] and four under the second and third pillars of the EU.[68]

Agencies and bodies have certain common characteristics. Most of them were created by a Community Regulation and have legal personality and a certain degree of organisational and financial autonomy. However, there is no single model for a European agency. As was noted above, a classification of agencies into three groups depending on their tasks has been adopted. The first group, data-collecting agencies, is composed of agencies whose main role involves the gathering and provision of specialised information, recommendations and opinions to the Commission and Member States, but not the adoption of individual decisions. An example of this first group is the European Environmental Agency and, recently, the European Railway Agency. The second group is made up of the regulatory agencies, which implement Union regimes established by EU regulations adopting individual decisions, such as the Office for Internal Market Harmonization, the Agency for Evaluation of Medicinal Products and the Community Plan Variety Office.[69]

[66] Almost every time it looks at the OJ of the European Communities one new agency is created, therefore, the following is not an exhaustive enumeration. European Centre for the Development of Vocational Training (Regulation (EEC) No 337/75 of 10 February 1975 [1975] OJ L39/1); European Foundation for the Improvement of Living and Working Conditions (Regulation (EEC) No 1365/75 of 26 May 1975 [1975] OJ L139/1); European Environment Agency (Regulation (EEC) No 1210/90 of 7 May 1990 [1990] OJ L120/1); European Training Foundation (Regulation (EEC) No 1360/90 of 7 May 1990 [1990] OJ L131/1); European Monitoring Centre for Drugs and Drug Addiction (Regulation (EEC) No 302/93 of 8 February 1993 [1993] OJ L36/1); European Agency for the Evaluation of Medicinal Products (Regulation (EEC) 2309/93 of 22 July 1993 [1993] OJ L214/1); OHIM (Regulation (EC) No 40/94 of 20 December 1993 [1994] OJ L11/1); European Agency for Safety and Health at Work (Regulation (EC) No 2062/94 of 18 July 1994 [1994] OJ L216/1); Community Plant Variety Office (Regulation (EC) No 2100/94 of 27 July 1994 [1994] OJ L227/1); Translation Centre for bodies of the European Union (Regulation (EC) No 2965/94 of 28 November 1994 [1994] OJ L314/1); European Monitoring Centre on Racism and Xenophobia (Regulation (EC) No 1035/97 of 2 June 1997 [1997] OJ L151/1); European Agency for Reconstruction (Regulation (EC) No 2454/1999 of 15 November 1999 [1999] OJ L299/1); European Food Safety Authority (Regulation (EC) No 178/2002 of 28 January 2002 [2002] OJ L31/1); European Maritime Safety Agency (Regulation (EC) No 1406/2002 of 27 June 2002 [2002] OJ L208/1); European Aviation Safety Agency (Regulation (EC) No 1592/2002 of 15 July 2002 [2002] OJ L240/1); Executive Agencies to be entrusted with certain tasks in the management of Community programmes (Council Regulation (EC) No 58/2003 of 19 December 2002 laying down the statute for executive agencies to be entrusted with certain tasks in the management of Community programmes [2003] OJ L11/1); European Railway Agency (Regulation (EC) No 881/2004 of 29 April 2004 [2004] OJ L164/1); and Community Fisheries Control Agency (Regulation (EC) No 768/2005 of 26 April 2005 [2005] OJ L128/2001). On European agencies see Chiti (2002).

[67] Euratom Supply Agency, Art 52(2)(b) of the Euratom Treaty (see also the Statutes of the Agency, published in OJEC No 534, 6 December 1958).

[68] European Union Institute for Security Studies (Joint Action of 20 July 2001, OJ [2001] L200/1); European Union Satellite Centre (Joint Action of 20 July 2001, OJ [2001] L200, 25 July 2001). European Police Office-Europol (Convention of 26 July 1995, OJEC No C 316, 27 November 1995); Eurojust (Decision of 28 February 2002 [2002] OJ L63/1).

[69] The White Paper on European Governance included, within the Regulatory Agencies, the European Agency for the Evaluation of Medicinal Products. White Paper on European Governance

Finally, the executive agencies, which were set up as a consequence of the reform of the Commission, are responsible for the management of the non-discretionary part of the Community's programmes. The administrative reform of the Commission highlighted the need to focus the Commission primarily on its institutional task[70] and, therefore, to delegate some of its tasks relating to the management of Community programmes to third parties. The executive agencies were set up to guarantee maximum responsibility and control by the Commission in the implementation of Community programmes. They have legal personality, but reviews of the legality of their acts are carried out by the Commission.[71] The Commission decision may be challenged through an annulment or an action for failure to act before the CFI.[72]

The White Paper on European Governance proposed a framework of conditions for the creation of agencies, focusing on the regulatory agencies under the EC.[73] While a legal framework for executive agencies was under discussion, the White Paper pointed out the need to establish a common set of conditions for the creation, operation and supervision of the regulatory agencies. According to the White Paper, the European Parliament, the Council and the Commission should respect certain criteria and conditions when creating new regulatory agencies. The implementation of the Community's policies would be more effective and controlled within that general framework.[74]

The Commission published a Communication on the Operating Framework for the European Regulatory Agencies, according to which these agencies must be created by a legislative act, which will specify the legal basis for the creation of the

COM (2001) 428 final, 25 July 2001 [2001] OJ C287/1, p 27. However, this Agency does not fulfil one characteristic of that category, which is the power to adopt individual decisions. According to its foundational act, it is for the European Commission to adopt the decision on the authorisation to place a medicinal product for human use and a veterinary medicinal product on the market, based on an expert committee draft decision. The applicant may appeal against the opinion of the committee for refusing its application. This appeal takes place before the final decision is adopted by the Commission (Arts 10, 32 and 73 of its Regulation, n 66). When the final decision is adopted by the Commission the applicant may challenge it before the CFI, via Art 230(4) EC. Although the Committee's opinion was favourable to the applicant, authorising a medicinal product for human use or a veterinary medicinal product, the Commission is not bound by it. In cases in which the Commission delays the adoption of a final decision, despite the Committee report being favourable, the CFI allowed compensation for damage caused to the applicant by the delay, but dismissed the action against the Commission for failure to act (Joined Cases T-344/00 and T-345/00 *CEVA Santé Animale SA y Pharmacia Entreprises SA v Commission* ECR [2003] II-229).

The Commission's Communication on the Operating Framework for the European Regulatory Agencies defined a European regulatory agency and an executive agency as follows: the first is one 'actively involved in exercising the executive function by enacting instruments which contribute to regulating a specific sector', whereas an executive agency is responsible for purely managerial tasks, ie 'assisting the Commission in implementing the Community's financial support programmes': COM (2002) 718 final, pp 3–4.

[70] White Paper on Commission Reform COM (2000) 200, 1 March 2000, p 6. See Craig (2000); Nieto Garrido (2002). For a summary of the administrative reform of the Commission see Harlow (2002) 53–57.

[71] Art 22 of its Regulation (n 66). With regard to the first executive agencies see Craig (2006) pp 43–50.

[72] Art 22(5) of its Regulation and Arts 230(4) and 232 EC.

[73] White Paper on European Governance (n 69), p 27.

[74] *Ibid*, p 35.

agency, its legal personality and its location.[75] The legal framework should also contain a provision establishing a board of appeal to deal with complaints by third parties arising from the decision it adopts prior to judicial control.[76]

2. Judicial Review of Agencies' Acts

Among other aspects to be included in the framework of European Regulatory Agencies adopted by the Commission, it emphasised the need to subject these agencies to an appropriate system of control. This involves not only drafting provisions, on the relationship between the agencies and the Commission, which must reconcile their autonomy with the Commission's ultimate responsibility within the Union system, but also drafting provisions on administrative, political, financial and judicial supervision.[77] In respect of judicial supervision, according to the Commission's Communication on the Operating Framework for the European Regulatory Agencies, the Member States and the institutions should be able to appeal to the Community Courts to rule on any breach of the principle of legality by the agencies. Furthermore, according to the Commission's Communication, it was necessary to provide an appeal mechanism by which interested third parties could apply to the CFI for annulment of the decision taken by an agency or for a declaration on its failure to act.[78]

The White Paper on Governance and the Communication of the Commission on the Operating Framework for the European Regulatory Agency seemed to be at the root of the modifications of Articles 230 and 232 of the EC. These provisions are silent on judicial review of the acts of the agencies. In the current EC, there is no general provision conferring jurisdiction on the Court to review the legality of acts of the agencies. The foundational act of an agency is used to confer powers on the Community Courts in order to review the legality of the agency's acts.[79] However, the foundational act of an agency may be silent on this aspect. An overview of the agencies' regulations reveals that most of them include a provision conferring jurisdiction on the Court. Nonetheless, it is a limited jurisdiction depending on the functions performed by the agency. The following paragraphs discuss the current situation depending on the tasks performed by the agencies.

Firstly, with respect to the data-collecting agencies, whose role involves the gathering and provision of specialised information to the Commission and

[75] COM (2002) 718 final (n 69). The legislative act shall determine the powers and scope of the agency, setting up an administrative board, a director and a board of appeal against the agency's act.

[76] The boards of appeal, currently set up at the OHIM, the Community Plant Variety Office and the European Aviation Safety Agency, would act as an initial internal control prior to any referral to the CFI. *Ibid*, 10.

[77] *Ibid*, 12–13.

[78] *Ibid*, 13.

[79] For example, in Council Regulation No 1035/97 of 2 June 1997 establishing a European Monitoring Centre on Racism and Xenphobia (Art 15) [1997] OJ L151/1; and Regulation No 1406/2002 of the European Parliament and Council of 27 January establishing a European Maritime Safety Agency (Art 8) [2002] OJ L208/1.

Member States, their foundational act (a regulation) usually grants jurisdiction to the Community Courts in disputes on contractual liability 'pursuant to an arbitration clause contained in a contract concluded by the Agency'.[80] In terms of non-contractual liability, the Community Courts will have jurisdiction in disputes relating to compensation for any damage caused by an Agency or its servants in the performance of their duties.[81] This clause is included in most agencies' foundational acts.[82] Therefore, the modifications of Articles 365 and 367 introduced by the Constitutional Treaty, granting jurisdiction to the CFI to review the legality of agencies' acts, is not a significant development from the previous scenario, because these data-collecting agencies do not have the power to adopt individual decisions with legal effects on third parties. It is the Commission that will adopt the acts based on the report provided by an agency. The applicant may challenge the decision adopted by the Commission if he fulfils the standing requirements under Articles 365 and 367 of the Constitutional Treaty.

Secondly, with respect to the regulatory agencies, whose role it is to implement a Union regime and, therefore, have the power to adopt individual decisions, the Constitutional Treaty will establish a general framework in order to enable the review of their acts.[83] Currently, their foundational acts establish boards of appeal against agencies' decisions and grant jurisdiction to the Community Courts to review these appeals, but their provisions on judicial protection of third parties are not uniform. For instance, some of their foundational acts grant standing to the Member States and to the institutions to appeal an agency's decision directly before the CFI, without a previous appeal before the internal board of appeal of the agency,[84] whereas others grant standing to individuals to appeal an agency's decision directly to the CFI.[85] With regard to regulatory agencies, an overview of their foundational acts reveals that the extent of the judicial review of their acts is also different. In most cases, the Community Courts have competence to annul an agency's decision but also, in some cases, to alter that decision.[86] Finally, among the regulatory agencies there is no single rule of standing before the Community Courts. For instance, the Regulation on the European Aviation Safety Agency establishes a rule of standing similar to that contained in Article 230(4) of the EC.[87] However, the Regulation on the Community Trade Mark contains a wider rule of

[80] Council Regulation on the establishment of the European Environment Agency and the European Environment Information and Observation Network (n 66), Art 18(1).

[81] *Ibid*, Art 18(2).

[82] For instance, Regulation establishing a European Maritime Safety Agency (n 66), Art 8; Regulation establishing a European Railway Agency (n 66), Art 34.

[83] OHIM, the European Aviation Safety Agency and the Community Plant Variety Office (n 66).

[84] European Aviation Safety Agency (Art 42 of its Regulation, n 66).

[85] Council Regulation on Community Plant Variety Rights (n 66), Art 74.

[86] Regulation on the Community Trade Mark (n 66), Art 63.

[87] 'Any natural or legal person may appeal against a decision addressed to that person, or against a decision which, although in the form of a decision addressed to another person, is of direct and individual concern to the former. The parties to proceedings may be party to the appeal proceedings.' Art 36 of the European Aviation Safety Agency Regulation (n 66).

standing which includes any party adversely affected by a decision of the Office for Internal Market Harmonization.[88]

Thirdly, with regard to the executive agencies, the amendment of Articles 230 and 232 of the EC by the Constitutional Treaty will not modify the previous situation because the legality of their decisions are subject to the control of the Commission. Article 22 of the Executive Agencies' Regulation[89] establishes an administrative appeal before the Commission on the legality of their acts. Therefore, the final decision is that of the Commission.

3. Standardising the Judicial Review of Acts of the EU's Agencies and Bodies

The lack of democratic and judicial control of bodies such as Europol and Eurojust and the differences in the level of judicial control exercised in respect of the acts of the agencies explain the debate within the discussion circle on the judicial control of bodies and agencies' acts. The aim of the members of the discussion circle was to guarantee the right to effective judicial protection and, in doing so, to fulfil the principle of legality within the EU.[90] The discussion circle suggested standardising the rule of judicial review by making Article 230 of the EC applicable to proceedings contesting the legal acts of all the agencies.[91]

Following the discussion circle's opinion, sections 1 and 5 of Article III-365 of the Constitutional Treaty establish that:

> The Court of Justice shall review the legality of European Laws and frameworks laws, of acts of the Council of Minister, of the Commission and of the European Central Bank . . . It also review the legality of acts of bodies or agencies of the Union intended to produce legal effects vis-à-vis third parties. . . .
>
> Acts setting up bodies and agencies of the Union may lay down specific conditions and arrangements concerning actions brought by natural or legal persons against acts of these bodies or agencies intended to produce legal effects.

An appeal against those acts of the EU's agencies and bodies will be admissible if the applicant fulfils the conditions set out in Article III-365 and if the act is a 'legal act' within the meaning of the case law of the Court.[92] Moreover, the foundational act of an agency or body may establish specific conditions and arrangements concerning actions brought by natural or legal persons against their acts which intend to produce legal effects.[93] For example, the rule of standing for individuals

[88] 'Any party to proceedings adversely affected by a decision may appeal. Any other parties to the proceedings shall be parties to the appeal proceedings as of right.' Art 58 of the Regulation on the Community Trade Mark (n 66).

[89] See n 66.

[90] The effectiveness of the right to judicial protection required, according to the discussion circle, that no contested act of an institution, body or agency escapes the judicial scrutiny of their legality. CONV 636/03 (n 47), para 25, p 9.

[91] CONV 636/03 (n 47), pp 8–10.

[92] An act that produces legal effects vis-à-vis third parties.

[93] Constitutional Treaty, Art III-365(5).

established in Article III-365 could not be applied to challenge the decisions of the Office for Internal Market Harmonization, because its foundational act establishes a wider ranging rule. A foundational act may establish the necessity of challenging an Agency's decision before the internal board of appeal prior to any judicial review[94] or establish the necessity of instituting proceedings before the Commission (eg a requirement established by the Regulation on Executive Agencies of the Union).[95]

Furthermore, the Constitutional Treaty not only standardised judicial review to ensure the legality of EU agencies' and bodies' acts, but also to review their failure to act. Article III-367 of the Constitutional Treaty, after establishing the action against the institutions for failure to act, reads: 'This Article shall apply, under the same conditions, to bodies, offices and agencies of the Union which fail to act.'[96]

This provision introduces an innovation recognising the jurisdiction of the Court to make a declaration in respect of EU agencies, bodies and offices' failure to act. As was seen above, the regulations of some agencies[97] include a provision granting jurisdiction to the Court to review the legality of acts of the agencies but not usually to rule upon their failure to act. For example, the Office for Internal Market Harmonization Regulation and the Community Plan Variety Office Regulation do not grant jurisdiction to the Community Courts to rule upon their failure to act.[98] The case law on both Offices shows that an appeal before the Community Courts, even before their boards of appeal, must be against decisions, not omissions.[99] An exception is the European Aviation Safety Agency, whose Regulation grants jurisdiction to the Community Courts to make a declaration for its failure to act.[100]

Taking this scenario into account, the modification introduced by Article III-367 of the Constitutional Treaty becomes relevant. It is not only the logical consequence of the reference to agencies and bodies within the action for annulment (Article III-365), being the other side of the coin for failure to act, but it will also fill a lacuna in the field of judicial protection. Currently there is no legal recourse for situations in which agencies do not take a decision or delay a decision without justification. Article III-367 of the Constitutional Treaty provides an answer to these cases in which an appeal before the Commission for failure to act was not possible, because

[94] European Aviation Safety Agency Regulation, Art 35; Regulation on Community Plant Variety Rights, Art 67; European Agency for the Evaluation of Medicinal Products Regulation, Art 31; Regulation on the Community Trade Mark, Art 57. All quoted at n 66.

[95] See n 66. See also Council Regulation establishing a European Agency for Safety and Health at Work (n 66), Art 22.

[96] Conditions relating to, firstly, the admissibility of the action (only when the agency or body has first been called upon to act and, after two months have elapsed, it persists in not defining its position) and, secondly, the rule of standing and its conditions imposed by Art III-365(4) Constitutional Treaty upon private parties.

[97] Regulatory agencies whose acts produce legal effects on third parties (n 83).

[98] Both Regulations speak of appeals against resolutions of the Agencies but they do not say anything about appeals against Agencies' omissions. See the Regulation on Community Plant Variety Rights, Art 73, and the Regulation on the Community Trade Mark, Art 63, both at n 66.

[99] Case T-122/01 *Best Buy Concepts Inc v OAMI* [2003] ECR II-2235; Case T-334/01 *MFE Marienfelde GmbH v OAMI* [2004] ECR 2787.

[100] European Aviation Safety Agency Regulation (n 66), Art 41.

the final decision was adopted by the agency and not by the Commission. In cases where the final decision is taken by the Commission, the mention of Article III-367 and reference to agencies and other bodies will have no effect. An action for failure to act will be a common action against an omission of the Commission or an agency, whereas currently the Commission is the defendant in proceedings for failure to act.[101]

4. Europol and Eurojust's Decision and its Judicial Review by the Community Courts

As we saw above, the White Paper on European Governance and the Commission's Communication were at the root of the extension of the Community Courts' jurisdiction. During the Convention, several documents in the field of Justice and Home Affairs expressed concern about Europol's activities, which are subject neither to democratic control by the European Parliament[102] nor to judicial control by the Community Courts.[103] Moreover, the control of Europol's activities by national courts was considered an option, but a very controversial one which was not as clear as the current controls exercised by national parliaments.[104] A large number of Convention members wanted to see the Community Court's power extended to control Europol's activities and even Eurojust's activities, and possible extensions in the future, with the introduction of an appeal for private individuals in these areas. To that end, various models were put forward for stricter control of these joint bodies but, eventually, the elimination of the pillars structure and the modification of the current Articles 230 and 232 of the EC was the option adopted by the drafters of the Constitutional Treaty in order to submit Europol's activities to judicial review.[105]

[101] Eg Case T-105/96 *Pharos SA v Commission* ECR [1998] II-285; Case T-212/99 *Intervet International BV v Commission* ECR [2002] II-1445; Cases T-344/00 and T-345/00 *CEVA Santé Animale SA and Pharmacia Enterprises SA versus Commission* ECR [2003] II-229.

[102] Currently, the adoption of a common position by the Council does not require consultation with the European Parliament (Art 32 TEU) in spite of a Protocol that amended the Europol Convention with the aim of introducing Parliamentary control on the actions of Europol (the Council Act of 27 November 2003 drew up a Protocol amending the Europol Convention on the basis of Art 43(1) of that Convention [2004] OJ C2/1). This Protocol imposed a duty on the President of the Council, assisted by the Director of Europol, to inform the European Parliament or discuss general questions relating to Europol with the Parliament (Art 34(2) Europol Convention). Prior to this Protocol, the Europol Convention established that the President of the Council must forward a special report to the European Parliament each year (n 68), Art 34.

[103] *Justice and Home Affairs—Progress Report and General Problems* CONV 69/02, 31 May 2002, pp 10–11. And *Note of the Plenary Meeting*, Brussels, 6 and 7 June 2002 CONV 97/02, 19 June 2002, pp 4–6.

[104] CONV 97/02, *ibid*, p 4; CONV 69/02, *ibid*, p 10.

[105] Among the models discussed by the European Parliament in a special parliamentary committee was the integration of the third pillar into a Community arrangement under the supervision of the Commission or the creation of a new High Representative of the Union acting as an interlocutor for national parliaments for third pillar issues and responsible for the proper functioning of those bodies. CONV 97/02 (*ibid*), p 5.

What is clear from the Convention's documents is that the strengthening of Europol went hand in hand with increased parliamentary and judicial control of its activities.[106] Article III-276 of the Constitutional Treaty reflects these concerns when it states that European laws shall lay down the procedures for the scrutiny of Europol's activities by the European Parliament together with national parliaments. However, what is more important from the perspective of private parties' judicial protection is the extension of the Court's jurisdiction to review its actions and omissions. Taking into account Europol's functions of collection, storage, processing and exchange of information, the provision in Article III-367 authorising the ECJ to review omissions on the part of the EU's bodies and agencies becomes functional.[107] The data subject may request access to his data stored by Europol and request its correction or deletion.[108] If the enquirer is not satisfied with Europol's reply he may challenge it before the CFI once he has fulfilled the conditions imposed by Articles III-365 and III-367.

Currently, the data subject has the right to ask Europol that his data be deleted when proceedings against him are dropped or when he is acquitted.[109] But, if the enquirer is not satisfied with Europol's reply or if there is no reply within three months, the only option is to refer the matter to a Joint Supervisory Body established by the Europol Convention.[110]

The same situation applies to Eurojust's processed data. Eurojust was set up by a Council Decision of 28 February 2002 on the basis of Articles 31 and 34(2)(c) of the TEU. This Decision developed the fight against serious organised crime, begun in the Tampere European Council summit of 15 and 16 October 1999. The Tampere conclusions set up a unit (Eurojust) composed of prosecutors, magistrates or police officers of equivalent competence, detached from each Member State according to its legal system.[111] Eurojust's task is to facilitate the proper co-ordination of national prosecuting authorities and of supporting criminal investigations in organised crime cases, based on Europol's analysis, as well as to co-operate closely

106 Art III-276 of the Constitution does not strengthen Europol competences but allows a European law to do so. However, that provision establishes one limit on the European law: the application of the coercive measure shall be the exclusive responsibility of the competent national authority (s 3). This was a limitation imposed by the Europol Convention in its amended version by Council Act of 28 November 2002 [2002] OJ C312/1 drawing up a Protocol amending the Convention on the establishment of a European Police Office (Europol Convention) and the Protocol on the privileges and immunities of Europol, the members of its organs, the deputy director and the employees of Europol, Art 3(a)(1), [2002] OJ C312/1.

107 Although Europol may participate in joint investigation teams, mainly assisting in all activities, and exchange information with all members of the joint investigation team, its officials cannot take part in the taking of any coercive measures (Art 3(a), n 106).

108 Europol Convention (n 68), Arts 19 and 20.

109 Europol Convention (n 68), Art 8(5).

110 *Ibid*, Art 20(4). A Joint Supervisory Body, with the function of reviewing the activities of Europol in order to ensure that the rights of the individual are not violated by the storage, processing and utilisation of the data held by Europol, is established by Art 24 of Europol's Convention. It is composed of members or representatives of each of the national supervisory bodies (not more than two for each Member State).

111 Tampere European Council of 15 and 16 October 1999. Presidency Conclusions, point 46, available at http://www.europarl.eu.int/summits/tam_en.htm.

with the European Judicial Network, particularly in order to simplify the execution of rogatory letters.[112] Insofar as it is necessary to achieve its objectives, Eurojust may process the personal data of someone subject to a criminal investigation or prosecution for one or more of the types of crime described by the Council Decision.[113] Every person has the right to access personal data concerning him or her in the possession of Eurojust and to ask for its correction and deletion if it is incorrect or incomplete.[114] If access is denied or the applicant is not satisfied with the reply given to his or her request, or no answer is given, he may appeal against that decision before a Joint Supervisory Body.[115] As we saw with the Europol Convention, the decision of the Joint Supervisory Body is final and binding on Eurojust.

The Constitutional Treaty not only improves parliamentary control on Eurojust but also improves judicial control. According to the Constitutional Treaty, a European law will determine Eurojust's structure, operation, field of action, tasks and the arrangements for involving the European Parliament and national parliaments in the evaluation of Eurojust's activities.[116] Currently, control of Eurojust's activities by the European Parliament is very limited. The Eurojust Decision imposed a duty on the Presidency of the Council to forward a report to the European Parliament on the work carried out by Eurojust and on the activities of the Joint Supervisory Body.[117]

Judicial control of the activities of Eurojust is also limited (eg Case C-160/03 *Kingdom of Spain v Eurojust*).[118] The Council Decision on Eurojust establishes that national courts are competent to determine the liability of Eurojust for any damage caused to an individual which results from the unauthorised or incorrect processing of data by it.[119] Within the Constitutional Treaty, the Community Courts will have jurisdiction to review the activities of Eurojust. As is the case with Europol, Eurojust's activities are included in Articles III-365 and III-367 of the Constitutional Treaty, conferring jurisdiction on the Court to declare the annulment of bodies' and agencies' activities or their failure to act. Furthermore, under the Constitutional Treaty, Europol and Eurojust's activities concerning data processing may fall under the supervision of the European Data Protection

[112] *Ibid.*

[113] Computer crime, fraud and corruption and any criminal offence affecting the European Community's financial interests, the laundering of the proceeds of crime, environmental crime and participation in a criminal organisation, Art 4(1)(b) Council Decision on Eurojust of 28 February 2002 (n 68). This Decision was modified by Council Decision 2003/659/JHA of 18 June 2003 that aims to bring into line the management of Eurojust general budget with the general Finalcial Regulation of the European Communities.

[114] Council Decision on Eurojust (n 68), Arts 19 and 20.

[115] The Joint Supervisory Body collectively monitors Eurojust's activities to ensure that the processing of personal data is carried out correctly. It is composed of one judge from each Member State. The judges should not be members of Eurojust. Council Decision on Eurojust (n 68), Art 23.

[116] Constitutional Treaty, Art III-273(1).

[117] Council Decision on Eurojust (n 68), Art 32.

[118] Case C 160/03 *Kingdom of Spain v Eurojust* [2005] ECR I-2077, in which the annulment action based on Art 230 EC was declared inadmissible because Eurojust's acts are not Community acts. Taking into account other factors (eg the Union as a community of law), AG Pollares Maduro was in favour of the admissibility of the case.

[119] *Ibid*, Art 24.

Supervisor. The European Data Protection Supervisor is an independent supervisory authority responsible for ensuring that the fundamental rights and freedoms of natural persons, and in particular their right to privacy, are respected by the Community institutions and bodies.[120] The European Law on Europol and Eurojust or the norms of legislative character that will regulate their powers and activities, may decide that these bodies should be under the supervision of the European Data Protection Supervisor. In that case, the legislative measure will have to decide what to do with the Joint Supervisory Bodies of Europol and Eurojust, whose role would be redundant. The European Data Protection Supervisor's decisions may be challenged before the Community Courts.[121]

IV MEMBER STATES' OBLIGATION TO PROVIDE APPROPRIATE REMEDIES TO ENSURE EFFECTIVE LEGAL PROTECTION IN THE FIELDS COVERED BY UNION LAW

1. Origin of the Provision

As we saw above, with respect to the reform of Article 230(4) of the EC, the discussion circle was divided into two groups. One group was in favour of a reform of its wording, which would allow individuals or legal persons to challenge a regulation when they were directly concerned by it if that regulation envisaged any further implementing measure. The other group had in mind the present decentralised system based on the subsidiarity principle, according to which the defence of individuals' rights would be ensured by national courts. For this group it was not necessary to make any substantive changes to Article 230(4). They thought that the Constitution should mention explicitly that:

> In accordance with the principle of loyal cooperation as interpreted by the Court of Justice, national courts are required, so far as possible, to interpret and apply national procedural rules governing the exercise of rights of action in a way that enables natural and legal persons to challenge before the courts the legality of any decision or other national measure relative to the application to them of a Community act of general application, by pleading the invalidity of such an act. It is in fact for the Member States to establish a system of legal remedies and procedures which ensures respect for the right of individuals to effective judicial protection as regards rights resulting from Union Law.[122]

This seems to be the origin of Article I-29(1)(2) of the Constitutional Treaty, which reads: 'Member States shall provide remedies sufficient to ensure effective legal protection in the fields covered by Union law.'

[120] Regulation (EC) No 45/2001 of the European Parliament and of the Council of 18 December 2000 on the protection of individuals with regard to the processing of personal data by the Community institutions and bodies and on the free movement of such data, Art 41 [2001] OJ L8/1.

[121] *Ibid*, Art 32.

[122] CONV 636/03 (n 47), para 18, p 6.

Nonetheless, this provision is directed at Member States generally and not only national courts. Therefore, this section analyses the possible implications of that provision for Member States, which, it is submitted, is more important than the principle of loyal co-operation under Article 10 EC.[123] Before analysing the implications of this, it is worth briefly commenting on the provision's wording. The draft of the Constitutional Treaty adopted by the Convention was worded differently in its English version than the current version signed in Rome in October 2004. Originally it read: 'Member States shall provide *rights of appeal* sufficient to ensure effective legal protection in the field of Union law.'

The Draft Constitutional Treaty adopted by the Convention was originally in French and was translated into the EU's official languages. The English version implied rights of appeal before national courts, whereas the aim of the original French draft was wider, providing for remedies not just before courts but also administrative authorities.[124]

2. Possible Implications of Article I-29(1)(2) of the Constitutional Treaty for Member States

The wording of Article I-29(1)(2) of the Constitutional Treaty (addressed not just to the national courts but to administrative authorities and referring to administrative and judicial appeals) raises the question of whether Article I-29(1)(2) of the Constitutional Treaty only consolidates pre-existing case-law, on the right of every person to obtain an effective remedy in a competent court against measures that he or she considers to be contrary to a provision of EU law, or whether it sets up a basis for the future development of the State liability action.

In the *Francovich* case, the ECJ, acting as a quasi-legislator, created the principle of State liability, in cases where the State had not fulfilled the duties imposed by Community law.[125] To that end, the ECJ recalled that the Community has a legal system, created by the EEC, which is integrated into the Member States' legal systems and which their national courts are bound to apply. Furthermore, the subjects of that legal system are not just Member States but also their nationals.[126] According to the Court, the effectiveness of Community law depends on the Member States' correct fulfilment of their obligations. This implies that individuals should be able 'to obtain redress when their rights are infringed by a breach of Community law for which a Member State can be held responsible'.[127]

[123] See below.

[124] 'Les États membres établissent les voies de recours nécessaires pour assurer une protection juridictionnelle effective dans les domaines couverts par le droit de l'Union', Art I-28 (1)(2), *Projet de traité établissant une Constitution pour l'Europe*, CIG 50/03, 25 November 2003.

[125] Joined Cases C-6/90 and 9/90 *A Francovich and D Bonifaci and others v Italian Republic* [1991] ECR I-5357. On this topic see, *inter alia*, Alonso García (1997); Cobreros Mendazona (1995); Guichot (2001).

[126] Case 26/62 *Van Gend en Loos v Nederlandse Administratie der Belastingen* [1963] ECR 3; (1963) 1 *CML Rev* 82–92.

[127] *Francovich* (n 125), para 33.

Furthermore, the liability of States is based not only on the principle of effectiveness of Community law, but also on the principle of loyal co-operation under Article 10 of the EC. This principle requires that Member States take all appropriate measures to ensure the fulfilment of their obligations under Community law. According to theECJ, 'among these is the obligation to nullify the unlawful consequences of a breach of Community law',[128] which means making good loss and damage to private parties caused by the unlawful acts of the State.

The principle of loyal co-operation was also relied on by the Court in the *UPA* case to hold that the principle imposes an obligation on national courts to interpret their procedural rules in such a way as to satisfy the right to effective judicial protection of private parties.[129] According to the ECJ, the Treaties established a complete system of legal remedies and procedures designed to ensure judicial review of the legality of institutions' acts and national courts should interpret national procedural rules in a way that facilitates the indirect challenge of the Union's regulation through a preliminary ruling.[130] Therefore, prior to the drafting of the Constitutional Treaty, national courts were obliged to find a way of guaranteeing private parties' right to effective judicial protection.[131]

Article I-29(1)(2) guarantees this right, and goes further than the obligation imposed by Article 10 of the EC.[132] It imposes a particular obligation on Member States that is more important and specific than the duty to interpret national procedural rules according to the *pro actione* principle. It is addressed not only to the judiciary but also to the legislature and executive.[133] The question is whether infringement of this provision by a Member State may provoke an action for damages before the ECJ, assuming that the requirements of the State's liability were fulfilled.[134]

Article I-29(1)(2) establishes a particular obligation for Member States that grants a legal right to the individual because it is a provision that has direct effect.[135]

[128] *Francovich* (n 125), para 36.

[129] On the principle of loyal co-operation see Due (1992) 15–35.

[130] Case C-50/00 *Unión de Pequeños Agricultores v Council* (n 2), paras 38–42.

[131] The ECJ held that 'In accordance with the principle of sincere co-operation laid down in Art 10 EC, national courts are required, so far as possible, to interpret and apply national procedural rules governing the exercise of rights of action in a way that enables natural and legal persons to challenge before the courts the legality of a Community act of general application, by pleading the invalidity of such an act'. Case C-263/02 *Commission v Jégo-Quéré & Cie SA* (n 2), para 32.

[132] It is accepted that the term 'Member States' in Art 10 EC applies also to state bodies such as the judiciary: Craufurd Smith (1999) 296.

[133] The *Francovich* case made no distinction with respect to whether the loss or damage ensues from an infringement attributable to omissions of the legislator or of the executive. AG Tesauro's Opinion, Cases C-46/93 and C-48/93 *Brasserie du Pêcheur SA v Bundesrepublik Deutschaland and the Queen v Secretary of State for Transport, ex parte Factortame Ltd and others* [1996] ECR I-1029, para 35.

[134] 'Community law confers a right to reparation where three conditions are met: the rule of law infringed must be intended to confer rights on individuals; the breach must be sufficiently serious; and there must be a direct causal link between the breach of the obligation resting on the State and the damage sustained by the injured parties': Joined Cases C-46/93 and C-48/93 *Brasserie du Pêcheur SA v Bundersrepublik Deutschland and The Queen v Secretary of State for Transport, ex parte Factortame Ltd and others*, *ibid*, para 51.

[135] Condition for State liability established by the *Francovich* case (n 125), para 40. On direct effect see Ross (1993).

It is submitted that the provision imposes an obligation on Member States to achieve a particular outcome.[136] The question is whether or not that provision implies discretionary powers conferred on Member States. It is submitted that the obligation to provide 'remedies sufficient' does not imply discretionary powers for Member States; it is an indeterminate concept that should be determined on a case-by-case basis in each Member State. Although it might be thought that Article I-29(1)(2) contains discretionary powers in favour of Member States, applying the manifest and serious breach test, the obligation has a clear and precise content.[137] In the Opinion of AG Tesauro:

> It has to be acknowledged that there will be State liability in principle whenever the State is constrained under Community law to achieve a precise result. This is precisely the case, as already held by the Court in *Francovich*, where there is a failure to implement a directive within the prescribed period, provided, of course, that the other conditions set out by the Court are fulfilled. *But this is also the case with all other provisions, including those of the Treaty, that are confined to imposing on the Member States precise, clearly identified obligations to refrain from some conduct (suffice it to mention the prohibition on the introduction of new customs duties laid down by Article 12 and, more generally, all the standstill clauses) which concurrently give rise to a right for individuals. So, in all those sectors and with regard to all those provisions which do not give Member States a significant margin of discretion, in the sense described above, there must be held to be liability and an obligation in damages simply on account of the infringement of a Community provision which confers on individuals a right which is precise and whose subject-matter is determinable; no other factors may be taken into account.*[138]

With respect to the meaning of 'remedies sufficient', it is submitted that the remedies must be effective to guarantee the right to effective judicial protection, but it is up to each Member State to give this term precise content.

Article I-29(2) contains a base for an action for damages that individuals may use when a national judge, legislator or executive does not establish the legal remedies guaranteeing their right to effective judicial protection. This provision introduces into primary law the ECJ's case law on the Member States' obligation to guarantee the right to effective judicial protection, extending that obligation to all public powers of the State.

[136] At this point it is appropriate to recall AG Tesauro's Opinion in the *Brasserie* and *Factortame* cases whereby, in order to establish the liability of the German and British Member States, he held that what is more important than the rank of the provision infringed by the Member State (Treaty or secondary legislation) and the measure (legislative or executive) that infringes it, is the discretion, that 'can and must be the decisive factor' (n 133), para 78. And 'the greater or lesser degree of discretion available to the State coincides, moreover—at least in most cases—with the greater or lesser degree of clarity and precision of the obligation to which [the Member State] is subject': *ibid.* On the conditions for State liability see Craig and De Búrca (2003) 259–68; see also Guichot (2001) 509–63.

[137] With regard to the meaning of a manifest and serious breach, AG Tesauro defined them in the following terms: 'obligations whose content is clear and precise in every respect but have not been complied with; the Court's case-law has provided sufficient clarification; the national authorities' interpretation of the relevant Community provisions in their legislative activity (or inactivity) is manifestly wrong' (n 133), para 84.

[138] AG Tesauro's Opinion (n 133), paras 79–80 (emphasis added).

V. EXTENSION OF THE COURT OF JUSTICE'S COMPETENCE TO THE PRESENT THIRD PILLAR

One conclusion reached by Working Group X of the Convention on Freedom, Security and Justice was that the limited jurisdiction of the Court was no longer acceptable with respect to acts adopted in areas that directly affect the fundamental rights of individuals, such as police co-operation and judicial co-operation in criminal matters.[139] One characteristic of the pillars structure, introduced by the TEU, has been the exclusion or limitation of the Community Courts' jurisdiction: in general terms, the second and the third pillars of the Union remained separate from the Community institutional and legal structure. However, one feature of the Constitutional Treaty is the 'communitarisation' of the pillars: the second pillar within 'Union external action' and the third under the heading of 'Freedom, Security and Justice', which includes police and judicial co-operation in criminal matters.[140] This 'communitarisation' means, firstly, the extension of the Court's jurisdiction to third pillar matters and, secondly, its regulation through the same normative instruments and procedures for adoption, with the intervention of the European Parliament, as in the first pillar.

The aim of this section is to analyse the extent to which the Constitutional Treaty grants jurisdiction on the ECJ in the area of Freedom, Security and Justice and its implications for Member States. To that end, this section deals, firstly, with the evolution of the area of Home Affairs and Justice under EU law and the extension of the Court's jurisdiction in those matters. Secondly, it analyses the Convention proposals in the area of Freedom, Security and Justice. Thirdly, it goes on to look at the provisions that were eventually included in the Constitutional Treaty which grant jurisdiction on the ECJ in the area of Freedom, Security and Justice.

It is worth noting that, according to the Conclusions of the Presidency of the Council of the European Union (Brussels, June 2007, p 16, n 2), the content of Title VI of EC, on police and judicial cooperation in criminal matters, will be included in the Title in the area of freedom, security and justice in the modified EC, which will be called the Treaty on the Functioning of the Union. Therefore, it will broaden the current competence of the Court of Justice in the present third pillar matters.

1. Freedom, Security and Justice in the Treaties: Evolution

To build an internal market without frontiers has been the aim of the Community since the very beginning. Nonetheless, the lack of agreement among those who want to exercise control over population movements into and within their territories (Ireland and UK) and those who perceived the Community as an area

[139] Final Report of Working Group X on Freedom, Security and Justice CONV 426/02, Brussels, 2 December 2002, p 25.

[140] Constitutional Treaty, Part Three, Title III, Chapter IV.

free of frontiers, in which Member States would cease to impose internal border controls, caused delays in the development of Article 14 of the EC.[141] This provision provides for the establishment of an internal market which 'shall comprise an area without internal frontiers in which the free movement of goods, persons, services and capital is ensured in accordance with the provision of this Treaty'.[142] It was not until 1995 that the Commission adopted proposals for two Directives based on this provision, one concerning the elimination of controls on crossing frontiers and another concerning the right of third-country nationals to travel within the Community.[143] Before those proposals, five of the Member States decided to do away with checks at their shared borders and co-operate on matters of visa policy by signing the Schengen Agreement of 1985 and the Schengen Implementing Convention of 1990.[144] That same year, the so-called Dublin Convention determining State responsibility for examining applications for asylum lodged in one of the Member States, was also signed.

As we know, the TEU introduced the pillars structure: the second pillar concerned Common Foreign and Security Policy (CFSP) and the third pillar dealt with co-operation in Justice and Home Affairs (JHA). The pillars remained separate from the Community institutional and legal structure. Dehousse suggests that their exclusion was designed by the negotiators as a way of ensuring that 'the institutional bridges set up between the Community and the intergovernmental pillars should not lead to a complete absorption of the latter into the former'.[145]

Originally both pillars were governed by the intergovernmental method, which required unanimity in decision-making using the instruments of classic international law (resolutions, joint positions and conventions), the implementation of which by the Member States was outside the jurisdiction of the ECJ. A review of the Treaty of Maastricht revealed that it was evident that the intergovernmental method was not working properly:[146] proposals from Member States and the need for unanimity led to the lowest common denominator which, in the form of an international agreement, took a long time for all Member States to ratify and enter into force. In addition, the third pillar instruments contained guidelines binding the executive but not the legislature or the judiciary.

The ToA represented the semi-communitarisation of the third pillar: a new title (IV) was introduced into the EC under the heading 'Visas, Asylum, Immigration

[141] The objective of the abolition of internal frontiers among Member States introduced by the SEA was framed as a challenge to sovereignty or security by some Member States. See Guild and Peers (2001) 268.

[142] Art 14 EC was introduced by the SEA as Art 8(a) of the EC, after renumbering by the TEU (Art 7(a)) and by the ToA (Art 14).

[143] COM (95) 347 final [1995] OJ C289/16 and COM (95) 346 final [1996] OJ C306/5.

[144] France, Germany, Belgium, Luxembourg and the Netherlands decided to abolish the checks at their shared borders and co-operate on matters of visa policy by signing the Schengen Agreement of 1985 and the Schengen Implementing Convention of 1990. In the same year the so-called Dublin Convention was signed; this concerned asylum applications and came into force on 1 September 1997 [1997] OJ C189/105.

[145] Dehousse (1994) ch 1, esp 10.

[146] Kuijper (2004).

and Other Policies related to Free Movement of Persons'.[147] This title on the free movement of persons covered visas, asylum, immigration and judicial co-operation in civil matters, whereas police and judicial co-operation in criminal matters remained within the TEU, using the intergovernmental method for adopting decisions on those matters. In addition, the Schengen Acquis was integrated by the ToA into EC law and EU law as secondary legislation.[148] The dispersion of its provisions in the EC and TEU and in secondary legislation attached *ex post* to the Treaties, its variable geometry in which some Member States were able to opt in or out of its provisions and, especially, the limited jurisdiction of the ECJ in these very sensitive matters provoked widespread criticism (see below).

Therefore, in 1999 the Tampere European Council created an area of freedom, security and justice in the Union, based on the principles of transparency and democratic control.[149] More transparency and accountability in this area was requested, specifically to increase the role of the European Parliament in the decision making-process and the jurisdiction of the Community Courts when reviewing actions taken on these matters: specifically because visas, immigration, asylum and border controls touch on fundamental rights and raise problems similar to those arising from the free movement provisions of the EC.[150]

The role of the ECJ in Justice and Home Affairs goes back to the 1970s, when the then six Member States granted the Court jurisdiction over a Convention on co-operation in civil matters.[151] Nonetheless, it was a very limited jurisdiction:[152] for instance, the Protocol did not permit courts or tribunals of first instance to refer questions for a preliminary ruling to the ECJ; only intermediate national courts had that option, and final national courts were under an obligation to refer questions for a preliminary ruling to the ECJ if they considered that it was necessary to their judgment. However, before the entry into force of the TEU, the Member States agreed a number of other conventions which did not give jurisdiction to the ECJ—for instance the Dublin Convention[153] and the Europol Convention, according to which disputes between Member States on its interpretation or application were to be discussed in the Council.[154]

[147] Arts 61–69 EC.

[148] On the consequences of that integration see Kuijper (2000) esp 349.

[149] Tampere European Council 15 and 16 October 1999, Presidency Conclusions (n 111), p 3. See also Editorial Comments, 'The Tampere Summit: The Ties that Bind, or The Policemen's Ball' (1999) 36 *CML Rev* 1120.

[150] Craig and De Búrca (2003) 39.

[151] First Protocol governing references for a preliminary ruling to the ECJ from national courts and tribunals on the Brussels Convention on Jurisdiction and the Enforcement of Judgments in Civil and Commercial Matters (consolidated text in [1998] OJ C/27/1 and, currently, Council Regulation (EC) No 44/2001 of 22 December 2000 [2001] OJ L12/1).

[152] Peers (1998) 340–1.

[153] Art 18 of the Dublin Convention establishes a Committee comprising one representative of the Government of each Member State to examine, at the request of one or more Member States, any question concerning the application or interpretation of the Convention.

[154] After six months without agreement in the Council, the Member States, with the exception of the UK, will submit the dispute to the ECJ. Declaration Cm 3060 [1995] OJ C316/1. See also Denza (2002) 314–15.

Under the TEU the situation was no better: the Court did not have jurisdiction in matters covered by the second and third pillars.[155] Nonetheless, Member States, through the Council, were able to draw up conventions stipulating the Court's jurisdiction to interpret their provisions or to rule on disputes regarding their application.[156]

Finally, the ToA, by introducing visas, asylum, immigration and civil co-operation polices into the EC, determined the extension of the Court's jurisdiction to those matters. Nonetheless, the preliminary ruling jurisdiction is more limited in these matters than in the original first pillar matters: firstly, only courts of last instance can use the preliminary ruling procedure; secondly, preliminary ruling jurisdiction is excluded in relation to certain measures or decisions relating to maintaining law and order or internal security; thirdly, a request for interpretation clause means that a preliminary ruling could be invoked not just by a national court but also by the Council, Commission or a Member State.[157] In addition, Title IV of the EC did not mention the jurisdiction of the Community Courts to rule on an annulment action or an action for failure to act relating to visas, asylum, immigration and civil co-operation.[158]

Although visas, immigration, asylum and border controls were moved into the first pillar, judicial and police co-operation in criminal matters was left within the third pillar. Nonetheless, the ECJ was given jurisdiction over certain measures adopted under this pillar. For instance, Article 35 of the TEU established a preliminary ruling procedure similar to that of Article 234 of the EC, but with the peculiarity that Member States should declare individually that they accept such jurisdiction in relation to specified national courts.[159] In addition, the ECJ was given jurisdiction to review the legality of framework decisions and decisions on the same grounds as Article 230 of the EC, but only the Commission or a Member State could ask for that review. Therefore, individuals were not given standing before the ECJ to challenge EU decisions or framework decisions even though such decisions touch on their fundamental rights. Furthermore, a provision similar to that contained in Article 68 of the EC was introduced, restricting the Court's jurisdiction on 'operations carried out by the police or other law enforcement services of a

[155] Peers (1998) explains that the belief that the Court did not have jurisdiction over the third pillar before the ToA entered into force is a myth: it did so, for instance, ruling a first-pillar act as *ultra vires* EC law because it entered into areas reserved for the third pillar TEU (p 343).

[156] Arts L and K3(2)(c) TEU (Maastricht version). See Albors-Llorens (1998).

[157] Art 68, EC.

[158] Peers (1998) has maintained that 'there is a presumption of full applicability that can only be outset by express language' (p 352).

[159] Only 14 Member States have opted in. COM (2006) 346 final (n 3), p 9. According to the *Pupino* case, once a Member State accepts such jurisdiction, 'the system under Art 234 EC is capable of being applied to the Court's jurisdiction to give preliminary ruling by virtue of Art 35 EU, subject to the conditions laid down by that provision' (Case C-105/03 *Maria Pupino* [2005] ECR I-5285, para 19). ECJ has extended its jurisdiction under Art 35 TEU in the judgment of 27 February 2007 in the *Segi* case (C-355/04 P, *Segi v Council* [2007] ECR p 0). According to this judgment, 'it has to be possible to make subject to review by the Court a common position which, because of its content, has a scope going beyond that assigned by the TEU to that kind of act'. This finding is a consequence of the right to an effective judicial protection that the applicant invoked.

Member State or the exercise of the responsibilities incumbent upon Member States with regard to the maintenance of law and order and the safeguarding of internal security', in which the review of the legality or proportionality of such operations was excluded. Finally, the Court was given jurisdiction to rule on any dispute between Member States regarding the interpretation or the application of common positions, framework decisions, decisions and conventions adopted under Article 34(2), whenever such a dispute cannot be settled by the Council within six months of its being referred to the Council by one of its members and, also, any dispute between Member States and the Commission on the interpretation of conventions adopted under Article 34(2)(d).

To conclude, the changes introduced by the ToA were welcome, due to the extension of the jurisdiction of the ECJ to the area of visas, asylum, immigration, civil co-operation and third pillar matters. However, the limitations imposed on the Court's jurisdiction by its provisions sparked widespread criticism, especially after the proclamation of the Charter of Fundamental Rights. At that stage the Charter was a soft law instrument, which had implications for EU law and the courts and tribunals of Member States. It was clear that the Constitutional Treaty, with a Charter of Fundamental Rights, could not continue with a limited jurisdiction of the ECJ in that sensitive area.

To sum up, the problems submitted to the Convention for revision were as follows:[160]

- In the area of criminal and police co-operation, the preliminary ruling system, established in Article 35 of the TEU, depended on the discretion of the Member States, which had to accept the Court's jurisdiction expressly.[161]
- The legal instruments of the third pillar (decisions and framework decisions) did not have direct effect and there was no form of infringement proceedings against Member States for breach of their obligations under Title VI of the TEU.[162]
- Only the Commission or a Member State had standing to bring annulment proceedings before the ECJ.[163] The European Parliament and private parties were excluded, which is more dramatic when one takes into account the fact that the subject-matter was criminal and police co-operation, where there is a high risk that human rights violations will occur.
- Finally, the clause limiting the Court's jurisdiction in terms of reviewing any measure or decision taken by a Member State 'relating to the maintenance of

160 Albors-Llorens (1998) 1281–2 and 1288–9.

161 At n 159.

162 It is worth noticing that in the *Pupino* case the ECJ held that 'the binding character of framework decisions, formulated in terms identical to those of the third paragraph of Article 249 EC [Directives], places on national authorities, and particularly national courts, an obligation to interpret national law in conformity with Community law' (Case 105/03 *Maria Pupino* [2005] ECR I-5285, para 34). Therefore, the Court retains the binding character of framework decisions that, according to the Court, are similar to that of Community directives.

163 Art 35(6) TEU.

the law and order and the safeguarding of internal security' not just in the TEU but, also, in the EC where originally the Court had full jurisdiction.[164]

2. The Convention's Proposals

Given the problems mentioned above, it was not surprising that the need for an amendment to the third pillar was raised at the first meeting of the Convention. The progress report presented to the Convention on Justice and Home Affairs by the Praesidium pointed out that the limited jurisdiction of the Court was just one of the concerns in this area. According to the report, there were five main problems:[165] the need to clarify which matters of criminal law should be dealt with at European level and which should remain within the Member States' competence; the lack of appropriate legal instruments within the third pillar (the delays and uncertainties caused during the ratification process of the Convention between Member States and the lack of direct effect of framework decisions and decisions); the absence of institutional accountability (the European Parliament does not have a role in the supervision of Europol's activities or in the adoption of a common position by the Council) and limited judicial control; the complexity of sharing a competence between the first and third pillars with different legal instruments, procedural rules and institutional roles; and, finally, the lack of mutual trust in sensitive matters such as police co-operation and Europol where many actors are involved. All of these issues were debated by the Convention,[166] which decided to create a Working Group on Freedom, Security and Justice.[167]

Working Group X held nine meetings and different experts were heard. Its proposals were underpinned by two 'golden rules':[168] firstly, the necessity of establishing a common general legal framework recognising the particularities of this area and, secondly, ensuring separation between legislative and operational task reforms.

On the first 'golden rule', the members of Working Group X agreed to get rid of the pillars structure. All provisions concerning the area of freedom, security and justice should be combined under a single title of the Constitutional Treaty, putting an end to the current uncertainty as to legal bases and the problems mentioned above.[169] Nonetheless, depending on the action envisaged at Union level, the procedure could be based on the Community method or reinforced

164 Art 35(5) TEU and Art 68(2) EC.

165 *Justice and Home Affairs—Progress Report and General Problems*, CONV 69/02, 31 May 2002, pp 9–12.

166 *Note on the Plenary Meeting*, CONV 97/02, 19 June 2002, pp 2–7.

167 Working Group X on Freedom, Security and Justice.

168 CONV 426/02 (n 139), pp 2–3.

169 Recent case law highlights the uncertainty as to legal bases that the pillars structure provokes, eg Case C-176/03 *Commission v Council* [2005] ECR I-7879; Joined Cases C-317/04 *European Parliament v Council of the European Union* [2005] ECR I-2457 and C-318/04 *European Parliament v Commission* [2005] ECR I-2467.

co-ordination.[170] To sum up, the Working Group proposal aimed to overcome the practical problems of the pillars structure; however, the result has gone further, dispensing with inter-governmentalism and giving a greater source of legitimacy to the measures in this area.

The second 'golden rule' of the Working Group work was separation between legislative and operational task reform proposals: in order to clarify the proposals of the Working Group, it was decided to separate, on the one hand, legal instruments and procedures and, on the other, the reform of Europol, Eurojust and the jurisdiction of the Court. With respect to legal instruments and procedures, the Working Group proposed the adoption of the legal instruments described in first part of the Constitutional Treaty. Their direct effect would avoid the problems of lack of effectiveness of the Council's decisions or framework decisions when a Member State did not fulfil its obligations under the TEU. The logical consequence of adopting the same legal instruments as those adopted in the first pillar is to follow the ordinary legislative procedure established by the Constitutional Treaty: co-decision with the intervention of the European Parliament and QMV as a general rule.[171] The adoption of this rule in this field would promote the effectiveness of EU law. Furthermore, it is submitted that the adoption of the co-decision procedure and QMV, as a general rule, has other implications: it adds legitimacy to the measure, avoiding the prevalence of national over transnational interests.

In terms of the reform of operational tasks, the Working Group proposed to enhance collaboration within the Council, the gradual development of an integrated system of external border control management (with the possible creation of a common European border guard unit) and the competences of Europol and Eurojust (see above). But what is more important for the purposes of this section is the Working Group's vision of the limited jurisdiction of the Court as 'no longer acceptable concerning acts adopted in areas (eg police co-operation, judicial co-operation in criminal matters) which directly affect fundamental rights of the individuals'.[172] The idea of having a Constitutional Treaty for Europe setting common values and including a Charter of Fundamental Rights as primary law impinged upon the limited jurisdiction of the Court in these very sensitive areas. In the first place, with respect to criminal and police co-operation, the Working Group mentioned the limited jurisdiction of the ECJ to give preliminary rulings. The ECJ has jurisdiction only if the Member States expressly accept it. The Working Group was also concerned about the Court's lack of jurisdiction to review acts of police forces and by its limited standing to bring annulment proceedings before the CFI on those matters that correspond only to the Commission or to the Member States. In

[170] CONV 426/02 (n 139) p 3.

[171] There are some exceptions, according to the Working Group recommendations, in which the unanimity rule would remain. For instance, it would request unanimity for the creation of new Union bodies with operational powers (such as a public prosecution office or a common border guard), for establishing rules on action by national policies authorities and joint investigative teams or for regulating law enforcement authorities acting in the territory of another Member State. CONV 426/02 (n 139), p 14.

[172] CONV 426/02 (n 139), p 25.

the second place, as regards the Court's jurisdiction in terms of visas, asylum, immigration and civil co-operation, the two main criticisms of the Working Group members were, firstly, that only supreme or last instance courts are able to request a preliminary ruling to the ECJ, whereas difficulties of interpretation usually arise before first instance courts,[173] and, secondly, the absence of justification for the absence of the Court's jurisdiction to review the legality of measures relating to the maintenance of law and order and the safeguarding of internal security, such as the control of persons crossing internal borders. Specially, it is difficult to justify the exclusion of that competence of the ECJ when it has jurisdiction to review other measures relating equally to the maintenance of law and order, such as the expulsion of EU citizens from one Member State to another.[174]

Bearing these criticisms in mind, Working Group X recommended that the Convention abolish the specific mechanisms established in Articles 35 of the TEU and 68 of the EC and extend the jurisdiction of the ECJ to the area of freedom, security and justice, including reviewing the actions of Union bodies in this field.[175] However, members of the Working Group agreed that, since Member States will carry on being responsible for the maintenance of law and order and internal security within their frontiers, national acts falling within these responsibilities would lie outside the scope of EU law and, therefore, outside the Court's jurisdiction. The question here would be what happens with national acts implementing Union law? Should these acts be reviewed by the ECJ? According to Working Group X the answer would be yes, because those acts are within the scope of EU law and therefore the Court should have competence to review them. As we will see in the following section, different drafts of the Constitutional Treaty have given various answers to this question.

3. Reforms Achieved by the Constitutional Treaty

In the field of freedom, security and justice, the Constitutional Treaty makes several improvements: firstly, this field would be ruled by European laws and framework laws adopted by the co-decision procedure and QMV as a general rule (for example, in policies on border checks, asylum, immigration, and judicial co-operation in civil matters). Nonetheless, the Constitutional Treaty contained many exceptions to that rule; for instance, for family law measures with cross-border implications, the establishment of a European Public Prosecutor's Office or the rule on operational co-operation between police authorities of all Member States it would be necessary to enact a European law or framework law with the Council acting unanimously after consulting the European Parliament. Secondly, under the Constitutional

[173] The implication of that rule is that the individual would have to appeal to the last instance in national courts in order to request a question of interpretation or validity bearing in mind that this is an area (particularly in asylum or immigration) where speedy legal proceedings are crucial.

[174] CONV 426/02 (n 139), p 25.

[175] *Ibid.*

Treaty the jurisdiction of the Community Courts on measures within the area of freedom, security and justice would be wider than it is currently. The abolition of the pillars structure would extend the Courts' jurisdiction to policies within that area, to the same extent that the Community Courts' jurisdiction has in the first pillar, including the competence to review acts of EU bodies such as Europol or Eurojust. The general rule would be that the Community Courts would have full jurisdiction to review measures under the scope of EU law unless there was an exception to that rule (eg Article III-377 of the Constitutional Treaty, see below). The wider jurisdiction of the Community Courts would be crucial in relation to, for example, policies relating to asylum, since the Union created a common European system establishing minimum standards for the qualification and status of third country nationals or stateless persons as refugees: for instance, regarding a national decision on the revocation of, or refusal to renew, refugee status.[176] The Constitutional Treaty does not establish limited jurisdiction in preliminary rulings. Therefore, a first instance court could request a preliminary ruling from the ECJ relating to asylum issues, which is a very welcome innovation.

Among the general provisions on freedom, security and justice, the Constitutional Treaty states that the establishment of that chapter 'shall not affect the exercise of responsibilities incumbent upon Member States with regard to the maintenance of law and order and the safeguarding of internal security'.[177] This provision is similar to those contained in Articles 68(2) of the EC and 35(5) of the TEU.[178] Its aim would be to stop any attempt by the ECJ to review the legality of a Member State measure regarding the maintenance of law and order and the safeguarding of internal security. However, the drafters at the Convention thought that it would be difficult to justify and maintain a provision similar to that of Article 35(5) of the TEU, especially taking into account the traditional jurisdiction of the Community Courts to review measures relating equally to the maintenance of law and order (eg the expulsion of EU citizens from one Member State to another).[179]

[176] Council Directive 2004/83/EC of 29 April 2004 on minimum standards for the qualification and status of third country nationals or stateless persons as refugees or persons who otherwise need international protection and the content of the protection granted, Art 14.

[177] Draft Constitutional Treaty of July 2003, Art III-163; Constitutional Treaty of October 2004, Art III-262.

[178] Art 68(2) EC establishes the following: 'In any event, the Court of Justice shall not have jurisdiction to rule on any measure or decision taken pursuant to Article 62(1) relating to the maintenance of law and order and the safeguarding of internal security.' Art 35(3) TEUestablishes that the ECJ does not have jurisdiction 'to review the validity or proportionality of operations carried out by the police or other law enforcement services of a Member State or the exercise of the responsibilities incumbent upon Member States with regard to the maintenance of law and order and the safeguarding of internal security'.

[179] Measures such as the expulsion of an EU citizen from Member State territory, taken on grounds of public policy and public security, shall comply with the principle of proportionality according to Art 27(2), Directive 2004/38/EC of the European Parliament and the Council of 29 April 2004 on the right of citizens of the Union and their family members to move and reside freely within the territory of the Member State, amending Regulation (EEC) No 1612/68 and repealing Directives 64/221/EEC, 68/360/EEC, 72/194/EEC, 73/148/EEC, 75/34/EEC, 75/35/EEC, 90/364/EEC, 90/365/EEC and 93/96/EEC: [2004] OJ L158/77.

Therefore, the Draft Constitutional Treaty of July 2003 added an important clause to the current Article 35(5) of the TEU:

> In exercising its powers regarding the provisions of Section 4 and 5 of Chapter IV of Title III concerning the area of freedom, security and justice, the Court of Justice shall have no jurisdiction to review the validity or proportionality of operations carried out by the police or other law-enforcement services of a Member State or the exercise of the responsibilities incumbent upon Member States with regard to the maintenance of law and order and the safeguarding of internal security, *where such action is a matter of national law.*[180]

By introducing that clause, the ECJ would have jurisdiction to review the validity or proportionality of operations carried out by the police or other law enforcement services of a Member State when implementing EU law (judicial authorities implementing the European arrest warrant)[181] or the measures adopted by a Member State with regard to the maintenance of law and order and the safeguarding of internal security when implementing EU law (eg when a third-country national or a stateless person is excluded from being eligible for subsidiary protection because he or she has committed a serious crime or constitutes a danger to the Member State in which he or she is present).[182]

This clause would bring added coherence and consistency to the jurisdictional system drawn by the Constitutional Treaty: all measures taken by Member States implementing EU law are under the jurisdiction of the ECJ, even measures relating to judicial co-operation in criminal matters and police co-operation. However, the Member States did not want a clause that imposed the parameters of control of EU law used by the Court on matters directly related to their sovereignty, such as police co-operation and the maintenance of law and order and the safeguarding of internal security. In the end, Article III-283 of the Draft Constitutional Treaty was rewritten and the last clause ('where such action is a matter of national law') disappeared. Therefore, the Constitutional Treaty, signed in Rome in October 2004, contains the following provision limiting the jurisdiction of the ECJ (as does Article 35.5 of the TEU):

> In exercising its powers regarding the provisions of Section 4 and 5 of Chapter IV of Title III [on judicial co-operation in criminal matters and police co-operation] relating to the area of freedom, security and justice, the Court of Justice of the European Union shall have no jurisdiction to review the validity or proportionality of operations carried out by the police or other law-enforcement services of a Member State or the exercise of the responsibilities incumbent upon Member States with regard to the maintenance of law and order and the safeguarding of internal security.[183]

180 Draft Constitutional Treaty of July 2003, IGC 50/03, Art III-283 (emphasis added).

181 2002/584/JHA Council Framework Decision of 13 June 2002 on the European arrest warrant and the surrender procedures between Member States [2002] OJ L190/1. Statements made by certain Member States on the adoption of the Framework Decision.

182 Council Directive 2004/83/EC of 29 April 2004 on minimum standards for the qualification and status of third country nationals or stateless persons as refugees or persons who otherwise need international protection and the content of the protection granted [2002] OJ L304/12.

183 Constitutional Treaty, Art III-377.

A *sensu contrario* reading would imply that the restriction on the Court's jurisdiction does not apply to the review of the validity or proportionality of operations carried out by Member States' police or other law-enforcement services in matters relating to border checks, asylum, immigration and judicial civil co-operation. Even if the Constitutional Treaty is ratified by all Member States, the ECJ would determine the scope of Article III-377, taking into account the right to effective judicial protection in a Union of citizens with stronger political integration.

In any event, due to the paralysis of the Constitutional Treaty ratification process and the need to guarantee the right to effective judicial protection, especially in sensitive fields such as border checks, asylum, immigration and judicial co-operation in civil matters, the Commission has adopted a Communication on the adaptation of the provisions of Title IV of the EC relating to the jurisdiction of the ECJ.[184] The Communication's purpose is to contribute to the adaptation of Article 68 of the EC[185] by aligning the jurisdiction of the ECJ to the general scheme of the EC. According to the Commission, that adaptation will ensure the uniform application and interpretation of Community law in that area and will strengthen judicial protection in fields that are particularly sensitive in terms of fundamental rights. Furthermore, it will remedy a paradoxical retrograde step in judicial protection as a result of the Amsterdam Treaty in civil matters covered by Article 65 of the EC.[186]

An Annex to the Communication includes a draft Council Decision, according to which,

> With effect from [1 January 2007], Article 234 of the Treaty shall apply to any request made to the Court of Justice by a national court to rule on a question concerning the interpretation of Title IV of Part Three of the Treaty or on the validity and interpretation of acts of the Community institutions on the basis of that Title, including requests made before [1 January 2007] on which the Court of Justice has not yet ruled at that date.[187]

[184] Communication from the Commission to the European Parliament, the Council, the European Economic and Social Committee, the Committee of the Regions and the Court of Justice of the European Communities, Adaptation of the provision of Title IV, COM (2006) 346 final (n 3).

[185] The adaptation of Title IV of the EC was initiated by Council Decision 2004/927/EC of 22 December 2004, providing for certain areas covered by Title IV of Part Three of the Treaty establishing the European Community to be governed by the procedure laid down in Art 251 of that Treaty [2004] OJ L396/45.

[186] COM (2006) 346 final (n 3), pp 3–9.

[187] *Ibid*, Single Art (1).

Bibliography

ALBORS-LLORENS, A (1998) 'Changes in the Jurisdiction of the European Court of Justice under the Treaty of Amsterdam' 35 *CML Rev* 1273.

—— (1996) *Private Parties in European Community Law* (Oxford, Clarendon Press).

ALCOCEBA GALLEGO, MA (2006) 'La subordinación del Acervo Schengen al de la Unión Europea. Comentario a la sentencia del TJCE de 31 de enero de 2006. As C-503/03, Comisión Europea c España' 10 *Revista General de Derecho Europeo* 1.

ALONSO GARCÍA, R (2005) 'El acto administrativo comunitario: imprecisión normativa, y luces y sombras al respecto en la doctrina del Tribunal de Justicia' in Colaço Antunes and Sáinz Moreno (eds), *O acto no contencioso administrativo. Tradição e reforma* (Coimbra, Almedina) 43.

—— (2002) 'Las cláusulas horizontales de la Carta de los Derechos Fundamentales de la Unión Europea' in E García de Enterría (ed), *La encrucijada constitucional de la Unión Europea* (Madrid, Civitas) 151.

—— (1997) *La responsabilidad de los Estados Miembros por infracción del Derecho comunitario* (Madrid, Civitas).

ANDENAS, M and TÜRK, A (eds) (2000) *Delegated Legislation and the Role of Committees in the EC* (Boston, Kluwer Law International).

ARNULL, A (2005) 'From Bit Part to Starring Role? The Court of Justice and Europe's Constitutional Treaty' 24 *Yearbook of European Law* 1.

—— (1999) *The European Court and its Court of Justice* (Oxford, OUP).

—— (1995) 'Private Applicants and the Action for Annulment under Article 173 of the EC Treaty' 32 *CML Rev* 7.

ARNULL, A and WINCOTT, D (eds) (2002) *Accountability and Legitimacy in the European Union* (Oxford, OUP).

ARZOZ SANTISTEBAN, X (1998) *Concepto y régimen jurídico del acto administrativo Comunitario* (Oñati, Instituto Vasco de Administración Pública).

AUBY, JB and DUTHEIL DE LA ROCHÈRE, J (eds) (2006) *Droit administrative européen* (Brussels, Bruylant).

BAÑO LEÓN, JM (2006) 'Las fuentes del Tratado de la Constitución Europea: un análisis prospectivo' 11 *Revista General de Derecho Administrativo* 1.

BARBIER DE LA SERRE, E (2006) 'Procedural Justice in European Community Case-law concerning the Rights of the Defence: Essentialist and Instrumental Trends' 12 *European Public Law* 225.

BARNÉS, J (2003) 'Acto y procedimiento administrativo', paper presented at *Diritto amministrativo ed integrazione europea*, Florence, 5 December.

—— (1993) *El procedimiento administrativo en el Derecho Comparado* (Madrid, Civitas).

BELLAMY, R and CASTIGLIONE, D (2000) 'Democracy, Sovereignty and the Constitution of the Europe Union: The Republican Alternative to Liberalism' in Z Bankowski and A Scott (eds), *The European Union and its Order: The Legal Theory of European Integration* (Oxford, Blackwell) 169.

Bering Liisberg, J (2006) 'The EU Constitutional Treaty and its Distinction between Legislative and Non-legislative Acts—Oranges into Apples?' *Jean Monnet Working Paper* 01/06, NYU School of Law.

Besselink, Leonard FM (2001) 'The Member States, the National Constitutions and the Scope of the Charter' 8 *Maastricht Journal of European and Comparative Law* 68.

Bieber, R and Amarelle, C (2000) 'Simplification of European Law' in F Snyder (ed), *The Europeanisation of Law: The Legal Effects of European Integration* (Oxford, Hart Publishing) 219.

Bieber, R and Salomé, I (1996) 'Hierarchy of Norms in European Law' 33 *CML Rev* 907.

Biglino Campos, P (2003) 'Derechos fundamentales en la Unión y en los Estados Miembros: algunos problemas de conexión' 69 *Revista Española de Derecho Constitucional* 387.

Bonnor, PG (2000) 'The European Ombudsman: A Novel Source of Soft Law in the European Union' 25 *EL Rev* 39.

Braibant, G (2001) *La Charte des droits fondamentaux de l'Union européenne* (Seuil, Éditions du Seuil).

Cabral, P (2006) 'Access to Member State Documents in EC Law' 31 *EL Rev* 378.

Caroli Casavola, H and Greco, S (2002) 'Il fondo agricolo europeo di orientamento e di garanzia-FEOGA' 2 *Rivista Giuridica del Mezzogiorno* 605.

Carreti, P (2006) 'La tutela dei diritti fondamentali nel nuovo Trattato che istituisce una Costituzione per l'Europa' in G Morbidelli and F Donati, *Una Costituzione per l'Unione Europea* (Torino, Giappichelli) 163.

Carrillo, M (2003) 'La Carta de Derechos Fundamentales de la Unión Europea' 65 *Revista Vasca de Administración Pública* 145.

Casini, L and Midena, E (2002) 'I fondi strutturali e il programma operativo multiregionale (POM) «Sviluppo locale-patti territoriali per l'occupazione»' 1 *Rivista Giuridica del Mezzogiorno* 97.

Cassese, S (2006) *La globalización jurídica* (Madrid, Marcial Pons-INAP).

—— (2003a) 'Il diritto amministrativo europeo presenta caratteri originali?' 1 *Rivista Trimestrale di Diritto Pubblico* 35.

—— (2003b) 'Il procedimento amministrativo europeo', paper presented at the Max-Planck-Institute, 9 October.

—— (2003c) 'Le basi costituzionali' in S Cassese (ed), *Trattato di diritto amministrativo. Diritto amministrativo generale*, vol I (Milan, Giuffrè) 213.

—— (2003d) *Lo spazio giuridico globale* (Rome-Bari, Laterza), translated into spanish by L Ortega, I Martín Delgado and I Gallego Córcoles, *La globalización jurídica* (Madrid, INAP-Marcial Pons, 2006).

Cassia, P (2002a) 'Quelles perspectives pour la recevabilité du recours en annulation des particuliers' 37 *Le Dalloz* 2825.

—— (2002b) *Accès des personnes physiques ou morales au juge de la légalité des actes communautaires* (Paris, Dalloz).

Chiti, E (2005) 'The Relationship between National Administrative Law and European Administrative Law in Administrative Procedures' in J Ziller (ed), *What's New in European Administrative Law?* EUI Working Paper (2005/10), Florence.

—— (2002) Le Agenzie Europee. Unità e Decentramento nelle Amministrazioni Comunitarie (Padova, CEDAM, 2002)

Chiti, E and Franchini, C (2003) *L'integrazione amministrativa europea* (Bologna, Il Mulino).

Chiti, MP (2002) *Derecho administrativo europeo* (Madrid, Civitas).
—— (2000) 'Il mediatore europeo e la buona amministrazione Communitaria' (2000) 2 *Rivista Italiana di Diritto Pubblico Communitario* 303.
—— (1995a) 'Are there Universal Principles of Good Governance?' 2 *European Public Law* 241.
—— (1995b) 'The Role of the European Court of Justice in the Development of General Principles and their Possible Codification' 3–4 *Rivista Italiana di Diritto Pubblico Comunitario* 661.
Cobreros Mendazona, E (2002) 'Nota al Código Europeo de Buena Conducta Administrativa' 64 *Revista Vasca de Administración Pública* 241.
—— (1995) *Incumplimiento del Derecho Comunitario y responsabilidad del Estado* (Madrid, Civitas).
Craig, P (2006) EU Administrative law (Oxford, Oxford University Press)
—— (2005) 'Process Rights in Adjudication and Rulemaking: Legal and Political Perspectives' in J Ziller (ed), *What's New in European Administrative Law?* EUI Working Paper (2005/10), Florence, 2005, 25.
—— (2004) 'The hierarchy of Norms' in T Tridimas and P Nebbia (eds), *European Union Law for the Twenty-First Century,* vol 1 (Oxford, Hart Publishing) 75.
—— (2000) 'The Fall and Renewal of the Commission: Accountability, Contract and Administrative Organisation' 2 *ELJ* 98.
—— (1998) 'Democracy and Rulemaking within the EC: An Empirical and Normative Assessment' in P Craig and C Harlow (eds), *Lawmaking in the European Union* (London, Kluwer Law International).
—— (1994) 'Legality, Standing and Substantive Review in Community Law' 14 *OJLS* 507.
Craig, P and De Búrca, G (2003) *EU Law. Text, Cases and Materials* 3rd edn (Oxford, OUP).
Craufurd-Smith, R (1999) 'Remedies for Breaches of EU Law in National Courts: Legal Variation and Selection' in P Craig and G De Búrca (eds), *The Evolution of EU Law* (Oxford, OUP) 287.
Curtin, D (1998) 'Democracy, Transparency and Political Participation: Some Progress Post-Amsterdam' in V Deckmyn and I Thomson (eds), *Openness and Transparency in the European Union* (Maastricht, European Institute for Public Administration) 107.
Curtin, D and Meijers, H (1995) 'Access to European Union Information: An Element of Citizenship and a Neglected Constitutional Right' in NA Neuwahl and A Rosas (eds), *The European Union and Human Rights* (Netherlands, Kluwer Law International) 77.
Curtin D, and van Ooik, R (2001) 'The Sting is Always in the Tail. The Personal Scope of Application of the EU Charter of Fundamental Rights' 8 *Maastricht Journal of European and Comparative Law* 102.
De Búrca, G (2003) 'Fundamental Rights and Citizenship' in B De Witte (ed), *Ten Reflections on the Constitutional Treaty for Europe* (Florence, European University Institute) 11.
—— (2001) 'The Drafting of the European Union Charter of Fundamental Rights' 26 *EL Rev* 126.
Dehousse, R (2002) 'Misfits: EU Law and the Transformation of EU Governance' in C Joerges and R Dehousse (eds), *Good Governance in Europe's Integrated Market* (Oxford, OUP) 207.
—— (ed) (1994) *Europe after Maastricht: An Ever Closer Union?* (Munich, Law Books in Europe).
Della Cananea, G (2005) 'Beyond the State: The Europeanization and Globalization of Procedural Administrative Law' in L Ortega (ed), *Studies on European Public Law* (Valladolid, Lex Nova) 69.

Della Canenea, G (2003a) 'I procedimenti composti dell'Unione Europea', paper presented at 'The European normative on administrative procedure', conference in Rome, 8 April.
—— (2003b) 'L'amministrazione europea' in S Cassese (ed), *Trattato di diritto administrativo*, II (Milan, Giuffrè) 1797.
—— (2003c) *L'Unione Europea. Uno ordinamento composito* (Rome, Editori Laterza).
—— (1997) 'I procedimenti amministrativi della Comunità Europea' in MP Chiti and G Greco (ed), *Trattato di diritto amministrativo europeo* (Milan, Giuffrè) 225.
—— (1995) 'From Judges to Legislators? The Codification of EC Administrative Procedures in the Field of State Aids' 5 *Rivista Italiana di Diritto Pubblico Comunitario* 967.
Denza, E (2002) *The Intergovernmental Pillars of the European Union* (Oxford, OUP).
Díez Picazo, LM (2005) *Sistema de derechos fundamentales* 2nd edn (Madrid, Civitas).
—— (2002) *Constitucionalismo de la Unión Europea* (Madrid, Cuadernos Civitas).
—— (2001) 'Glosas a la nueva Carta de Derechos Fundamentales de la Unión Europea' 5 *Tribunales Superiores de Justicia* 21.
Due, O (1992) 'Article 5 du traité CEE. Une disposition de caractère federal?' Academy of European Law (ed), *Collected Courses of the Academy of European Law*, vol II book 1 (Netherlands, Kluwer Academic Publishers) 15.
Dutheil De La Rochère, J (2004) 'The EU and the Individual: Fundamental Rights in the Draft Constitutional Treaty' 41 *CML Rev* 345.
—— (2000) 'La Convention sur la Charte des Droits Fondamentaux et le processus de construction européenne' 437 *Revue du Marché commun et de l'Union européenne* 223.
Fernández Tomás, A (2001) *La Carta de Derechos Fundamentales de la Unión Europea* (Valencia, Tirant lo Blanch).
Fraile Ortiz, M (2003) *El significado de la ciudadanía europea* (Madrid, Centro de Estudios Políticos y Constitucionales).
Franchini, C (2003) 'I principi applicabili ai procedimenti amministrativi europei' 5 *Rivista Italiana di Diritto Pubblico Communitario* 1037.
Galera Rodrigo, S (1998) *La aplicación administrativa del Derecho Comunitario* (Madrid, Civitas).
García de Enterría, E (1993) 'La ampliación de la competencia de las jurisdicciones contencioso-administrativas nacionales por obra del Derecho Comunitario' 78 *Revista Española de Derecho Administrativo* 317.
García-Trevijano Garnica, E (2002) *Los procedimientos comunitarios de control de ayudas de Estado* (Madrid, Cuadernos Civitas).
Guichot, E (2001) *La responsabilidad extracontractual de los poderes públicos según el Derecho Comunitario* (Valencia, Tirant lo Blanch).
Guild, E and Peers, E (2001) 'Deference or Defiance? The Court of Justice's Jurisdiction over Immigration and Asylum' in E Guild and C Harlow (eds), *Implementing Amsterdam. Immigration and Asylum Rights in EC Law* (Oxford, Hart Publishing) 267.
Guillermin, G (1992) 'Le principe de l'équilibre institutionnel dans la jurisprudence de la Cour de Justice des Communautés Européennes (1)' 2 *Journal du Droit International* 319.
Haibach, G (2000) 'Separation and Delegation of Legislative Powers: A Comparative Analysis' in M Andenas and A Turk (eds), *Delegated Legislation and the Role of Committees in the EC* (Boston, Kluwer Law International) 58.
Harlow C (2002) *Accountability in the European Union* (Oxford, OUP).
—— (1996) 'Codification of EC Administrative Procedures? Fitting the Foot to the Shoe or the Shoe to the Foot' 1 *ELJ* 3.

Harlow, C and Rawlings, A (1997) *Law and Administration* (London, Butterworths).
Hartley, TC (1998) *The Foundations of European Community Law* 2nd edn (Oxford, Clarendon Press).
Isaac, G (2000) *Manual de Derecho Comunitario general* (Barcelona, Ariel).
Jacobs, FG (2004) 'The Evolution of the European Legal Order' 41 *CML Rev* 310.
—— (2002) 'The EU Charter of Fundamental Rights' in A Arnull and D Wincott (eds), *Accountability and Legitimacy in the European Union* (Oxford, OUP) 275.
Jacqué, JP (2004) 'The Principle of Institutional Balance' 41 *CML Rev* 383.
—— (2002) 'Présentation générale' in LS Rossi (ed): *Carta dei diritti fondamentali e Costituzione dell'Unione Europea* (Milan, Giuffrè) 55.
Kanska, K (2004) 'Towards Administrative Human Rights in the EU. Impact of the Charter of Fundamental Rights' 3 *ELJ* 296.
Koukoulis-Spiliotopoulos, S (2002) 'Towards a European Constitution: Does the Charter of Fundamental Rights "maintain in full" the *acquis communautaire*?' 14 *European Review of Public Law* 57.
Kranenborg, HR (2006) 'Is it Time to Revise the European Regulation on Public Access to Documents?' 12 *EL Rev* 251.
Kuijper, PJ (2004) 'Evolution of the Third Pillar from Maastricht to the European Constitution: Institutional Aspects' 41 *CML Rev* 609.
—— (2000) 'Some Legal Problems Associated with the Communitarization of the Policy on Visas, Asylum and Immigration under the Amsterdam Treaty and Incorporation of the Schengen Acquis' 37 *CML Rev* 345.
Ladeur, KH (2002) 'Conflict and Co-operation between European Law and the General Administrative Law of the Member States' in K-H Ladeur (ed), *The Europeanisation of Administrative Law. Transforming National Decision-making Procedures* (Aldershot, Ashgate-Dartmouth) 1.
Ladenburger, C (2006) 'Fundamental Rights and Citizenship of the Union' in G Amato, H Bribosia and B De Witte (eds), *The European Constitution: Retrospective and Prospects* (Florence, EUI) 30.
—— (2005a) 'Introductory Comments on the Convention Method, and on some Features of an Improved Constitutional Charter' in L Ortega (ed), *Studies on European Public Law* (Valladolid, Lex Nova) 131.
—— (2005b) 'La implementación del Derecho de la Unión por los Estados Miembros y la Carta de Derechos Fundamentales de la Unión', paper presented at *Jornadas sobre las implicaciones del Tratado Constitucional para los ciudadanos y las Administraciones Públicas*, Centro de Estudios Políticos y Constitucionales, Madrid.
—— (2002) 'L'application pratique de la Charte des Droits Fondamentaux par la Commission Europèenne' 14 *European Review of Public Law* 817.
Lauwaars, RH (1994) 'Rights of Defence in Competition Cases' in D Curtin and T Heukels (eds), *Institutional Dynamics of European Integration. Essays in Honour of Henry G Schermers*, vol II (London, Martinus Nijhoff Publishers) 497.
Lenaerts, K (2004) 'In the Union we Trust: Trust-Enhancing Principles of Community Law' 41 *CML Rev* 317.
—— (1991) 'Some Reflections on the Separation of Powers in the European Community' 28 *CML Rev* 11.
Lenaerts, K and Corthautm, T (2004) 'Judicial Review as a Contribution to the Development of European Constitutionalism' in T Tridimas and P Nebbia (eds), *European Union Law for the Twenty-First Century* (Oxford, Hart Publishing) 43.

Lenaerts, K and de Smijter, E (2001) 'A "Bill of Rights" for the European Union' 38 *CML Rev* 273.

Lenaerts, K and Desomer, M (2003) 'Simplification of the Union's Instruments' in B De Witte (ed), *Ten Reflections on the Constitutional Treaty of the European Union* (Florence, EUI, Robert Schuman Centre 107.

Lenaerts, K and Vanhamme, J (1997) 'Procedural Rights of Private Parties in the Community Administrative Process' 34 *CML Rev* 531.

Lenaerts, K and Verhoeven, A (2002) 'Institutional Balance as a Guarantee for Democracy in EU Governance' in C Joerges and R Dehousse (eds), *Good Governance in Europe's Integrated Market* (Oxford, OUP) 35.

Levitt, M (1997) 'Access to the File: The Commission's Administrative Procedure in Cases under Articles 85 and 86' 34 *CML Rev* 1413.

Maeso Seco, LF (2005) 'La ejecución administrativa del Derecho Comunitario: ejecución indirecta y procedimientos compuestos' in L Ortega Álvarez (ed), *La seguridad integral europea* (Valladolid, Lex Nova) 35.

—— (2004) 'I procedimenti composti comunitari: riflessioni intorno alla problematica della impossibilità a difendersi ed eventuali alternative' in G della Cananea and M Gnes (eds), *I procedimenti amministrativi dell'Unione Europea. Un'indagine* (Torino, Giappichelli) 11.

Martín Delgado, I (2004) *El procedimiento por inejecución en la justicia europea* (Madrid, Centro de Estudios Políticos y Constitucionales).

Martín-Retortillo Baquer, L (2006) *Vias concurrentes para la protección de los derechos humanos. Perspectivas española y europeas* (Madrid, Civitas).

—— (2002) 'Dos notas sobre la Carta' in E García de Enterría, *La encrucijada constitucional de la Unión Europea* (Madrid, Civitas) 183.

Morbidelli, G (2001) 'Il procedimento amministrativo' in L Mazzarolli *et al*, *Diritto amministrativo*, vol II, 3rd edn (Bologna, Monduzzi Editore) 1225.

Moreno Molina, AM (2000) 'La administración pública de los Estados Miembros como administración Comunitaria. Referencia a la situación española' in Parejo Alfonso *et al* (eds), *Manual de Derecho administrativo Comunitario* (Madrid, Centro de Estudios Ramon Areces) 145.

—— (1998) *La ejecución administrativa del Derecho Comunitario. Régimen europeo y español* (Madrid, Marcial Pons).

Muñoz Machado, S (1992) 'Los principios generales del procedimiento administrativo comunitario y la reforma de la legislación española' 75 *Revista Española de Derecho Administrativo* 329.

Nehl, HP (1999) *Principles of Administrative Procedure in EC Law* (Oxford, Hart Publishing).

Nieto Garrido, E (2004) 'The Strengthening of the Commission's Competences by the Constitutional Treaty and the Principle of Balance of Power', *EUI Working Papers*, RSCAS No 2005/03. Published under the title 'La Reforma Constitucional de la Comisión Europea' in 17 *Revista de Derecho Comunitario Europeo* 193.

—— (2002) 'El Proceso de reforma de la Comisión Europea' 218 *Gaceta Jurídica de la Unión Europea y de la Competencia* 66.

Nieto Garrido, E and Martín Delgado, I (2002) 'EU Charter of Fundamental Rights' 1 *European Review of Public Law* 681.

Ortega Álvarez, L (2005) 'Fundamental Rights in the European Constitution' in L Ortega (ed), *Studies on European Public Law* (Valladolid, Lex Nova) 113.

—— (2004) 'I caratteri dell'amministrazione Communitaria' in G della Cananea and M Gnes (eds), *I procedimenti amministrativi dell'Unione Europea. Un'indagine* (Torino, Giappichelli) 85.

—— (1993) 'Formalised Procedure has Become a Generalized Form of Carrying Out Public Activities' Special Issue *European Public Law Review* 71 'Principles of Administrative Procedure'.

PAREJO, L (2000a) 'El procedimiento administrativo Comunitario' in L Parejo Alfonso *et al* (eds), *Manual de Derecho administrativo Comunitario* (Madrid, Centro de Estudios Ramón Areces) 229.

—— (2000b) 'Los principios generales del Derecho administrativo Comunitario' in L Parejo Alfonso *et al* (eds), *Manual de Derecho administrativo Comunitario* (Madrid, Centro de Estudios Ramón Areces) 39.

PEERS, S (1998) 'Who's Judging the Watchman? The Judicial System of the Area of Freedom, Security and Justice' in P Eeckhout and T Tridimas (eds), *Yearbook of European Law* 18 (Oxford, OUP) 337.

PESCATORE, P (1978) 'L'executif communautaire: justification du quadripartisme institué par les traités de Paris et de Rome' 4 *Cahiers de Droit Européen* 387.

PICOZZA, E (1994) 'Il regime giuridico del procedimento amministrativo Communitario' 324 *Rivista Italiana di Diritto Pubblico Communitario* 321.

PIÑAR MAÑAS, JL (2006) 'ECJ Case-Law on the Right to Protection of Personal Data: Part 1' 1 *BNA International World Data Protection Report* 3.

—— (2005) 'The Fundamental Right to Data Protection. Essential Content and Current Challenges' in *Personal Data Protection. Yesterday, Today and Tomorrow* (Varsobia, Biuro Generalnego Inspectora Ochrony Danych Osobowych) 337.

—— (2005) 'Derecho fundamental a la protección de datos personales. Algunos retos de presente y futuro? 13 *Revista Parlamentaria de la Asamblea de Madrid* 21.

PONCE SOLE, J (2002) 'Good Administration and European Public Law' 4 *European Review of Public Law* 1503.

—— (2001) *Deber de buena administración y derecho al procedimiento debido* (Valladolid, Lex Nova).

DE LA QUADRA, T (2000) 'Acto Administrativo Comunitario' in L Parejo Alfonso *et al* (eds), *Manual de Derecho administrativo Comunitario* (Madrid, Centro de Estudios Ramón Areces) 193.

REQUEJO ISIDRO, M (2004) 'La Carta de los Derechos Fundamentales de la Unión Europea: ámbito de aplicación' in C Ruiz Miguel (co-ord), *Estudios sobre la Carta de los Derechos Fundamentales de la Unión Europea* (Santiago de Compostela, Universidade de Santiago de Compostela) 211.

RODRÍGUEZ BEREIJO, A (2002) 'El valor jurídico de la Carta de los Derechos Fundamentales de la Unión Europea después del Tratado de Niza' in E García de Enterría, *La encrucijada constitucional de la Unión Europea* (Madrid, Civitas) 199.

RODRÍGUEZ PONTÓN, FJ (2004) 'La aplicación de las garantías del proceso equitativo al procedimiento administrativo: elementos de la jurisprudencia europea para el debate' in J Montoro Chiner (co-ord), *La justicia administrativa, Homenaje al Prof Dr D Rafael Entrena Cuesta* (Barcelona, Atelier) 93.

ROSS, M (1993) 'Beyond *Francovich*' 56 *MLR* 55.

ROSSI, LS (2002) '«Costituzionalizzazione» dell'UE e dei diritti fondamentali' in LS Rossi (ed), *Carta dei diritti fondamentali e Costituzione dell'Unione Europea* (Milan, Giuffrè) 249.

Rubio Llorente, F (2002) 'Mostrar los derechos sin destruir la Unión' 64 *Revista Española de Derecho Constitucional* 13.

Saiz Arnáiz, S (2001) 'La Carta de los Derechos Fundamentales de la Unión Europea y los ordenamientos nacionales: ¿qué hay de nuevo?' 13 *Cuadernos de Derecho Público* 153.

Saltari, L and Savino, M (2002) 'Il caso dei Fondi strutturali in materia di ambiente' 1 *Rivista Giuridica del Mezzogiorno* 143.

Sandulli, MA (ed) (20002) *Il procedimento amministrativo in Europa* (Milano, Giuffrè).

Sarmiento, D (2004) *Poder judicial e integración europea. La construcción de un modelo jurisdiccional para la Unión* (Madrid, Civitas).

Schmidt-Assmann, E (1993) 'El procedimiento administrativo, entre el principio del Estado de Derecho y el principio democrático' in J Barnés (ed), *El procedimiento administrativo en el Derecho Comparado* (Madrid, Civitas) 317.

—— (2001) 'El Derecho Administrativo General desde una perspectiva europea' 13 *Justicia Administrativa* 5.

—— (2002) *La teoría general del Derecho Administrativo como sistema* (Madrid, Marcial Pons-INAP).

Schwarze, J (2006) 'The Treaty establishing a Constitution for Europe—Some General Reflections on its Character and its Chances of Realisation' 12 *European Public Law* 200.

—— (2004) 'The Legal Protection of Individuals against Regulation in the European Union Law. Remarks on the ECJ Judgment in the case *UPA* of 25 July 2002 in view of the European Constitutional Reform' 10 *European Public Law* 285.

—— (1992) *European Administrative Law* (London, Sweet & Maxwell).

—— (1991) 'Tendencies towards a Common Administrative Law in Europe' 16 *EL Rev* 3.

Shapiro, M (2002a) 'The Giving Reasons Requirement' in M Shapiro and A Stone Sweet (eds), *On Law, Politics and Judicialization* (Oxford, OUP) 228.

—— (2002b) 'Two Transformations in Administrative Law: American and European?' in K-H Ladeur (ed), *The Europeanisation of Administrative Law. Transforming National Decision-making Procedures* (Aldershot, Ashgate-Dartmouth) 14.

—— (1996) 'Codification of Administrative Law: The US and the Union' 1 *ELJ* 26.

de la Sierra, S (2005) 'The Constitutional Bases of European Administrative Law', EUI Working Paper (2005/10), Florence.

Smismans, S (2002) 'Institutional Balance as Interest Representation. Some Reflections on Lenaerts and Verhoeven' in C Joerges and R Dehousse (eds), *Good Governance in Europe's Integrated Market* (Oxford, OUP) 89.

Söderman, J (2001) 'El derecho fundamental a la buena administración' 214 *Gaceta Jurídica de la Unión Europea y de la Competencia* 8.

—— (1998) 'The Role and Impact of the European Ombudsman in Access to Documentation and the Transparency of Decision-Making' in V Deckmyn and I Thomson (eds), *Openness and Transparency in the European Union* (Maastricht, European Institute of Public Administration) 75.

Stewart, RB (1975) 'The Reformation of American Administrative Law' 8 *Harvard Law Review* 1669.

Tomás Mallén, B (2004) *El derecho fundamental a una buena administración* (Madrid, Instituto Nacional de Administración Pública).

Vitorino, A (2000) 'La Charte des Droits Fondamentaux de l'Union Européenne' 3 *Revue du Droit de l'Union Européenne* 499.

Vos, E (1999) *Institutional Frameworks of Community. Health & Safety Regulation. Committees, Agencies and Private Bodies* (Oxford, Hart Publishing).

—— (1997) 'The Rise of Committees' 3 *ELJ* 210.

WARD, A (2000) *Judicial Review and the Rights of Private Parties in EC Law* (Oxford, OUP).

WEBER, A (2002) 'La Carta de los Derechos Fundamentales de la Unión Europea' 64 *Revista Española de Derecho Constitucional* 79.

—— (1993) 'Comunidad Europea: el procedimiento administrativo en el Derecho Comunitario', in J Barnés (ed), *El procedimiento administrativo en el Derecho Comparado* (Madrid, Civitas) 57.

—— (1992) 'Il diritto amministrativo procedimentale nell'ordinamento della Communità Europea' 2 *Rivista Italiana di Diritto Pubblico Communitario* 393.

WEILER, JH (1999) *The Constitution of Europe, "Do the New Clothes Have an Emperor?" and Other Essays on European Integration* (Cambridge, CUP).

DE WITTE, B (2001) 'The Legal Status of the Charter: Vital Question or Non-Issue?' 8 *Maastricht Journal of European and Comparative Law* 81.

ZAMPINI, F (1999) 'Convention europèenne des droits de l'homme et Droit Communautaire de la concurrence' 432 *Revue du Marché commun et de l'Union européenne* 628.

Index

www.ingramcontent.com/pod-product-compliance
Ingram Content Group UK Ltd.
Pitfield, Milton Keynes, MK11 3LW, UK
UKHW020142290926
15471UKWH00004B/650

9 781841 135120